Wordfinder

Publishers ● Grosset & Dunlap ● New York
A Filmways Company

Introduction

The Grosset & Dunlap *Wordfinder* is a problem-solving refe
ence work. Writers, editors, proofreaders, secretaries, student
and typesetters can all use this guide when faced with question
of spelling, pronunciation, or word division. It lists the prope
spelling for more than 20,000 words, shows how to hyphenat
each one, and indicates the correct syllabic stress.

Man's need to express himself in written form has led to auxi
iary necessities such as spelling and word division. Proper divi
sion of any word is actually an integral part of its spelling. As
quick and reliable reference, *Wordfinder* is unbeatable—prope
word division, spelling, and pronunciation have never been easie
to locate.

Hyphenation rules are included as the initial instruction fe
using this guide. The reader who reviews these rules will quickl
become familiar with the subject and eventually will be able t
predict how a word might be divided.

Introduction copyright © 1977 by Grosset & Dunlap, Inc.
All rights reserved
ISBN 0-448-14334-8
First Grosset & Dunlap printing 1977
Printed in the United States of America

WORDBREAK RULES

1. Division of words should be minimized in leaded matter and avoided in double-leaded matter.

2. Except in narrow measures, wordbreaks should be avoided at the ends of more than two lines. Similarly, no more than two consecutive lines should end with the same word, symbol, group of numbers, etc.

3. In two-line centerheads, the first line should be centered and set as full as possible, but it is not set to fill the measure by unduly wide spacing. Wordbreaks should be avoided. Flush sideheads are set full measure and wordbreaks are permitted if unavoidable. They are not set ragged unless so indicated on copy.

4. The final word of a paragraph should not be divided.

5. Words should preferably be divided according to pronunciation; and to avoid mispronunciation, they should be divided so that the part of the word left at the end of the line will suggest the whole word: *capac-ity,* not *capa-city; extraor-dinary,* not *extra-ordinary; Wednes-day,* not *Wednesday; physi-cal,* not *phys-ical; service-man,* not *serviceman.*

6. Although WORD DIVISION lists beginning and ending one-letter syllables for pronunciation purposes, under no circumstances are words to be divided on a single letter (e.g., *usu-al-ly,* not *u-su-al-ly; imag-i-nary,* not *i-mag-i-nar-y*).

7. Division of short words (of five or fewer letters) should be avoided; two-letter divisions, including the carryover of two-letter endings *(ed, el, en, er, es, et, fy, ic, in, le, ly, or,* and *ty);* should also be avoided. In narrow measure, however, a sounded suffix (e.g., paint-*ed;* not rained) or syllable of two letters may be carried over—only if unavoidable. (See rule 10.)

8. Words of two syllables are split at the end of the first

syllable: *dis-pelled, con-quered;* words of three or more syllables, with a choice of division possible, divide preferably on the vowel: *particu-lar, sepa-rate.*

9. In words with short prefixes, divide on the prefix; e.g., *ac, co, de, dis, ex, in, non, on, pre, pro, re, un,* etc. (e.g., *non-essential,* not *nones-sential; pre-selected,* not *prese-lected*).

If possible, prefixes and combining forms of more than one syllable are preserved intact: *anti, infra, macro, micro, multi, over, retro, semi,* etc. (e.g., *anti-monopoly,* not *antimo-nopoly; over-optimistic,* not *overop-timistic*). (For chemical prefixes, see rule 30.)

10. *Words ending in* -er.—Although two-letter carry-overs are to be avoided (rule 7), many *-er* words which are derived from comparatives *(coarse, coarser; sharp, sharper)* have been listed to prevent a wrong wordbreak; e.g., *coars-er,* not *coar-ser.*

Nouns ending in *-er (adviser, bracer, keeper, perceiver, reader)* derived from action verbs are also listed to prevent a wrong division; e.g., *perceiv-er,* not *percei-ver.*

Except in narrow measure and if unavoidable, the above *-er* words are not divided unless division can be made on a prefix; e.g., *per-ceiver.*

11. *Words ending in* -or.— Generally, *-or* words with a consonant preceding are divided before the preceding consonant; e.g., *advi-sor* (legal), *fabrica-tor, guaran-tor, interve-nor, simula-tor, tai-lor;* but *bail-or, bargain-or, consign-or, grant-or.*

12. The following suffixes are not divided: *ceous, cial, cient, cion, cious, scious, geous, gion, gious, sial, tial, tion, tious,* and *sion.*

13. The suffixes *-able* and *-ible* are usually carried over intact; but when the stem word loses its original form, these suffixes are divided according to pronunciation: *comfort-able, corrupt-ible, manage-able;* but *dura-ble,*

audi-ble.

14. Words ending in *-ing*, with stress on the primary syllable, are preferably divided on the base word; e.g., *appoint-ing, combat-ing, danc-ing, engineer-ing, processing, program-ing, stencil-ing, trac-ing*, etc. However, present participles, such as *control-ling, forbid-ding, refer-ring* with stress placed on the second syllable, divide between the doubled consonants (see also rule 16).

15. When the final consonant sound of a word belongs to a syllable ending with a silent vowel, the final consonant or consonants become part of the added suffix: *chuck-ling, han-dler, twin-kling;* but *rollick-ing.*

16. When the addition of *-ed, -er, -est,* or a similar ending, causes the doubling of a final consonant, the added consonant is carried over: *pit-ted, rob-ber, thin-nest, gladden, control-lable, transmit-table;* but *bless-ed* (adj.), *dwell-er, gross-est.*

17. Words with doubled consonants are usually divided between these consonants: *clas-sic, ruf-fian, neces-sary, rebel-lion;* but *call-ing, mass-ing.*

18. If formation of a plural adds a syllable ending in an *s* sound, the plural ending should not be carried over by itself: *hor-ses, voi-ces;* but *church-es, cross-es,* thus not breaking the base word (see also rule 7).

19. The digraphs *ai, ch, ck, dg, gh, gn, ng, oa, ph, sh,* and *th* are not split.

20. Do not divide contractions: *doesn't, haven't.*

21. Solid compounds are divided preferably between the members: *bar-keeper, hand-kerchief, proof-reader, humming-bird.*

22. Avoid a division which adds another hyphen to a hyphen compound: *court-martial,* not *court-mar-tial; tax-supported,* not *tax-sup-ported.*

23. A word of one syllable is not split: *tanned, shipped, quenched, through, chasm, prism.*

3

24. Two consonants preceded and followed by a vowel are divided on the first consonant: *abun-dant, advan-tage, struc-ture;* but *attend-ant, accept-ance, depend-ence.*

25. When two adjoining vowels are sounded separately, divide between them: *cre-ation, gene-alogy.*

26. In breaking homonyms, distinction should be given to their relative functions: *pro-ject* (v.), *proj-ect* (n.); *pro-duce* (v.), *prod-uce* (n.); *stran-ger* (n.), *strang-er* (comparative adjective); *rec-ollect* (recall), *re-collect* (collect again); but *proc-ess* (n., v.); *pro-test* (n., v.).

27. *Words ending in* -meter.—In the large group of words ending in *-meter,* distinction should be made between metric system terms and terms indicating a measuring instrument. When it is necessary to divide metric terms, preserve the combining form *-meter;* e.g., centi-meter, deca-meter, hecto-meter, kilo-meter. But measuring instruments divide after the *m: al-tim-e-ter, ba-rom-e-ter, mi-crom-e-ter, mul-tim-e-ter,* etc. Derivatives of these *-meter* terms follow the same form; e.g., *mul-tim-e-ter, mul-tim-e-try.*

For orthographic reasons, however, several measuring instruments do not lend themselves to the general rule; e.g., *flow-meter, flux-meter, gauss-meter, taxi-meter, torque-meter, volt-meter, water-meter, watt-meter,* etc.

28. *Foreign languages.*–Rules for word division in foreign languages, by language, are printed in the 1967 GPO Style Manual (unabridged), pages 387–492.

29. *Chemical formulas.*—In chemical formulas, the hyphen has an important function. If a break is unavoidable in a formula, division is preferably made after an original hyphen to avoid the introduction of a misleading hyphen. If impractical to break on a hyphen, division may be made after an original comma, and no hyphen is added to indicate a runover. The following formula shows original hyphens and commas where division may be made. No

letterspacing is used in a chemical formula, but to fill a line, a space is permitted on both sides of a hyphen.

$$\text{1-(2,6,6-trimethylcyclohex-1-en-yl)-3,7,12,16}$$

30. *Chemical combining forms, prefixes, and suffixes.*—If possible, and subject to rules of good spacing, it is desirable to preserve as a unit such combining forms as follows:

aceto, anhydro, benzo, bromo, chloro, chromo, cincho, cyclo, dehydro, diazo, flavo, fluoro, glyco, hydroxy, iso, keto, methyl, naphtho, phospho, poly, silico, tetra, triazo.

The following suffixes are used in chemical printing. For patent and narrow measure composition, two-letter suffixes may be carried over.

al, an, ane, ase, ate, ene, ic, id, ide, in, ine, ite, ol, ole, on, one, ose, ous, oyl, yl, yne.

31. *Mineral elements.*—When it is necessary to break mineral constituents, division should preferably be made before a center period and beginning parenthesis, and after inferior figures following a closing parenthesis; but elements within parentheses are not separated. In cases of unavoidable breaks, a hyphen is not added to indicate a runover.

$$Mg(UO_2)_2(SiO_3)_2(OH)_2 \cdot 6H_2O$$

32. The em dash is not used at the beginning of any line of type, unless it is required before a credit line or signature, or in lieu of opening quotation marks in foreign languages. (See rules 9.52, 9.53, p. 142, 1967 GPO Style Manual.)

33. Neither periods nor asterisks used as an ellipsis are overrun alone at the end of a paragraph. If necessary, run over enough preceding lines to provide a short word or part of a word to accompany the ellipsis. If a runback is possible, subject to rules of good spacing and word division, this method may be adopted.

34. Abbreviations and symbols should not be broken at the end of a line: *A.F. of L., A.T. & T., C. Cls. R., f.o.b.,*

n.o.i.b.n., R. & D., r.p.m., WMAL. Where unavoidable in narrow measures and AGO's, long symbols may be broken after letters denoting a complete word. Use no hyphens. COM SUB A C LANT (Commander Submarine Allied Command Atlantic.)

35. Figures of less than six digits, decimals, and closely connected combinations of figures and abbreviations should not be broken at the end of a line: *$15,000, 34,575, 31,416, £8 4s. 7d., $10.25, 5,000 kw.-hr., A.D. 1952, 9 p.m., 18° F., NW¼.* If a break in six digits or over is unavoidable, divide on the comma or period, retain it, and use a hyphen.

36. Closely related abbreviations and initials in proper names and accompanying titles should not be separated, nor should titles, such as *Rev., Mr., Esq., Jr., 2d,* be separated from surnames.

37. Avoid dividing proper names, but if inescapable, follow general rules for word division.

38. Divisional and subdivisional paragraph reference signs and figures, such as § *18, section (a) (1), page 363(b),* should not be divided, nor should such references be separated from the matter to which they pertain.

In case of an unavoidable break in a lengthy reference (e.g., *7(B)(1)(a)(i)),* division will be made after elements in parentheses, and no hyphen is used.

39. In dates, do not divide the month and day, but the year may be carried over.

40. In case of an unavoidable break in a land-description symbol group at the end of a line, use no hyphen and break after a fraction.

41. Avoid breaking longitude and latitude figures at the end of a line; space out the line instead. In case of an unavoidable break at end of line, use hyphen.

WORD DIVISION*

A

Aar-on
Aa-ron-ic
ab-a-ca
ab-a-cus
ab-a-lo-ne
a-ban-don
a-ba-si-a
a-bat-a-ble
ab-a-tis
ab-at-toir
a-bet-ter
a-bet-tor (law)
ab-bre-vi-a-tor
ab-di-ca-tor
ab-do-men
ab-dom-i-nal
ab-dom-i-no-per-i-ne-al
ab-dom-i-nos-co-py
ab-duc-tor
a-be-ce-dar-i-an
A-bed-ne-go
ab-en-ter-ic
ab-er-om-e-ter
ab-er-ra-tion
a-bey-ance
ab-hor-rence
ab-hor-ri-ble
a-bid-ance
ab-i-ent
ab-i-e-tate
ab-i-et-ic
Ab-i-gail
Ab-i-lene
a-bil-i-ty
a-bi-ot-ic
a-bi-ot-ro-phy
ab-ju-ra-tion
ab-jur-a-to-ry
ab-la-tive
a-blep-si-a
ab-ne-ga-tor
ab-nor-mal-i-ty
ab-nor-mi-ty

a-bol-ish
ab-o-li-tion-ist
a-bom-i-na-ble
ab-o-rig-i-nes
a-bor-ti-cide
a-bort-in
a-bor-tive
ab-ra-ca-dab-ra
a-brad-ant
A-bra-ham
a-bran-chi-ate
ab-ra-si-om-e-ter
ab-ra-sion
ab-ra-sive
a-bridg-ment
ab-ro-ga-tive
ab-rupt
ab-scess
ab-scis-sa
ab-scis-sion
ab-scond
ab-sence
ab-sen-tee-ism
ab-sinthe
ab-sin-thin
ab-so-lu-tion
ab-so-lut-ism
ab-so-lu-tive
ab-so-lu-tize
ab-sol-u-to-ry
ab-sol-vent
ab-solv-er
ab-sorb-ate
ab-sorb-ent
ab-sorp-tance
ab-sorp-ti-om-e-ter
ab-ste-mi-ous
ab-sten-tious
ab-ster-gent
ab-sti-nence
ab-stract-er
ab-strac-tive
ab-struse

ab-surd-i-ty
a-bu-lo-ma-ni-a
a-bun-dance
a-bus-age
a-bu-sive
a-but-ting
a-bys-mal
a-byss-al
Ab-ys-sin-i-an
a-ca-cia
ac-a-dem-i-cal
a-cad-e-mi-cian
a-cad-e-my
a-camp-si-a
ac-a-na-ceous
ac-an-tha-ceous
a-can-thoid
ac-an-tho-ma
a-can-thus
a cap-pel-la
a-cap-su-lar
a-ca-pul-co
a-car-dite
ac-a-ri-a-sis
a-car-i-cid-al
ac-a-roid
a-cau-date
ac-ced-ence
ac-cel-er-ans
ac-cel-er-a-tive
ac-cel-er-a-tor
ac-cel-er-om-e-ter
ac-cend-i-ble
ac-cen-tu-a-tor
ac-cept-a-ble
ac-cept-ance
ac-cep-ta-tion
ac-cept-er
ac-cep-tor (law)
ac-ces-si-ble
ac-ces-so-ri-al
ac-ciac-ca-tu-ra

*Although Word Division lists beginning and ending one-letter syllables for pronunciation purposes, under no circumstances are words to be divided on a single letter. (See rule 6.)

ac-ci-den-tal
ac-cla-ma-tion
ac-clam-a-to-ry
ac-cli-mate
ac-cli-ma-ti-za-tion
ac-cliv-i-ty
ac-cli-vous
ac-co-lade
ac-com-mo-dat-ing
ac-com-pa-ni-ment
ac-com-pa-nist
ac-com-plice
ac-com-plish
ac-cord-ance
ac-cor-di-on-ist
ac-couche-ment
ac-cou-cheur
ac-count-a-ble
ac-count-an-cy
ac-cou-ter
ac-cred-i-ta-tion
ac-cres-cence
ac-cre-tive
ac-cul-tur-ate
ac-cum-bent
ac-cu-mu-la-tive
ac-cu-mu-la-tor
ac-cu-ra-cy
ac-cursed (v.)
ac-curs-ed (adj.)
ac-cus-a-ble
ac-cus-a-tive
ac-cus-a-to-ry
ac-cus-er
ac-cus-tomed
ac-e-naph-thy-lene
a-ceph-a-lous (adj.)
a-ceph-a-lus (n.)
ac-er-bate
a-cer-bi-ty
ac-er-ose
ac-e-tab-u-lum
ac-et-al-de-hyde
a-cet-a-mide
ac-et-am-i-dine
ac-et-a-mi-do-cin-nam-ic
ac-et-an-i-lide
ac-et-ar-sone
ac-e-tate
ac-e-ta-to-so-da-lite
a-ce-tic
a-ce-ti-fy

ac-e-tin
ac-e-to-ac-et-an-i-lide
a-cet-o-in
ac-e-tol-y-sis
ac-e-tom-e-ter
ac-e-tom-e-try
ac-e-tone
ac-e-ton-yl-i-dene
ac-e-to-phe-net-i-dide
ac-e-to-phe-none
ac-e-to-pro-pi-o-nate
ac-e-to-pur-pu-rine
ac-e-tous
ac-e-tox-yl
a-ce-tum
ac-e-tyl-ac-e-tone
a-cet-y-late
a-cet-y-la-tor
ac-e-tyl-cho-line
a-cet-y-lene
a-cet-y-lide
ac-e-tyl-meth-yl-car-bi-
  nol
ac-e-tyl-phen-yl-hy-dra-
  zine
ac-e-tyl-sa-lic-y-late
ac-e-tyl-sal-i-cyl-ic
Ach-il-le-an
A-chil-les
a-chol-ic
ach-ro-mat-ic
ach-ro-ma-tic-i-ty
a-chro-ma-tin
a-chro-ma-tism
a-cic-u-lar
ac-i-dif-er-ous
ac-i-dim-e-ter
ac-i-dim-e-try
a-cid-i-ty
a-cid-o-phil
ac-i-doph-i-lus
ac-i-do-sis
a-cid-u-lous
ac-i-na-ceous
ac-knowl-edge-a-ble
ac-knowl-edg-ment
ac-o-lyte
a-con-ic
ac-o-nite
ac-o-nit-ic
a-con-i-tine
a-cou-me-ter

a-cou-me-try
a-con-ti-um
a-cous-tic
ac-ous-ti-cian
a-cous-ti-con
ac-quaint-ance
ac-quaint-ed
ac-qui-es-cence
ac-quire
ac-qui-si-tion
ac-quis-i-tive
ac-quit-tal
a-cre-age
ac-ri-bom-e-ter
ac-rid
ac-ri-dine
ac-ri-din-i-um
a-crid-i-ty
ac-ri-mo-ni-ous
ac-ro-bat-ic
ac-ro-gen
a-crog-e-nous
a-cro-le-in
ac-ro-lith
ac-ro-nym
a-crop-e-tal
ac-ro-pho-bi-a
a-croph-o-ny
a-crop-o-lis
a-cros-tic
a-crot-ic
ac-ryl-am-ide
ac-ry-late
a-cryl-ic
ac-ry-lo-ni-trile
a-cryl-o-yl
ac-ry-lyl
ac-tin-ic
ac-tin-ism
ac-tin-i-um
ac-ti-no-bac-il-lo-sis
ac-ti-noid
ac-tin-o-lite
ac-ti-nom-e-ter
ac-ti-no-my-cin
ac-ti-no-my-co-sis
ac-ti-nos-co-py
ac-tion-om-e-ter
ac-ti-va-ble
ac-ti-va-tor
ac-tiv-ism
ac-tiv-ist

8

ac-tiv-i-ty
ac-to-my-o-sin
ac-tor
ac-tress
ac-tu-al-i-ty
ac-tu-ar-y
ac-tu-a-tor
a-cu-i-ty
a-cu-men
a-cu-mi-nate
a-cute-ness
a-cy-clic
ac-yl-ate
ad ab-sur-dum
ad-age
a-da-gio
ad-a-mant
ad-a-man-tine
A-dam-si-a
ad-ams-ite
Ad-am-son
a-dapt-a-ble
a-dapt-a-bil-i-ty
ad-ap-ta-tion
a-dapt-er
a-dapt-ive
ad-ap-tom-e-ter
a-dap-tor
a-dax-i-al
add-a-ble
add-ed
ad-den-da
add-er (one who adds)
ad-der (snake)
ad-dict-ed
ad-dic-tion
ad-dit-a-ment
ad-di-tion
ad-di-tive
ad-di-to-ry
ad-dress-ee
ad-dress-er
Ad-dres-so-graph
ad-dres-sor (law)
ad-du-cent
ad-duc-i-ble
ad-duc-tor
Ad-e-la
Ad-e-laide
Ad-el-bert
ad-e-nase
a-de-ni-a

a-den-i-form
ad-e-nine
ad-e-ni-tis
ad-e-no-car-ci-no-ma
ad-e-no-fi-bro-ma
ad-e-noi-dal
ad-e-no-ma
ad-e-nom-a-tous
ad-e-nop-a-thy
a-den-o-sine
ad-e-not-o-my
ad-e-nyl
ad-ept
a-dept-ness
ad-e-qua-cy
a-der-min
ad-her-ence
ad-her-ent
ad-he-res-cent
ad-he-sion
ad-he-sive
ad-i-a-bat-ic
ad in-fi-ni-tum
ad-i-nole
a-dip-a-mide
ad-i-pate
a-dip-ic
ad-i-po-ni-trile
ad-i-po-sis
ad-i-pos-i-ty
ad-i-po-so-gen-i-tal
ad-i-po-yl
ad-ja-cent
ad-jec-ti-val
ad-jec-tive
ad-ju-di-cate
ad-junc-tive
ad-ju-ra-tion
ad-jur-er
ad-just-a-ble
ad-just-er
ad-jus-tor (zoology)
ad-ju-tage
ad-ju-tant
ad-ju-vant
Ad-le-ri-an
ad lib-i-tum
ad-min-is-tra-tor
ad-min-is-tra-trix
ad-mi-ra-ble
ad-mi-ral-ty
ad-mi-ra-tion

ad-mir-er
ad-mis-si-ble
ad-mit-tance
ad-mon-ish
ad-mo-ni-tion
ad-mon i-to-ry
ad nau-se-am
a-do-be
ad-o-les-cent
Ad-olph
A-do-nis
a-dopt-er
a-dop-tive
a-dor-a-ble
ad-o-ra-tion
a-dor-er
a-dorn-ment
ad-re-nal
A-dren-a-lin
a-dren-er-gen
ad-re-ner-gic
a-dre-no-chrome
a-dre-no-cor-ti-co-troph-
    ic
A-dri-an
A-dri-at-ic
a-droit-ness
ad-sorb-ate
ad-sorb-ent
ad-sorp-tive
ad-u-la-tion
a-dul-ter-a-tor
a-dult-i-cide
ad-um-brate
ad va-lo-rem
ad-vanc-er
ad-van-ta-geous
ad-vec-tive
ad-ven-ience
Ad-vent-ist
ad-ven-ti-tious
ad-ven-tur-er
ad-verb-i-al
ad-ver-sar-y
ad-ver-si-ty
ad-vert-ence
ad-ver-tise-ment
ad-ver-tis-er
ad-vis-a-ble
ad-vis-er
ad-vi-sor (law)
ad-vi-so-ry

9

ad-vo-ca-cy
ad-voc-a-to-ry
Ae-ge-an
ae-o-li-an
aer-ate
aer-a-tor
aer-i-al
ae-rie
aer-if-er-ous
aer-i-fi-ca-tion
aer-o-bac-ter
aer-o-bat-ics
aer-o-bic
aer-o-dy-nam-ic
aer-ol-o-gy
aer-om-e-ter
aer-o-mo-tor
aer-o-nau-tics
aer-on-o-my
aer-o-scope
aer-os-co-py
ae-rose
aer-o-sol
aer-o-stat
Aes-chy-le-an
af-fa-ble
af-fec-ta-tion
af-fect-er
af-fect-i-ble
af-fec-tion-ate
af-fer-ent
af-fi-anced
af-fi-da-vit
af-fil-i-ate
af-fin-i-ty
af-firm-ance
af-fir-ma-tion
af-firm-a-tive
af-fla-tus
af-flict-ive
af-flu-ent
Af-ghan-i-stan
a-fi-ci-o-na-do
a-for-ti-o-ri
Af-ri-can-ize
af-ter
a-gam-ic
ag-a-ric
a-gar-i-cin-ic
ag-a-rin-ic
Ag-as-siz
ag-ate

Ag-a-thin
a-ga-ve
a-gen-cy
a-gen-da
a-gen-ti-val
a-geu-si-a
ag-er-a-tum
ag-glom-er-ate
ag-glu-ti-nant
ag-glu-ti-noid
ag-gran-dize
ag-gra-vate
ag-gre-gate
ag-gres-sive
ag-gres-sor
ag-griev-ance
ag-ile
a-gil-i-ty
ag-i-ta-tive
ag-i-ta-tor
ag-it-prop
a-glo-mer-u-lar
ag-no-si-a
ag-nos-te-rol
ag-nos-ti-cism
ag-o-niz-ing
ag-o-ra-pho-bi-a
a-grar-i-an
ag-ri-cul-tur-al
ag-ri-mo-ny
ag-ro-nom-ic
a-gron-o-mist
a-gron-o-my
ag-ros-tol-o-gy
ag-ryp-not-ic
a-gu-ish
aide me-moire
ai-grette
ai-le-ron
ai-lu-ro-phobe
air-i-ness
air-om-e-ter
Ak-ti-en-ge-sell-schaft
A1-a-bam-i-an
al-a-bas-ter
a-lac-ri-ty
a-la-me-da
al-a-mo
a-la-mode
a-la-nine
a-la-nyl
a-larm-ist

A-las-kan
Al-ba-ni-an
al-ba-tross
al-be-dom-e-ter
al-be-rene
al-bes-cent
al-bin-ic
al-bi-nism
al-bi-nos
al-bo-lite
Al-bu-quer-que
al-bu-men (egg)
al-bu-min (chemical)
al-bu-mi-nate
al-bu-mi-nom-e-ter
al-bu-mi-no-sis
al-bu-mi-nu-ri-a
al-bur-num
al-ca-mine
al-chem-ic
al-che-mist
al-che-my
al-co-hol-ism
al-co-hol-om-e-ter
al-co-hol-om-e-try
al-co-hol-y-sis
Al-deb-a-ran
al-de-hyd-ic
al-de-hy-drol
al-der-man
Al-der-ney
Al-dine
al-do-fu-ran-o-side
al-dol-ase
al-don-ic
a-le-a-to-ry
a-lem-bi-cate
a-lep-ric
a-lert-ness
al-eu-drin
al-eu-rit-ic
al-eu-rom-e-ter
al-eu-rone
A-leu-tian
a-lex-i-a
a-lex-in
al-ge-bra-i-cal
al-ge-fa-cient
Al-ge-ri-an
al-ge-si-a
al-ge-sim-e-ter
al-gi-nate

al-gin-ic
al-gol-o-gy
al-gom-e-ter
Al-go-rab
al-go-rism
al-gra-phy
a-li-as
al-i-bi
al-i-cy-clic
al-i-dade
al-ien-ate
al-ien-ist
a-lif-er-ous
al-i-men-ta-ry
al-i-mo-ny
a-line-ment
a-lin-er
al-i-phat-ic
al-i-quot
al-i-vin-cu-lar
a-liz-a-rin
al-ka-li
al-ka-lim-e-ter
al-ka-lin-i-ty
al-ka-loi-dal
al-ke-nyl
alk-ox-ide
alk-ox-yl-ate
al-kyl-ate
al-kyl-ene
al-kyl-ic
al-kyl-ize
al-lan-to-in-ase
al-le-ga-tion
Al-le-ghe-ni-an
Al-le-ghe-ny
al-le-giance
al-le-gor-i-cal
al-le-go-ry
al-le-gro
al-ler-gen-ic
al-ler-gic
al-le-vi-ate
al-le-vi-a-tor
al-li-a-ceous
al-li-ga-tor
al-lit-er-a-tive
al-lo-ca-ble
al-lo-ca-tor
al-log-a-my
al-lom-er-ism
al-lom-e-try

al-lo-path
al-lop-a-thy
al-loph-a-nate
al-lo-se-mat-ic
al-lo-troph-ic
al-lot-ro-py
al-lot-ted
al-lot-tee
al-lot-ting
al-lur-ing
al-lu-sive
al-lu-vi-al
al-lu-vi-um
al-lyl-a-mine
al-lyl-ic
al-ma-nac
al-might-y
al-mond
al-mon-er
a-lo-di-um
al-o-et-ic
al-o-gism
al-o-in
al-o-pe-ci-a
Al-o-ys-i-us
al-pac-a
al-pha-bet-i-cal
al-pha-bet-ize
al-pha-mer-ic
al-pha-tron
Al-pine
Al-pin-ism
al-read-y
al-sike
al-tar
al-ter
al-ter-na-tive
al-ter-na-tor
al-tim-e-ter
al-tim-e-try
al-ti-tu-di-nar-i-an
al-to-geth-er
al-trose
a-lu-mi-na
a-lu-min-i-um
a-lu-mi-nize
a-lu-mi-nous
a-lu-mi-num
a-lum-nus
a-lun-dum
al-u-nite
al-ve-o-lar

Al-ve-o-li-tes
a-lys-sum
a-mal-ga-mate
a-mal-ga-ma-tor
a-man-u-en-sis
am-a-ranth
am-a-ran-thine
am-a-roid
am-a-ryl-lis
am-a-teur-ish
am-a-tol
am-a-to-ry
a-maze-ment
Am-a-zo-ni-an
am-bas-sa-do-ri-al
am-ber-gris
am-ber-oid
am-bi-dex-trous
am-bi-ent
am-bi-gu-i-ty
am-big-u-ous
am-bip-a-rous
am-bi-tious
am-biv-a-lence
am-bling
am-blys-to-ma
am-bro-si-a
am-bu-lance
am-bu-la-to-ry
am-bus-cad-er
a-me-ba
a-me-bi-a-sis
a-me-bic
A-mel-ia
a-me-lio-ra-tive
am-e-lo-blas-to-ma
a-me-na-ble
a-mend-a-to-ry
a-men-i-ty
a-men-or-rhe-a
am-ent (botany)
am-en-ta-ceous
A-mer-i-can-a
A-mer-i-can-ism
am-er-i-ci-um
ames-ite
am-e-thyst
a-mi-a-ble
am-i-ca-ble
a-mi-cus cu-ri-ae
am-i-dase
am-ide

11

a-mid-ic
a-mi-do
a-mi-do-gen
am-i-dol
am-i-dox-ime
a-mi-go
am-i-nate
a-mine
a-mi-no
a-mi-no-ben-zo-ic
am-i-nol-y-sis
am-i-nop-ter-in
a-mi-no-sal-i-cyl-ic
am-me-ter
am-mo-ni-a
am-mo-ni-ate
am-mo-nite
Am-mon-ites (Biblical)
am-mo-ni-um
am-mu-ni-tion
am-ne-sia
am-nes-ty
a-mo-le
am-o-rous
a-mor-phism
am-or-ti-za-tion
A-moy-ese
am-per-age
am-pere-me-ter
am-per-o-met-ric
am-per-om-e-try
am-per-sand
am-phet-a-mine
am-phib-i-an
am-phib-i-ol-o-gy
am-phib-i-ous
am-phi-bol-ic
am-phib-o-lite
am-phib-o-lous
am-phi-dip-loi-dy
am-phi-ge-net-ic
am-phig-e-nous
am-phi-kar-y-on
Am-phip-o-da
am-pho-ter-ic
am-phot-er-ism
am-pli-fi-er
am-pli-tude
am-poule
am-pu-ta-tor
Am-ster-dam
am-u-let

a-mu-si-a
a-mus-ing
a-myg-da-la-ce-ae
a-myg-da-lin
a-myg-da-loi-dal
am-y-la-ceous
am-y-lase
am-yl-ene
am-y-loi-dal
am-y-loi-do-sis
am-y-lol-y-sis
am-y-lo-pec-tin
am-y-lose
a-nab-a-sine
an-a-bi-o-sis
an-a-bol-ic
a-nab-o-lism
a-nach-ro-nism
A-nac-re-on
a-nad-ro-mous
an-aer-o-bi-a
an-aer-o-bic
a-nag-ly-phy
an-a-glyp-tics
an-a-gog-ic
a-nal-cite
an-a-lep-tic
an-al-ge-si-a
an-al-ge-sic
an-a-log-i-cal
a-nal-o-gous
a-nal-o-gy
a-nal-y-sis
an-a-lyst
an-a-lyt-i-cal
an-a-lyz-er
an-a-mor-pho-sis
An-a-ni-as
an-a-phy-lax-is
an-ar-chism
an-ar-chis-tic
an-ar-chy
a-nas-to-mo-sis
a-nas-to-mot-ic
an-a-tase
a-nath-e-ma
an-a-tom-i-cal
a-nat-o-mist
a-nat-o-my
an-ces-tral
an-chor-age

an-cho-rite (hermit)
an-chor-ite (rock)
an-cho-vy
an-cient
an-cil-lar-y
an-cy-lo-sto-mi-a-sis
An-da-lu-sian
an-da-lu-site
An-da-man
an-de-site
and-i-ron
An-dor-ran
an-dor-ite
An-do-ver
an-dro-gen-ic-i-ty
an-drog-y-nous
An-drom-e-da
An-dro-mede
an-dro-sin
an-dro-stane
an-dros-te-rone
an-ec-dot-al
a-ne-mi-a
a-ne-mic
a-nem-o-gram
an-e-mom-e-ter
a-nem-o-ne
a-nem-o-scope
an-er-oid
an-es-the-sia
an-es-the-sim-e-ter
an-es-the-si-ol-o-gy
an-es-thet-ic
an-es-the-tist
a-neu-ri-a
an-eu-rin
an-eu-rysm
an-ga-ry
an-gel-ic
an-ger
an-gi-i-tis
an-gi-na pec-to-ris
an-gi-o-car-di-og-ra-p
an-gi-o-cyst
an-gi-om-e-ter
an-gi-op-a-thy
an-gi-o-sis
an-gi-os-to-my
an-gi-o-to-nin
an-gler
An-gli-can
an-gli-cize

An-go-lese
An-go-ra
an-gos-tu-ra
an-gry
ang-strom
an-guish
an-gu-lar-i-ty
an-he-dral
an-hi-dro-sis
an-hi-drot-ic
an-hy-dride
an-hy-dro-bi-o-sis
an-hy-drous
an-i-lide
an-i-line
a-nil-i-ty
an-i-mad-ver-sion
an-i-mal-cule
an-i-mal-ism
an-i-ma-tion
an-i-mism
an-i-mos-i-ty
an-i-on-ic
an-i-on-ot-ro-py
an-is-ate
an-ise
an-i-seed
an-is-ette
a-nis-ic
a-nis-i-dine
an-i-sot-ro-py
an-klet
an-ky-lo-sis
an-ky-los-to-ma
an-nal-ist
An-nam-ese
an-neal-er
an-ni-hi-late
an-ni-ver-sa-ry
an-no-ta-tor
an-nounc-er
an-nu-al
an-nu-i-tant
an-nu-lar
an-nu-let
an-nun-ci-a-to-ry
an-ode
an-od-ic
an-od-ize
an-o-dyne
a-noint-ment
a-nom-a-lis-tic

a-nom-a-lous
a-nom-a-ly
an-o-nym-i-ty
a-non-y-mous
an-o-op-si-a
A-noph-e-les
an-ox-i-a
an-ser-ine
an-swer
ant-ac-id
an-tag-o-nism
Ant-arc-tic
An-tar-es
an-te-ced-ent
an-te-di-lu-vi-an
an-te-lope
an-te-pe-nul-ti-mate
an-te-ri-or
ant-he-lion
ant-hel-min-tic
an-them
an-ther-al
an-tho-cy-an-i-din
an-thog-e-nous
an-tho-log-i-cal
an-thol-o-gy
An-tho-ny
an-thra-cene
an-thra-cif-er-ous
an-thra-cite
an-thra-co-sil-i-co-sis
an-thra-nil-ic
an-thran-o-yl
an-thra-pur-pu-rin
an-thra-qui-no-nyl
an-thrax
an-thro-poi-dal
an-thro-po-log-i-cal
an-thro-pol-o-gy
an-thro-pom-e-ter
an-thro-po-met-ric
an-thro-poph-a-gy
an-ti-bi-ot-ic
an-ti-cal
an-tic-i-pa-to-ry
an-ti-cli-nal
an-ti-dot-al
an-ti-gen-ic
an-ti-ge-nic-i-ty
An-tig-o-ne
An-ti-guan
an-ti-his-ta-min-ic

An-til-le-an
an-til-o-gism
an-ti-mo-ny
an-ti-pas-to
an-ti-pa-thet-ic
an-tip-a-thy
an-tiph-o-nal
an-tip-o-dal
an-ti-pode
an-tip-o-de-an
an-tip-o-des
an-ti-quar-i-an
an-ti-quate
an-tique
an-tiq-ui-ty
an-ti-sep-tic
an-tith-e-sis
an-ti-thet-i-cal
ant-ler
an-to-nym
Ant-werp
an-u-re-sis
anx-i-e-ty
anx-ious
a-or-tic
a-pache (Paris thug)
A-pach-e (Indian tribe)
a-pa-re-jo
a-part-heid
ap-as-tron
ap-a-thet-ic
ap-a-thy
ap-a-tite
Ap-en-nine
a-pe-ri-ent
a-pe-ri-od-ic
a-per-i-tif
ap-er-tom-e-ter
ap-er-tur-al
aph-a-nite
aph-a-nit-ic
a-pha-sia
a-phe-lion
aph-i-cide
aph-o-rism
a-phra-si-a
aph-ro-dis-i-ac
Aph-ro-di-te
a-pi-a-rist
a-pi-ar-y
ap-i-cal
a-pi-ose

ap-ish
a-piv-o-rous
ap-neu-sis
a-poc-a-lyp-tic
a-poc-o-pe
a-poc-ry-phal
Ap-o-des
ap-o-dic-tic
a-pog-a-my
ap-o-ge-an
ap-o-gee
a-pog-e-ny
A-pol-li-nar-is
A-pol-lo
a-pol-o-get-ic
ap-o-lo-gi-a
a-pol-o-gist
ap-o-pho-rom-e-ter
ap-o-phyl-lite
ap-o-plec-tic
ap-o-plex-y
a-pos-ta-sy
a-pos-tate
a-pos-ta-tize
a-pos-te-ri-o-ri
a-pos-tle
a-pos-to-late
ap-os-tol-ic
a-pos-tro-phe
ap-os-troph-ic
a-poth-e-car-y
a-poth-e-o-sis
Ap-pa-lach-ian
ap-pall-ing
ap-pa-nage
ap-pa-ra-tus
ap-par-eled
ap-par-ent
ap-pa-ri-tion
ap-pear-ance
ap-pel-lant
ap-pel-la-tion
ap-pend-age
ap-pend-ant
ap-pen-dec-to-my
ap-pen-di-cal
ap-pen-di-ci-tis
ap-pen-dix
ap-per-cep-tion
ap-pet-i-ble
ap-pe-tiz-er
ap-pe-tiz-ing

ap-pli-ca-ble
ap-pli-ca-tor
ap-pli-ca-to-ry
ap-pli-que
ap-pog-gia-tu-ra
ap-point-ee
ap-point-ive
ap-po-site
ap-pos-i-tive
ap-prais-al
ap-pre-ci-a-tive
ap-pre-hen-si-ble
ap-pre-hen-sive
ap-pren-tice
ap-proach-ing
ap-pro-ba-tion
ap-pro-pri-a-tive
ap-prov-al
ap-prox-i-mate
ap-pui
ap-pur-te-nance
a-pri-cot
A-pril
a pri-o-ri
ap-ro-pos
ap-sis
ap-te-ri-um
ap-ter-ous
ap-ti-tude
aq-ua-plane
aq-ua-relle
a-quar-i-um
A-quar-i-us
a-quat-ic
aq-ua-tint
aq-ua-vit
aq-ue-duct
a-que-ous
aq-ui-fer
aq-ui-line
ar-a-besque
A-ra-bi-an
Ar-a-bic
a-rab-i-nose
Ar-ab-ize
ar-a-ble
A-rach-ni-da
ar-ach-noi-dal
Ar-a-go-nese
a-rag-o-nite
ar-al-kox-y
ar-al-kyl-ate

Ar-a-ma-ic
A-rap-a-ho
A-rau-ca-ni-an
ar-bi-ter
ar-bi-tra-ble
ar-bi-trag-er
ar-bit-ra-ment
ar-bi-trar-y
ar-bi-tra-tor
ar-bo-re-al
ar-bo-res-cent
ar-bo-re-tum
ar-bo-ri-cul-tur-al
ar-bo-rize
ar-bor-vi-tae
ar-bu-tus
ar-cade
Ar-ca-di-an
ar-ca-num
ar-cha-ic
ar-che-o-log-i-cal
ar-che-ol-o-gy
arch-er-y
ar-che-typ-al
ar-che-us
Ar-chi-bald
ar-chi-e-pis-co-pa-cy
Ar-chi-me-de-an
ar-chi-pel-a-go
ar-chi-tec-tur-al
ar-chi-trave
ar-chives
ar-chi-vist
Arc-tic
Arc-tu-rus
ar-cu-ate
ar-dent
ar-dor
ar-du-ous
ar-e-al
a-re-na
ar-e-na-ceous
a-re-o-la
ar-gen-tal
ar-gen-te-ous
ar-gen-tif-er-ous
Ar-gen-ti-na
ar-gen-tite
ar-gen-tous
ar-gen-tum
ar-gil-la-ceous
ar-gil-lif-er-ous

ar-gil-lite
ar-gi-nine
ar-gol
ar-gon
Ar-go-naut
ar-go-sy
ar-gu-men-ta-tive
Ar-gy-rol
a-rid-i-ty
Ar-i-el
A-ri-es
A-ri-on
a-ris-tate
ar-is-toc-ra-cy
a-ris-to-crat-ic
Ar-is-to-te-li-an
Ar-is-tot-le
ar-ith-met-ic (adj.)
a-rith-me-tic (n.)
ar-ith-met-i-cal
ar-ith-mom-e-ter
Ar-i-zo-nan
Ar-kan-san
ark-ite (mineral)
ar-ma-da
ar-ma-dil-los
Ar-ma-ged-don
ar-ma-ment
ar-ma-men-tar-i-um
ar-ma-ture
Ar-me-ni-an
ar-mi-stice
ar-mor-er
ar-mo-ri-al
ar-mo-ry
ar-ni-ca
a-ro-ma
ar-o-mat-ic
ar-o-ma-ti-za-tion
a-rous-al
a-rous-ing
ar-raign
ar-range-ments
ar-rear-age
ar-rest-er
ar-res-tive
ar-rhyth-mi-a
ar-riv-al
ar-ro-gant
ar-ron-disse-ment
ar-roy-o
ar-se-nal

ar-se-nate
ar-se-nic (n.)
ar-sen-ic (adj.)
ar-sen-i-cal
ar-se-nide
ar-se-ni-ous
ar-se-ni-o-sid-er-ite
ar-se-no-ben-zene
ar-sine
ar-son-ist
ar-so-ni-um
ars-phen-a-mine
ar-te-ri-al
ar-te-ri-og-ra-phy
ar-te-ri-o-lar
ar-te-ri-o-scle-ro-sis
ar-te-ri-ot-o-my
ar-te-ri-tis
ar-ter-y
ar-te-sian
ar-thrit-ic
ar-thri-tis
ar-thro-dese
ar-throd-e-sis
ar-throg-e-nous
ar-throg-ra-phy
ar-throm-e-ter
ar-throp-a-thy
ar-thro-pod
Ar-throp-o-da
ar-ti-choke
ar-ti-cle
ar-tic-u-la-tor
ar-ti-fact
ar-ti-fice
ar-tif-i-cer
ar-ti-fi-cial
ar-til-ler-y
ar-ti-nite
ar-ti-san
art-ist
ar-tiste
ar-tis-ti-cal
ar-tist-ry
A-run-del (Maryland)
Ar-y-an-ize
ar-yl-am-ine
ar-yl-ate
ar-yl-ene
as-a-fet-i-da
as-bes-to-sis
as-ca-ri-a-sis

as-car-i-dole
as-cend-an-cy
as-cend-ant
as-cend-er
as-cer-tain
as-cet-i-cism
as-cid-i-an
as-ci-tes
a-scor-bic
as-cribe
a-sep-sis
a-sep-tic
Ash-ke-na-zi
A-si-at-ic
as-i-nin-i-ty
a-skance
a-skew
as-pa-rag-i-nase
as-par-a-gine
as-par-a-gus
as-par-tic
as-pect
as-pen
as-per-ate
as-perge
as-per-gil-lus
as-per-i-ty
as-per-sion
as-phal-tene
as-phal-tic
as-phyx-i-ate
As-pi-dis-tra
as-pi-rant
as-pi-ra-tor
as-pi-ra-to-ry
as-pi-rin
As-ple-ni-um
as-sail-ant
As-sam-ese
as-sas-si-nate
as-sem-bla-ble
as-sem-bler
as-sem-bly
as-sen-tor
as-sert-i-ble
as-ser-tive
as-sess-ee
as-ses-sor
as-ses-so-ri-al
as-sev-er-ate
as-si-du-i-ty
as-sid-u-ous

as-si-ette
as-sign-a-ble
as-sig-nat
as-sig-na-tion
as-sign-ee
as-sign-or
as-sim-i-la-ble
as-sist-ant
as-so-ci-a-ble
as-so-ci-ate
as-so-nance
as-suage
as-sump-sit
as-sur-ance
As-syr-i-an
as-ta-tine
as-ter
as-te-ri-al
as-ter-isk
as-ter-oid
as-ter-oi-dal
as-the-ni-a
as-then-ic
asth-mat-ic
as-tig-mat-ic
a-stig-ma-tism
as-tig-mom-e-ter
as-ton-ish
as-tound-ing
as-tra-gal
as-trag-a-lus
as-tra-khan
as-tral
as-tric-tion
as-trin-gent
as-tri-on-ics
as-tro-ga-tor
as-trog-o-ny
as-troid
as-tro-labe
as-trol-o-ger
as-tro-log-i-cal
as-trol-o-gy
as-trom-e-try
as-tro-naut
as-tro-nau-tics
as-tron-o-mer
as-tro-nom-i-cal
as-tron-o-my
as-tro-sphere
As-tu-ri-an
as-tute

a-sun-der
a-sy-lum
a-sym-met-ri-cal
as-ymp-tote
as-ymp-tot-ic
a-syn-ap-sis
a-sys-to-le
At-a-brine
at-a-rac-tic
at-a-vism
at-a-vis-tic
a-tax-i-a
at-e-lier
a-the-is-ti-cal
ath-e-ne-um
A-the-ni-an
Ath-ens
ath-er-o-ma
ath-er-om-a-tous
ath-er-o-scle-ro-sis
ath-let-i-cal-ly
a-threp-si-a
ath-ro-cyte
ath-ro-gen-ic
At-lan-tic
at-lan-tite
at-mol-y-sis
at-mom-e-ter
at-mos-pher-i-cal
at-oll
a-tom-ic
a-tom-i-cal
at-o-mic-i-ty
at-om-ism
at-om-is-tic
at-om-iz-er
a-ton-al
a-tone-ment
at-o-ny
at-o-py
a-tre-si-a
a-tri-o-ven-tric-u-lar
a-tri-um
a-tro-cious
a-troc-i-ty
a-troph-ic
at-ro-phy
at-ro-pine
at-ro-pin-ize
at-ta-ché
at-tain-der
at-tem-per-a-tor

at-tend-ant
at-ten-tive
at-ten-u-a-tor
at-test-ant
at-tes-ta-tion
at-test-er
at-ti-tu-di-nize
at-tor-ney
at-tract-ant
at-trac-tive
at-trac-tor
at-trib-ut-a-ble
at-trib-ute (n.)
at-trib-ute (v.)
at-trib-u-tive
at-tri-tus
auc-tion-eer
auc-to-ri-al
au-da-cious
au-dac-i-ty
au-di-ble
au-di-ence
au-di-o-gen-ic
au-di-om-e-ter
au-di-om-e-try
au-di-to-ri-um
au-di-to-ry
Au-du-bon
au-gan-ite
au-ger
au-gite
au-gi-tite
aug-men-ta-tion
aug-men-ta-tive
aug-men-tor
au-gu-ry
au-gust
Au-gus-tin-i-an
au-ral
au-ra-mine
au-re-ate
au-re-li-an
au-re-o-e
Au-re-o-my-cin
au-ri-cle
au-ric-u-lar
au-ric-u-lo-pa-ri-e-tal
au-ro-ra bo-re-al-is
au-rum
aus-cul-tate
aus-pic-es
aus-pi-cious

aus-ten-it-ic
aus-ter-i-ty
Aus-tra-la-sian
Aus-tra-lian
Aus-tri-an
au-tar-chic
au-tar-chy
au-then-ti-cal-ly
au-then-ti-ca-tor
au-then-tic-i-ty
au-thor-i-tar-i-an
au-thor-i-ta-tive
au-thor-i-za-tion
au-thor-iz-er
au-tism
au-toc-ra-cy
au-to-crat
au-to-ge-net-ic
au-to-gen-ic
au-tog-e-nous
au-to-gi-ro
au-to-graph
au-tog-ra-pher
au-tol-y-sate
au-to-mat-i-cal
au-to-ma-tic-i-ty
au-tom-a-tin
au-to-ma-tion
au-tom-a-tism
au-tom-a-tist
au-tom-a-ti-za-tion
au-tom-a-ton
au-tom-a-tous
au-tom-ne-si-a
au-to-net-ics

au-to-nom-ic
au-ton-o-mous
au-toph-a-gous
au-toph-o-ny
au-top-sy
au-tos-co-py
au-tot-o-my
au-tox-i-diz-a-ble
au-tum-nal
aux-a-nom-e-ter
aux-il-ia-ry
aux-in
aux-o-chrom-ic
aux-om-e-ter
av-a-lanche
av-a-ri-cious
av-a-tar
av-e-nue
av-er-age
a-ver-sion
a-vert-i-ble
a-vi-an-ize
av-i-a-rist
a-vi-ar-y
a-vi-a-tor
a-vi-a-trix
av-i-din
a vid-i-ty
A-vi-gnon-ese
a-vi-on-ics
av-o-ca-dos
av-o-ca-tion
a-voc-a-to-ry
a-void-ance
av-oir-du-pois

a-vow-al
a-vun-cu-lar
a-wak-en
awk-ward
awn-ing (n., v.)
ax-i-al-ly
ax-il-lar-y
ax-i-o-mat-ic
Ax-min-ster
ax-o-lotl
ax-om-e-ter
a-za-lea
az-e-la-ic
a-ze-o-trop-ic
a-ze-ot-ro-py
Az-er-bai-ja-ni
az-ide
az-i-do-a-ce-tic
az-i-mi-no
az-i-muth-al
az-ine
az-o-im-ide
az-ole
az-o-meth-ane
a-zo-ni-um
A-zo-to-bac-ter
az-o-tom-e-ter
az-ox-y-ben-zene
Az-tec-an
az-u-lene
az-ure
az-u-rin
az-ur-ite
az-y-gous

B

ba-bas-su
bab-bitt
bab-bling
Ba-bel
bab-i-ru-sa
ba-boon
ba-bush-ka
Bab-y-lo-ni-an
bac-ca-lau-re-ate
bac-cha-na-lian
bac-chant
bac-cif-er-ous
bach-e-lor
bac-il-lar-y
ba-cil-li
ba-cil-lus

bac-i-tra-cin
ba-con
Ba-co-ni-an
bac-te-ri-a
bac-te-ri-cid-al
bac-te-ri-cid-in
bac-ter-id
bac-te-ri-o-log-i-cal
bac-te-ri-ol-o-gy
bac-te-ri-ol-y-sis
bac-te-ri-o-lyt-ic
bac-te-ri-os-co-py
bac-te-ri-um
bac-te-roi-dal
badg-er
bad-i-nage

Bae-de-ker
baf-fling
ba-gasse
bag-a-telle
ba-gel
ba-guette
Ba-ha-i
Ba-ha-ma
bail-ee
bail-er
Bai-ley
bail-iff
bail-i-wick
ba-ke-lite
bak-er-y
bak-sheesh

17

Ba-la-kla-va
bal-a-lai-ka
bal-anc-er
ba-la-ta
bal-brig-gan
bal-co-ny
bal-der-dash
bal-dric
Bal-e-ar-ic
ba-leen
Ba-li-nese
Bal-kan
balk-y
bal-lad-eer
bal-le-ri-na
bal-lis-tics
bal-lo-net
bal-loon-ist
bal-ma-caan
balm-i-ness
Bal-mor-al
bal-ne-al
ba-lo-ney
bal-sam
Bal-tic
Bal-ti-mor-e-an
bal-us-trade
bam-bi-no
bam-boo-zle
ba-nal (commonplace)
ban-al (governor)
ba-nal-i-ty
ba-nan-a
Ban-bury
ban-dag-er
ban-dan-na
ban-deau
band-er
ban-dit-ry
ban-do-leer
ban-dy-ing
ban-ga-lore
ban-gle
ban-ish
ban-is-ter
bank-er
bank-rupt-cy
ban-quet-er
ban-shee
ban-tam
ban-ter
bant-ling

ban-zai
bap-tis-mal
bap-tis-ter-y
bap-tiz-er
Bar-ab-bas
Bá-rá-ny
bar-a-the-a
Bar-ba-dos
bar-bar-i-an
bar-bar-ic
bar-ba-rism
bar-ba-rous
Bar-ba-ry
bar-be-cue
bar-ber
bar-bette
bar-bi-tal
bar-bi-tu-rate
bar-bi-tu-ric
bar-gain-er
bar-gain-or (law)
bar-ing
bar-ite
bar-i-tone
bar-i-to-sis
bar-i-um
bar-ken-tine
bark-er
Bark-hau-sen
Bar-kis
bark-om-e-ter
Bar-na-bas
bar-na-cle
bar-o-graph
ba-rom-e-ter
bar-o-met-ric
bar-o-met-ro-graph
bar-o-me-trog-ra-phy
ba-rom-e-try
bar-on-ess
bar-on-et
ba-ro-ni-al
ba-roque
bar-o-scope
ba-rouche
bar-ra-cu-da
bar-rage
bar-ra-try
bar-reled
bar-ren
bar-rette
bar-ri-cade

bar-ring
bar-ris-ter
bar-ter
Bart-lett
bar-y-lite
ba-ry-ta
ba-ryt-ic
bar-y-tron
ba-sal
ba-salt
ba-sal-tic
ba-sic
ba-si-cal-ly
ba-sic-i-ty
ba-sid-i-um
bas-il
ba-sil-i-ca
bas-i-lisk
ba-sin
ba-sis
Bas-ker-ville
bas-ket-ry
bas-si-net
bas-tar-dy
bas-tille
bas-ti-na-do
Ba-ta-vi-an
ba-teau
bath-o-lith-ic
ba-thom-e-ter
ba-thos
ba-thym-e-ter
bath-y-met-ric
ba-thym-e-try
bath-y-scaphe
ba-thys-mal
ba-tik
ba-tiste
ba-ton (n.)
bat-on (v.)
ba-tra-chi-um
bat-tal-ion
bau-ble
Bau-mé
baux-ite
baux-it-ic
Ba-var-i-an
bay-ard
bay-o-net
Ba-yonne
bay-ou
ba-zoo-ka

bdel-li-um
bea-con
bead-er
bea-dle
bea-gle
beak-er
bé-ar-naise
beat-er
be-a-tif-ic
be-at-i-fy
be-at-i-tude
Be-a-trice
beau-sé-ant
beau-te-ous
bea-ver
be-bee-rine
Bech-u-a-na-land
beck-on
Bec-que-rel
be-di-zen
Bed-ou-in
Be-el-ze-bub
Be-er-she-ba
Bee-tho-ven
bee-tle
beg-gar-y
be-gin-ning
beg-ohm
be-go-nia
be-hav-ior-al
be-he-moth
be-hold-en
bei-del-lite
be-lat-ed
be-lea-guered
bel-fry
Bel-gian
be-liev-er
bel-la-don-na
bel-li-cos-i-ty
bel-lig-er-ent
Be-na-res
ben-e-fac-tor
be-nef-i-cent
be-ne-fi-cial
ben-e-fi-ci-ar-y
ben-e-fi-ci-ate
ben-e-fit-ed
be-nev-o-lence
be-nign
be-nig-nant
be-ni-to-ite

Ben-ja-min
ben-ton-ite
benz-al-de-hyde
ben-zald-ox-ime
benz-am-ide
Ben-ze-drine
ben-zene-di-a-zo-ni-um
ben-ze-noid
ben-zil-ic
benz-im-id-a-zole
ben-zo-ate
ben-zo-fla-vine
ben-zo-ic
ben-zo-in
ben-zo-i-nat-ed
ben-zo-phe-none
ben-zo-sul-fi-mide
benz-ox-y-a-ce-tic
ben-zo-yl-ate
ben-zyl-ate
ben-zyl-ox-y
ber-ba-mine
ber-ber-ine
be-ret
ber-ga-mot
berg-schrund
ber-i-ber-i
Ber-ing
Berke-ley
berke-li-um
Ber-mu-da
Bern-ese
Ber-noul-li
Ber-tha
berth-ing
Ber-tram
be-ryl-li-um
ber-yl-loid
Bes-sa-ra-bi-an
Bes-se-mer
bes-tial
bes-ti-al-i-ty
be-stride
be-ta-cism
be-ta-ine
be-ta-tron
be-tel
Be-tel-geuse
Be-thes-da
be-troth-al
Beu-lah
bev-a-tron

bev-eled
bev-er-age
be-wil-der
bez-el
Bhu-ta-nese
Bi-a-fra
bi-ased
bi-be-lot
Bi-ble
Bib-li-cal
bib-li-o-graph-ic
bib-li-og-ra-phy
bib-li-o-phile
bib-u-lous
bi-car-bon-ate
bi-ceph-a-lous
bi-chlo-ride
bi-chro-mate
bick-er-ing
bi-cus-pid
bi-cy-clist
bi-cy-clo-al-kane
bi-fur-cat-ed
big-a-mous
big-ot-ry
bi-gua-nide
Bi-ki-ni
bil-i-ar-y
bil-i-cy-a-nin
bil-i-fi-ca-tion
bil-ious
bil-i-ru-bin
bil-i-ru-bi-ne-mi-a
bil-liards
bi-loc-u-lar
bi-met-al-lism
bi-na-ry
bin-au-ral
bind-er-y
bin-na-cle
bin-oc-u-lar
bi-no-mi-al
bi-og-e-ny
bi-o-graph-i-cal
bi-og-ra-phy
bi-o-log-i-cal
bi-ol-o-gist
bi-ol-y-sis
bi-om-e-ter
bi-o-met-ric
bi-om-e-try
bi-on-o-my

bi-op-sy
bi-os-co-py
bi-os-o-phy
bi-os-ter-ol
bi-ot-ic
bi-o-tin
bi-o-tite
bi-o-vu-lar
bip-a-rous
bi-par-ti-ble
bi-par-ti-ent
bi-par-tite
Bir-ming-ham
bis-cuit
bish-op-ric
bis-muth-ate
bis-muth-yl
bi-son
bit-er
bi-tu-men
bi-tu-mi-nous
bi-u-ret
bi-va-lent
biv-ouacked
bi-zarre
black-ened
blad-ed
blam-a-ble
Blan-chard
blanch-er
blan-dish
blan-ket
blar-ney
blas-phe-mous
blas-te-ma
blast-er
blas-tog-e-ny
Blas-to-my-ce-tes
blas-to-my-co-sis
blas-tu-la
bla-tant
blath-er-ing
blaz-er
bla-zon
blem-ish
blend-er
bleph-a-ral
bless-ed (adj.)
blessed (v.)
blind-er
blink-er
blis-ter

bloat-er
block-ade
blon-dine
bloom-er
bloop-er
blu-cher
bludg-eon
bluff-ing
blu-ing
blun-der-er
blus-ter
boat-swain
bob-bi-net
bo-cac-cio
bo-dhi-satt-va
bod-ice
bod-i-ly
bo-gey (golf term)
bo-gie (cart)
bo-gy (specter)
Bo-he-mi-an
boil-er
bois-ter-ous
bo-le-ro
bo-le-tus
Bo-liv-i-an
Bo-lo-gna
bo-lom-e-ter
Bol-she-vi-ki
bol-she-vism
Bol-she-vist
bol-ster
bom-bard-ier
bom-bas-ti-cal
bom-ba-zine
bom-bi-nate
bo-na fi-de
bo-nan-za
Bo-na-parte
bond-age
Bond-er-ize
bo-ni-to
bo-nus
boo-by
boo-dler
Bool-e-an
boo-mer-ang
boor-ish
boost-er
boo-tee
boo-ty
booz-er

bo-rac-ic
bo-ra-cite
bo-rat-ed
bo-rax
Bor-deaux
bor-der
bo-re-al
Bor-ghe-se
bo-ric
bo-ride
Bor-ne-an
bor-ne-ol
born-ite
bor-nyl
bo-ron
bor-ough
Bor-zoi
bos-om
Bos-po-rus
boss-ism
Bos-to-ni-an
bo-tan-i-cal
bot-a-nist
bot-a-ny
both-er-a-tion
bo-tog-e-nin
bot-ry-oi-dal
Bot-swa-na
bot-u-lin-ic
bot-u-lism
bou-cle
bou-doir
Bou-gain-vil-le-a
bouil-la-baisse
bouil-lon
boul-der
bou-le-vard
bound-a-ry
boun-te-ous
bou-quet
Bour-bon-ism
bour-geois
bour-geoi-sie
bou-ton-niere
bo-vine
bowd-ler-ize
bow-ie
boy-sen-ber-ry
bra-ce-ro
brach-i-al
bra-chi-o-la
Brach-i-op-o-da

20

brach-y-ceph-a-lous
bra-chyp-ter-ous
brach-ysm
bra-chyt-ic
brac-ing
brack-et
brack-ish
brac-te-al
brag-ga-do-ci-o
Brah-man-ism
bram-ble
bran-chi-al
bran-chif-er-ous
Bran-chi-op-o-da
brand-er
bran-dish
bra-se-ro
Bra-sí-lia
bras-sid-ic
bras-siere
bra-va-do
brav-er-y
bra-vo
bra-vu-ra
bray-er
bra-zen
bra-zier
braz-il (mining term)
bra-zil (wood, nut)
Bra-zil
Bra-zil-ian
breath-er
brec-ci-a
breez-i-ness
Bre-men
brems-strah-lung
brem-sung
brenn-schluss
breth-ren
Bret-on
bre-vet
bre-vi-ar-y
bre-vier
brev-i-ty
brew-er-y
Brew-ster
brib-er-y
brid-al
bri-dle
bri-dling
bri-er

bri-gade
brig-a-dier
brig-and-age
brig-an-tine
Brigh-ton
bril-liant
brin-dle
Bri-nell
bri-quet-ted
bri-sance
brisk-en
bris-ket
bris-tle
bris-tly
Brit-ain
Bri-tan-ni-a
Brit-ish
broad-cast-er
bro-cade
broc-co-li
bro-chure
broil-er
bro-ken
bro-ker-age
brom-ar-gy-rite
bro-mate
bro-me-lin
bro-mide
bro-mid-ic
bro-mi-dro-sis
bro-min-ate
bro-mi-na-tion
bro-mine
bro-mo-cre-sol
bro-mo-i-o-dide
bro-mo-met-ric
bro-mom-e-try
bron-chi-al
bron-chi-tis
bron-choph-o-ny
bron-chos-co-py
bron-co
bron-tom-e-ter
brood-er
broth-el
broth-er
brows-er
bru-cel-lo-sis
bruc-ine
bruc-ite
bruis-er

bru-tal-ize
brut-ish
bu-bon-ic
buc-ca-neer
buc-ci-na-tor
Bu-chan-an
Bu-cha-rest
buck-et-ful
buck-ler
buck-ling
bu-col-ic
Bu-da-pest
Bud-dha
budg-er-i-gar
budg-et-ar-y
budg-et-eer
Bue-nos Ai-res
buf-fa-lo
buff-er
buf-fet
buff-ing
buf-foon-er-y
bu-gle
bul-ba-ceous
bul-bar
bul-bo-cap-nine
bul-bous
Bul-gar-i-an
bulg-er
bulk-er
bul-late
bull-doz-er
bul-le-tin
bul-lion
bull-ish
bul-lock
bul-ly-ing
bul-rush
bum-bling
bump-er
bump-i-ness
bump-om-e-ter
bump-tious
bun-combe
Bun-des-rat
bun-dler
bun-ga-low
bun-gee
bun-gler
bun-ion
bun-ker-age

bun-kum
bunt-ing (v.)
bun-ting (bird, flag)
buoy-ant
bur-bled
bur-den
bu-reau
bu-reauc-ra-cy
bu-reau-crat-ic
bu-ret
bur-gee
bur-geon
bur-gess
bur-gher
bur-glar-ize
bur-gla-ry
bur-go-mas-ter
Bur-gun-di-an
bur-i-al
bur-ied
bur-lesque

ca-bal
cab-a-la
cab-a-lis-ti-cal
ca-ban-a
ca-bane
cab-a-ret
cab-bage
ca-ber-net
cab-e-zon
cab-i-net
ca-bling
cab-o-chon
ca-boose
cab-o-tage
cab-ri-o-let
ca-bu-ya
ca-ca-o
cach-a-lot
ca-chec-tic
ca-chet
cach-in-na-tion
ca-chou
ca-cique
cack-ling
cac-o-dyl-ic
ca-cog-ra-phy
cac-o-mis-tle
ca-coph-o-ny
cad-a-lene
ca-das-tral

bur-ley
Bur-mese
burn-ers
bur-nish-er
bur-sar
bur-si-tis
Bu-run-di-an
bur-y-ing
bus-es
bush-el
bus-i-ly
busi-ness
bus-kin
bust-er
bus-tling
bu-ta-di-ene
bu-tal-de-hyde
bu-tane
bu-ta-no-ic
bu-ta-nol
butch-er

C

ca-dav-er-ous
ca-delle
ca-dence
ca-den-za
ca-det
cad-i-nene
Ca-diz
cad-mi-um
cad-re
ca-du-ca-ry
ca-du-ce-us
Cae-sar
cae-si-ous
caf-e-te-ri-a
caf-feine
Ca-ga-yan
cais-son
ca-jol-er-y
ca-la-di-um
cal-a-mine
ca-lam-i-tous
ca-lan-dri-a
ca-lash
cal-a-ver-ite
cal-car-e-ous
cal-cif-er-ol
cal-cif-er-ous
cal-ci-fi-ca-tion
cal-cim-e-ter
cal-ci-mine

bu-te-nyl
bu-tox-yl
but-tress
bu-tyl-a-mine
bu-tyl-ene
bu-tyr-a-ceous
bu-tyr-ate
bu-tyr-ic
bu-tyr-in-ase
bu-tyr-o-lac-tone
bu-tyr-om-e-ter
bu-tyr-yl
bux-om
buzz-ard
buzz-er
Byel-o-rus-sia
By-ron-ic
bys-si-no-sis
Byz-an-tine

cal-ci-na-tion
cal-cite
cal-ci-um
cal-cu-la-ble
cal-cu-la-tor
cal-cu-la-to-ry
cal-cu-lus
cal-dron
cal-e-fa-cient
cal-en-dar
cal-en-der
ca-len-du-lin
ca-les-cent
cal-i-ber
cal-i-brat-er
cal-i-bra-tor
ca-li-che
Cal-i-for-ni-an
cal-i-for-ni-um
ca-lig-i-nous
cal-i-per
ca-liph
cal-is-then-ics
calk-er
cal-li-graph-ic
cal-lig-ra-phy
cal-li-o-pe
cal-lous (adj.)

cal-lus (n.)
cal-lus-es
cal-o-mel
cal-o-res-cence
ca-lor-ic
cal-o-rie
ca-lor-i-fa-cient
cal-o-rif-ic
cal-o-rim-e-ter
cal-o-ri-met-ri-cal
cal-o-rize
ca-lum-ni-ate
cal-um-ny
Cal-va-ry
Cal-vin-ism
ca-ly-coid
ca-lyp-so
ca-lyp-tra
ca-lyx
ca-ma-ra-de-rie
cam-a-ril-la
ca-ma-ta
cam-ber
cam-bi-um
Cam-bo-di-an
cam-bric
cam-el-eer
ca-mel-o-pard
Cam-em-bert
cam-e-o
cam-er-a
Cam-e-roon
ca-mion
cam-i-sole
cam-o-mile
Ca-mor-ra
cam-ou-flage
cam-pa-ni-le
camp-er
cam-pha-nyl
cam-phoid
cam-pho-len-ic
cam-pho-ra-ceous
cam-phor-ene
cam-phor-ic
cam-pim-e-ter
cam-pus
Ca-naan
Can-a-da
Ca-na-di-an
ca-nai-gre
ca-naille

ca-nal-i-za-tion
ca-na-pe
ca-nard
ca-nar-y
ca-nas-ta
Ca-nav-er-al
can-celed
can-cel-ing
can-cel-la-tion
can-cer-ous
can-croid
can-de-la
can-de-la-brum
can-de-li-lla
can-did
can-di-date
can-died
can-dling
can-dor
ca-nes-cent
ca-nic-o-la
ca-nine
can-is-ter
can-ker
can-na-bi-nol
can-na-bis
can-ner-y
can-ni-bal-ize
can-non-ade
can-nu-lar
ca-noe-ist
can-on
ca-ñon (Spanish form for canyon)
can-on-ess
ca-non-i-cal
can-on-i-za-tion
Ca-no-pus
can-o-py
can-ta-bi-le
can-ta-loup
can-tan-ker-ous
can-ta-ta
can-ter (v.)
cant-er (n.)
can-thar-i-des
can-tha-ris
can-thus
can-ti-cle
can-ti-le-ver
can-ton-ment
Ca-nuck

can-vassed
can-vass-er
caou-tchouc
ca-pa-ble
ca-pa-cious
ca-pac-i-tance
ca-pac-i-tor
ca-par-i-son
cap-e-lin
ca-per
ca-pi-as
cap-il-la-ros-co-py
cap-il-lar-y
cap-i-tal-ist
cap-i-tal-i-za-tion
ca-pi-tan
ca-pit-u-la-tor
cap-no-di-um
ca-pon-ette
ca-pote
cap-ric
ca-pric-cio
ca-price
ca-pri-cious
Cap-ri-cor-nis
cap-ro-ate
ca-pro-ic
cap-ry-late
ca-pryl-ic
cap-ry-lyl
cap-sa-i-cin
cap-si-cum
cap-stan
cap-su-lar
cap-ti-va-tor
cap-u-chin
cap-y-bar-a
car-a-bao
car-a-bi-neer
Ca-ra-cas
car-a-cul
ca-rafe
car-a-mel
car-a-pace
car-at
car-a-van-sa-ry
car-a-way
carb-ac-i-dom-e-ter
carb-alk-ox-yl
car-ba-mate
car-bam-ic
car-bam-ide

23

carb-am-i-do-hy-dan-to-in
car-ba-mine
carb-am-i-no
car-bam-o-yl
car-ba-nil-ic
car-ba-nil-ide
car-bar-sone
car-baz-ic
car-ba-zole
car-beth-ox-y1
car-bine
car-bi-nol
car-bo-cy-a-nine
car-bo-cy-clic
car-bo-di-i-mide
car-bol-ic
car-bo-lize
Car-bo-loy
car-bo-na-ceous
car-bon-ate
car-bon-ic
car-bon-if-er-ous
car-bo-ni-um
car-bon-ize
car-bon-yl
car-bon-y-late
Car-bo-run-dum
car-box-yl-ase
car-box-yl-ic
car-bun-cle
car-bu-rant
car-bu-ret-ed
car-bu-ret-or
car-bu-riz-er
car-byl-a-mine
car-cass
car-cin-o-gen
car-ci-no-gen-ic
car-ci-noid
car-ci-no-ma
car-ci-no-ma-to-sis
car-ci-nom-a-tous
car-ci-no-sis
car-da-mom
car-di-ac
Car-di-a-zol
car-di-nal
card-ing
car-di-o-gen-ic
car-di-og-ra-phy
car-di-oid
car-di-ol-o-gy

car-di-om-e-ter
car-di-ot-o-my
car-di-tis
ca-reen
ca-reer
ca-ress-ive
car-et
Car-ib-be-an
car-i-bou
car-i-ca-tur-al
car-ies
car-il-lon-neur
ca-ri-na
car-i-nate
car-i-ous
Car-list
Car-mel-ite
car-min-a-tive
car-min-ic
car-nage
car-nal-i-ty
car-nau-ba
Car-ne-gie
car-ne-lian
car-ni-tine
car-ni-val
car-niv-o-rous
car-no-tite
car-oled
Car-o-lin-i-an
car-om
car-o-tene
ca-rot-e-noid
ca-rot-id
ca-rous-al
Car-pa-thi-an
car-pel
car-pen-try
carp-er
car-pho-lite
car-pho-sid-er-ite
car-po-go-ni-um
car-riage
car-ri-on
car-ron-ade
car-rou-sel
cart-age
car-tel-ize
car-ti-lag-i-nous
car-tog-ra-phy
car-ton
car-toon-ist

car-touche
car-tridge
car-un-cle
car-vene
carv-er
Car-ver
car-y-at-id
car-y-op-sis
ca-sa-ba
Ca-sa-blan-ca
cas-car-a
ca-sein-ate
ca-se-ous
cash-ew
cash-ier
cas-ing
ca-si-no
cas-ket
cas-se-role
cas-si-mere
Cas-si-o-pe-ian
cas-sit-er-ite
cas-ta-net
cas-tel-late
cast-er
cas-ti-ga-tor
cas-tile
Cas-til-ian
cas-tle
cas-tor-ite
cas-tra-tive
cas-u-al-ty
cas-u-ist-ry
ca-sus bel-li
cat-a-bol-ic
ca-tab-o-lism
cat-a-clys-mic
cat-a-di-op-tric
cat-a-falque
cat-a-lase
cat-a-lec-tic
cat-a-lep-tic
cat-a-loged
cat-a-log-ing
ca-tal-y-sis
cat-a-lyst
cat-a-lyt-i-cal-ly
cat-a-lyz-er
cat-a-ma-ran
cat-a-me-ni-al
cat-a-pult
cat-a-ract

24

ca-tarrh-al
ca-tas-tro-phe
cat-a-stroph-ic
Ca-taw-ba
cat-e-che-sis
cat-e-chet-i-cal
cat-e-chism
cat-e-chu-men-al
cat-e-chol
ca-te-na
cat-e-gor-i-cal
cat-e-go-rize
cat-e-nar-y
cat-e-noid
ca-ter-er
cat-er-pil-lar
cat-er-waul
ca-thar-sis
ca-thar-tic
Ca-thar-ti-dae
ca-thec-tic
ca-the-dral
ca-thep-sin
cath-e-ter-i-za-tion
cath-e-tom-e-ter
cath-ode
ca-thod-ic
cath-o-lic-i-ty
ca-thol-i-cism
cat-i-on-ic
Cau-ca-sian
cau-cus
cau-dal
cau-di-llo
cau-li-flow-er
caus-al
cau-sal-i-ty
cau-sa-tion
caus-a-tive
cause ce-le-bre
cau-se-rie
caus-tic-i-ty
cau-ter-i-za-tion
cav-al-cade
cav-a-lier
cav-al-ry
cav-a-ti-na
ca-ve-at
cav-ern-ous
cav-i-ar
cav-iled
cav-il-er

cav-i-ta-tion
Ca-vi-te
cav-i-ty
ca-vort
cay-enne
Ca-yu-ga
Cay-use
ce-cum
ce-dar
ce-drat
ce-drol
ce-du-la
ceil-om-e-ter
Cel-an-ese
Cel-e-bes
cel-e-brate
ce-leb-ri-ty
ce-ler-i-ty
cel-er-y
ce-les-tial
cel-es-tite
ce-li-ac
cel-i-ba-cy
ce-li-ot-o-my
ce-lite
cel-lif-er-ous
cel-lo-phane
cel-lu-lar
cel-lu-loid
cel-lu-lose
cel-lu-los-ic
Cel-si-us
Celt-ic
cel-ti-um
ce-men-ta-tion
ce-ment-er
ce-ment-ite
ce-men-ti-tious
cem-e-ter-y
ce-no-bi-an
cen-o-bite
Ce-no-zo-ic
cen-so-ri-ous
Cen-tau-rus
cen-ta-vo
cen-te-nar-i-an
cen-te-nar-y
cen-ten-ni-al
cen-tes-i-mal
cen-te-si-mo
cent-ge-ner
cen-ti-me-ter

cen-ti-pede
cen-tral-ize
cen-trif-u-gal
cen-tri-fuge
cen-trip-e-tal
cen-troi-dal
cen-tu-ry
ce-phal-ic
ceph-a-lin
ceph-a-lo-di-um
ceph-a-lom-e-ter
ceph-a-lom-e-try
Ceph-e-id
ce-ram-ic
ce-ram-ist
ce-ram-i-um
ce-ra-ti-um
cer-a-to-sau-rus
Cer-ber-us
ce-re-al
cer-e-bel-lo-ru-bral
cer-e-bel-lum
cer-e-bral
cer-e-brate
cer-e-bro-side
cer-e-bro-spi-nal
cer-e-brum
cere-ment
cer-e-mo-ni-al
Ce-ren-kov
Ce-res
cer-e-sin
ce-rise
ce-rite
ce-ri-um
ce-ro-graph
ce-rog-ra-phy
ce-roid
ce-ro-lite
ce-rot-ic
cer-tain-ly
cer-tif-i-cate
cer-ti-fi-ca-tion
cer-ti-o-ra-ri
cer-ti-tude
ce-ru-le-an
ce-ru-men
ce-russ-ite
cer-van-tite
cer-vi-cal
ce-sar-e-an
ce-si-um

25

ces-sa-tion
Ce-ta-ce-a
ce-tane
ce-tene
ce-tyl
Cha-blis
Chad-i-an
chaf-er
chaff-er (one who chaffs or banters)
chaf-fer (trade term— buying and selling)
Cha-gres
cha-grin
chair-maned
chaise longue
chal-ced-o-ny
chal-ce-don-yx
chal-co-py-rite
chal-dron
cha-let
chal-ice
chal-i-co-sis
cha-lyb-e-ate
cham-ber-lain
cham-bray
cha-me-le-on
cham-fer
cham-ois
cham-pi-gnon
cham-pi-on
chan-cel-ler-y
chan-cel-lor
chan-cer-y
chan-cre
chan-croi-dal
chan-de-lier
chan-delle
chan-dler
change-a-ble
chang-er
chan-neled
chan-teur
chan-ti-cleer
cha-ot-ic
chap-ar-ral
cha-peau
chap-el
chap-er-on
chap-lain
char-a-banc
char-ac-ter-is-tic

cha-rade
charge-a-ble
char-gé d'af-faires
charg-er
char-i-ly
char-i-ness
char-i-ot-eer
cha-ris-ma
char-is-mat-ic
char-i-ta-ble
cha-ri-va-ri
Char-ley
Char-lotte
charm-er
char-nel
char-ter
char-treuse
Cha-ryb-dis
chas-er
chas-sis
chas-ten
chas-tis-er
chas-ti-ty
cha-teau
cha-te-laine
Chat-ham
cha-toy-an-cy
Chau-ce-ri-an
chau-tau-qua
chau-vin-ism
check-ered
chedd-ite
Che-ha-lis
chei-li-tis
Che-ka
che-la-tion
chel-i-do-ni-um
che-li-form
che-lo-ne
Chel-ten-ham
chem-i-at-ric
chem-i-cal
che-mig-ra-phy
che-mise
chem-i-sette
chem-is-try
chem-o-sphere
chem-o-ther-a-py
che-mot-ro-pism
che-mur-gic
chem-ur-gy
che-nille

Che-no-po-di-um
cher-ish
cher-no-zem
Cher-o-kee
che-root
cher-ub
che-rub-ble
cher-u-bim
Chesh-ire
Ches-ter
chev-a-lier
chev-i-ot
chev-ron
Chey-enne
chi-a-ro-scu-ro
chi-ca-ner-y
chick-en
chi-cle
chic-o-ry
chif-fon
chif-fo-nier
chi-gnon
chil-dren
Chil-e-an
chi-me-ra
chi-mer-i-cal
chim-pan-zee
Chi-nese
chi-noi-se-rie
Chi-nook
chin-qua-pin
Chi-ri-qui
chi-ro-graph
chi-rog-ra-pher
chi-ro-man-cy
chi-rop-o-dy
chi-ro-prac-tor
chi-rur-gi-cal
chis-eled
chis-el-ing
chi-tin-oid
chiv-al-rous
chlo-ral
chlor-al-um
chlor-a-lu-mi-nite
chlor-am-ide
chlor-am-ine
chlor-am-phen-i-col
chlo-rate
chlor-az-ide
chlor-co-sane
Chlo-rel-la

26

chlor-e-mi-a
chlor-en-chy-ma
Chlo-re-tone
chlo-ric
chlo-ride
chlo-ri-dize
chlor-im-ide
chlo-ri-nate (v.)
chlo-rin-ate (n.)
chlo-rine
chlo-rit-ic
chlo-ro-form
chlo-ro-gen-ic
chlo-rom-e-ter
chlo-rom-e-try
Chlo-ro-my-ce-tin
chlo-ro-phyll
chlo-ro-prene
chlo-ro-sis
chlo-ro-then
chlo-rous
choc-o-late
choic-est
chok-er
cho-lan-ic
chol-an-threne
cho-le-ate
cho-le-cal-cif-er-ol
cho-le-cys-tec-to-my
cho-le-cys-ti-tis
cho-le-cys-tog-ra-phy
cho-le-cys-to-ki-nin
cho-le-cys-tos-to-my
cho-le-ic
cho-le-mi-a
chol-er
chol-er-a
cho-le-ret-ic
chol-er-ic
cho-les-tane
cho-les-ta-nol
cho-les-ter-ic
cho-les-ter-ol
cho-lic
cho-lin-er-gic
cho-lin-es-ter-ase
chol-o-ge-net-ic
cho-los-co-py
chon-dri-o-som-al
chon-dri-o-some
chon-drit-ic
chon-dro-dite

chon-dro-dit-ic
chon-dro-ma
chon-drom-a-tous
chon-drot-o-my
chon-drule
cho-ral
cho-rale
chord-al
chor-date
chor-di-tis
chor-dot-o-my
cho-re-a
cho-re-og-ra-pher
cho-ri-o-men-in-gi-tis
cho-ri-sis
cho-ris-ter
cho-roi-dal
cho-roid-i-tis
cho-rol-o-gy
chor-tle
cho-rus
cho-sen
chow-der
chres-tom-a-thy
chris-ten
Chris-tian
Chris-ti-an-i-ty
chro-ma-mom-e-ter
chro-mate
chro-mat-ic
chro-ma-tic-i-ty
chro-ma-tin
chro-mat-o-gram
chro-ma-tog-ra-phy
chro-ma-tol-y-sis
chro-mat-o-lyt-ic
chro-mat-o-scope
chro-ma-to-sis
chro-mic
chro-mif-er-ous
chro-mi-nance
chro-mite
chro-mi-um
chro-mo-gen-ic
chro-mo-i-so-mer-ic
chro-mom-e-ter
chro-mos-co-py
chro-mo-som-al
chro-mo-trop-ic
chro-mous
chron-i-cler
chron-o-graph

chro-nog-ra-pher
chro-nol-o-ger
chron-o-log-i-cal-ly
chro-nol-o-gy
chro-nom-e-ter
chron-o-met-ri-cal
chro-nom-e-try
chron-o-scope
chro-nos-co-py
chrys-a-lis
chrys-a-loid
chrys-an-the-mum
chrys-a-ro-bin
chrys-a-zin
chry-sene
chrys-o-er-i-ol
chrys-o-graph
chry-sog-ra-phy
chry-so-i-dine
chrys-o-lite
chrys-o-phyll
chuck-ling
Church-ill
churl-ish
chut-ist
chy-la-ceous
chy-lo-sis
chy-mi-fy
chy-mo-tryp-sin
ci-ca-da
cic-a-tri-sive
cic-a-trix
cic-a-trize
cic-e-ro-ne (n.)
cic-e-rone (v.)
ci-der
ci-gar
cig-a-rette
cil-i-ar-y
cil-i-um
ci-mi-cid
cim-o-lite
cin-cho-loi-pon
cin-cho-me-ron-ic
cin-cho-na
cin-chon-a-mine
cin-cho-nine
cin-cho-phen
cinc-ture
Cin-der-el-la
cin-e-ma
cin-e-mat-o-graph

27

cin-e-ma-tog-ra-pher
cin-e-ole
cin-e-rar-i-a
ci-ne-re-ous
cin-na-bar
cin-nam-ic
cin-nam-o-yl
ci-pher
ci-pho-ny
cir-ci-nate
cir-clet
cir-cling
circ-o-var-i-an
cir-cuit-al
cir-cuit-er
cir-cu-i-tous
cir-cuit-ry
cir-cu-lar-ize
cir-cu-la-to-ry
cir-cum-e-ter
cir-cum-fer-en-tial
cir-cum-lo-cu-tion
cir-cum-loc-u-to-ry
cir-cum-scrib-a-ble
cir-cum-stan-tial
cir-rho-sis
cis-tern
cit-a-ble
ci-ta-to-ry
cit-i-fy
cit-i-zen
cit-ral
cit-rate
cit-ric
cit-ri-nin
cit-ron
cit-ron-el-la
cit-rus
civ-et
civ-il
ci-vil-ian
civ-i-li-za-tion
claim-ant
clam-or-ous
clan-des-tine
clang-or
cla-queur
Clar-ence
clar-et
clar-i-fi-ca-tion
clar-i-net
clar-i-on

clas-si-cal
clas-si-fy
clas-tic
claus-tro-pho-bi-a
clav-a-cin
clav-i-cle
cla-vic-u-lar
cleans-er
cleans-ing
clear-ance
cleav-age
Clem-a-tis
clem-en-cy
Clem-en-tine
Cle-o-pa-tra
cler-gy-man
cler-i-cal
clev-er
clev-is
cli-an-thus
click-er
cli-ent-age
cli-en-tele
cli-mac-ter-ic
cli-mac-tic
cli-mat-ic
cli-ma-tize
cli-ma-to-log-i-cal
cli-ma-tol-o-gy
cli-ma-tom-e-ter
cli-max
climb-er
clin-i-cal
cli-ni-cian
clin-i-co-path-o-log-ic
clin-i-co-pa-thol-o-gy
clink-er
cli-no-he-dral
cli-nom-e-ter
cli-quish
clit-o-ris
cloi-son-ne
clois-ter
Clo-rox
Clos-trid-i-um
clo-sure
cloth-ier
clo-ture
clo-ven
clo-ver
clown-ish
clum-si-ness

clus-ter
cne-mi-al
co-ad-ju-tor
co-ag-u-la-tor
co-ag-u-lom-e-ter
co-a-les-cence
co-a-lite (v.)
Coal-ite (n.)
co-a-li-tion
co-arc-ta-tion
coast-al
coast-er
co-bal-a-min
co-bal-tic
co-balt-if-er-ous
co-bal-ti-ni-trite
co-bal-to-cal-cite
co-bal-tom-e-nite
co-bal-tous
cob-bler
co-bra
co-caine
coc-cid-i-oi-dal
coc-cid-i-oi-din
coc-cid-i-o-sis
coc-cin-ic
coc-ci-nite
coc-cyg-e-al
co-chin
coch-i-neal
coch-le-ar
cock-ade
cock-er-el
cock-le-bur
co-coa
co-co-nut
co-coon
co-deine
codg-er
cod-i-cil
cod-i-fy
co-di-mer
cod-ling
co-erc-i-ble
co-er-cive
co-e-val
co-gen-cy
cog-i-ta-tive
co-gnac
cog-na-tus
cog-ni-tive
cog-ni-za-ble

cog-no-men
co-gno-scen-ti
cog-nos-ci-ble
co-her-ence
co-he-si-ble
co-he-sive
co-in-ci-den-tal
col-an-der
col-chi-cine
Col-chi-cum
co-lec-ti-vo
col-ec-to-my
Co-le-op-te-ra
col-ick-y
col-i-se-um
co-li-tis
col-lab-o-ra-tor
col-la-gen-ase
col-lag-e-nous
col-laps-i-ble
col-lat-er-al
col-la-tor
col-league
col-lect-a-ble
col-lec-ta-ne-a
col-lec-tive
col-lec-tor
col-le-gi-ate
col-lier
col-li-ma-tor
col-li-sion
col-lo-di-on
col-loi-dal
col-lo-qui-al-ism
col-lo-quy
col-lu-sive
col-lu-vi-um
co-logne
Co-lom-bi-an
co-lo-met-ric
co-lom-e-try
co-lon
colo-nel
co-lo-ni-al
co-lon-ic
col-o-nize
col-on-nade
col-o-ny
col-o-phon
col-o-pho-ny
col-or
Col-o-rad-an

Col-o-ra-do
col-or-a-tu-ra
col-or-im-e-ter
col-or-i-met-ric
col-or-im-e-try
co-los-sal
Col-os-se-um
co-los-sus
co-los-to-my
co-los-trum
col-por-teur
Co-lum-bi-a
col-um-bif-er-ous
col-um-bine
co-lum-bite
co-lum-bi-um
col-umn
co-lum-nar
col-um-nist
co-lure
Co-man-che
co-ma-tose
co-mat-u-la
com-bat-ant
com-bat-ed
com-bat-ing
com-bat-ive-ness
com-ba-tiv-i-ty
comb-er
com-bin-a-ble
com-bi-na-tive
com-bu-rim-e-ter
com-bus-ti-ble
com-bus-tor
co-me-di-an
com-e-dy
co-mes-ti-ble
com-e-tar-y
co-met-ic
com-fort-a-ble
com-fort-er
com-i-cal
Com-in-form
com-ing
co-mique
com-i-ty
com-man-dant
com-man deer
com-mand-er
com-man-do
com-mem-o-ra-tor
com-mend-a-ble

com-men-da-tion
com-mend-a-to-ry
com-men-su-ra-ble
com-men-tar-y
com-men-ta-tor
com-mer-cial
com-mi-na-to-ry
com-min-gle
com-mi-nute
com-mis-er-ate
com-mis-sar-i-at
com-mis-sar-y
com-mis-sion
com-mis-sur-al
com-mis-sur-ot-o-my
com-mit-ta-ble
com-mit-tee
com-mo-di-ous
com-mod-i-ty
com-mon-er
com-mon-sen-si-ble
com-mo-rant
com-mu-nal
com-mu-ni-ca-tive
com-mu-ni-ca-tor
com-mun-ion
com-mu-ni-que
com-mu-nism
Com-mu-nist
com-mu-nis-tic
com-mu-ni-ty
com-mut-a-ble
com-mu-ta-tion
com-mu-ta-tor
com-mut-er
com-pact-er
com-pact-i-ble
com-pac-tor
com-pan-ion
com-pa-ny
com-pa-ra-ble
com-par-a-tive
com-par-a-tor
com-par-i-son
com-par-o-scope
com-part-men-tal-ize
com-pat-i-ble
com-pel-ling
com-pen-di-um
com-pen-sa-ble
com-pen-sat-ing
com-pen-sa-to-ry

com-pe-tent
com-pe-ti-tion
com-pet-i-tor
com-pi-la-tion
com-pil-er
com-pla-cent
com-plain-ant
com-plai-sance
com-ple-men-tal
com-ple-men-ta-ry
com-ple-tive
com-plex-ion
com-pli-cate
com-plic-i-ty
com-pli-men-ta-ry
com-po-nent
com-pos-er
com-pos-ite
com-po-si-tion
com-pos-i-tor
com-po-sure
com-pound-er
com-pre-hend-i-ble
com-pre-hen-si-ble
com-press-i-ble
com-press-ing
com-pres-sive
com-pres-som-e-ter
com-pres-sor
com-pris-al
com-pro-mise
Comp-tom-e-ter
comp-trol-ler
com-pul-so-ry
com-put-er
com-put-ist
co-nal
co-na-tion
con-cat-e-na-tion
con-cav-er
con-ceiv-a-ble
con-cen-tra-tor
con-cen-tri-cal
con-cen-tric-i-ty
con-cep-tu-al
con-cer-ti-na
con-cert-ize
con-ces-sion-aire
con-chi-form
con-choi-dal
con-cho-log-i-cal
con-chol-o-gy

con-chyl-i-um
con-cil-i-a-to-ry
con-clu-sive
con-coct-er
con-com-i-tant
con-cord-ance
con-cord-ant
con-cres-cence
con-cret-er
con-cu-bi-nage
con-cu-pis-cence
con-cu-pis-ci-ble
con-dem-na-to-ry
con-den-sa-ble
con-den-sa-tion
con-dens-er
con-dens-ing
con-de-scen-sion
con-di-ment
con-do-lence
con-do-min-i-um
con-don-ance
con-duc-i-ble
con-du-cive
con-duct-ance
con-duct-ed
con-duct-i-ble
con-duc-tiv-i-ty
con-duc-tom-e-ter
con-duc-tor
con-duit
con-du-ran-gin
con-dy-loid
con-el-rad
Con-es-to-ga
con-fec-tion-er-y
con-fed-er-a-tion
con-fes-sor
con-fi-dant (n.)
con-fi-dent (adj.)
con-fig-u-ra-tion
con-fin-er
con-firm-a-ble
con-fir-ma-tion
con-firm-a-to-ry
con-firm-er
con-fis-ca-to-ry
con-fla-gra-tion
con-flic-tive
con-flux-i-ble
con-form-a-ble
con-for-ma-tion

con-form-i-ty
Con-fu-cian-ism
con-fus-a-ble
con-fut-a-ble
con-fu-ta-tion
con-ge-la-tive
con-gel-i-fract
con-ge-ner
con-ge-nial
con-ge-ni-al-i-ty
con-gen-i-tal
con-ge-ries
con-gest-i-ble
con-glom-er-at-ic
Con-go-lese
con-grat-u-la-to-ry
con-gre-ga-tor
con-gres-sion-al
con-gru-i-ty
con-i-cal
co-nic-e-ine
co-nid-i-um
con-i-fer
co-nif-er-ous
Co-ni-oph-o-ra
co-ni-um
con-jec-tur-al
con-ju-gal
con-ju-gate
con-junc-ti-vi-tis
con-ju-ra-tion
con-jur-er
con-nect-a-ble
con-nect-er
Con-nect-i-cut-er
con-nec-tive
con-niv-ance
con-nois-seur
con-nu-bi-al
co-noi-dal
co-no-phor
con-quer-or
con-quin-a-mine
con-san-guin-e-ous
con-sci-en-tious
con-scion-a-ble
con-scious
con-se-cra-tor
con-sec-u-tive
con-se-nes-cence
con-sen-sus
con-se-quen-tial

con-ser-va-tion
con-serv-a-tive
con-ser-va-tor
con-serv-a-to-ry
con-sid-er-ate
con-sig-na-tion
con-sign-ee
con-sign-or
con-sist-ent
con-sis-to-ry
con-so-la-tion
con-sol-i-date
con-som-me
con-so-nant
con-sor-ti-um
con-spi-cu-i-ty
con-spic-u-ous
con-spir-a-cy
con-spi-ra-tion
con-sta-ble
con-stab-u-lar-y
con-stan-cy
con-stant-an
con-ster-na-tion
con-sti-pa-tion
con-stit-u-ent
con-sti-tu-tive
con-stric-tor
con-struc-tor
con-sul-ar
con-sul-ate
con-sult-ant
con-sul-ta-tion
con-sult-a-tive
con-sult-er
con-sum-er
con-sum-mate
con-sum-ma-to-ry
con-sump-ti-ble
con-tac-tor
con-ta-gious
con-tam-i-na-tor
con-tem-pla-tor
con-tem-po-ra-ne-ous
con-tempt-i-ble
con-temp-tu-ous
con-tend-er
con-ten-tious
con-test-ant
con-tes-ta-tion
con-tex-tur-al
con-ti-gu-i-ty

con-tig-u-ous
con-ti-nence
con-ti-nen-tal
con-tin-gen-cy
con-ti-nu-i-ty
con-tin-u-ous
con-tin-u-um
con-tor-tive
con-tra-band
con-tract-a-ble
con-tract-ile
con-trac-tor
con-tra-dict-er
con-tra-dic-tor
con-tra-dic-to-ry
con-trail
con-tra-ri-e-ty
con-trar-i-wise
con-tras-tive
con-trib-ut-ing
con-tri-bu-tion
con-trib-u-tor
con-triv-ance
con-triv-er
con-trol-la-ble
con-tro-ver-sy
con-tro-vert-i-ble
con-tu-ma-cious
con-tu-me-li-ous
con-tu-me-ly
con-tu-sion
co-nun-drum
co-nus
con-va-les-cence
con-vec-tor
con-ven-ience
con-ven-ien-cy
con-ver-gent
con-verg-ing
con-vers-a-ble
con-ver-sant
con-ver-sive
con-vert-er
con-vert-i-ble
con-vey-or
con-vic-tive
con-vin-ci-ble
con-vinc-ing
con-viv-i-al
con-vo-lute
con-vul-sive
con-y-rine

cool-ant
cool-er
Coo-lidge
coo-lie
coop-er-age
co-op-er-a-tive
co-or-di-na-tor
coot-ie
co-pai-ba
co-pal-ite
Co-pen-ha-gen
Co-per-ni-cus
cop-ies
co-pi-ous
co-pla-nar
co-pol-y-mer
co-po-lym-er-ize
co-pra
cop-ro-por-phy-rin
cop-ro-stane
co-pros-ta-nol
co-pros-ter-ol
cop-u-la-tive
co-quet-ry
co-quet-tish
co-qui-na
cor-al
Cor-a-mine
cord-age
cor-date
cor-dial
cor-dial-i-ty
cor-dil-le-ra
cord-ite
Cor-do-ba
cor-don
cor-do-van
cor-du-roy
cor-dyl-ite
co-re-op-sis
co-re-spond-ent
co-ri-a-ceous
co-ri-an-der
Cor-i-ci-din
Cor-inth
Co-rin-thi-an
cor-i-o-lis
cor-mo-rant
cor-mus
cor-ne-al
cor-nered
cor-net-ist

cor-nice
cor-nif-ic
Cor-nish
cor-nu-co-pi-a
co-rol-la
cor-ol-lar-y
co-ro-na
cor-o-nal
cor-o-nar-y
cor-o-na-tion
cor-o-nene
cor-o-ner
cor-o-net
co-ro-ni-um
cor-po-ral
cor-po-ra-tive
cor-po-re-al
cor-pu-lent
cor-pus-cle
cor-pus-cu-lar
cor-rect-a-ble
cor-rect-ant
cor-rec-tive
cor-rec-tor
cor-re-late
cor-rel-a-tive
cor-re-spond-ence
cor-ri-dor
cor-ri-gen-dum
cor-ri-gi-ble
cor-rob-o-ra-to-ry
cor-rod-i-ble
cor-ro-si-ble
cor-ro-sive
cor-ru-ga-tor
cor-rupt-i-ble
cor-rup-tive
cor-sage
corse-let
cor-tege
cor-ti-cate
cor-ti-cip-e-tal
cor-ti-ci-um
cor-ti-co-ad-re-nal-o-
    trop-ic
cor-ti-cos-ter-one
cor-ti-sone
co-run-dum
co-rus-cant
cor-us-ca-tion
cor-vus-ite
co-ryd-a-line

cor-ym-bose
cor-y-phee
co-ry-za
co-sa-lite
co-se-cant
co-sine
cos-me-col-o-gy
cos-met-i-cal
cos-me-ti-cian
cos-me-tol-o-gy
cos-mi-cal-i-ty
cos-mism
cos-mo-gon-ic
cos-mog-o-ny
cos-mog-ra-pher
cos-mo-graph-ic
Cos-mo-line
cos-mol-o-gy
cos-mo-naut
cos-mo-pol-i-tan
cos-mop-o-lite
cos-mo-ra-ma
cos-mo-ram-ic
cos-mos-o-phy
cos-mo-tron
Cos-ta Ri-can
cos-tive
cos-tum-er
co-tar-nine
co-te-rie
co-ter-mi-nous
co-til-lion
co-to-ne-as-ter
cot-tag-er
cot-y-le-don
couch-ant
cou-lomb
cou-lom-e-ter
cou-ma-rin
cou-ma-rone
coun-cil-or
coun-seled
coun-sel-or
coun-te-nance
count-er (who counts)
coun-ter (other mean-
    ings)
coun-ter-feit
count-ess
coun-try
coun-ty
cou-pler

cou-plet
cou-pling
cou-pon
cour-age
cou-ra-geous
cou-rant
cou-ri-er
cours-er
cour-te-ous
cour-te-san
cour-te-sy
cour-tier
cous-in
cou-tu-ri-er
cou-vert
cov-e-nant-er
cov-e-nan-tor (law)
Cov-en-try
cov-er-age
cov-ert-ly
cov-et-ous
cov-ey
cox-i-tis
Cox-sack-ie
cow-ard-ice
cowl-ing
coy-ote
coz-en
co-zi-ness
crack-ers
crack-ling
cra-dling
cra-nid-i-um
cra-ni-ec-to-my
cra-ni-o-graph
cra-ni-og-ra-pher
cra-ni-ol-o-gy
cra-ni-om-e-ter
cra-ni-os-co-py
cra-ni-um
cra-ter-i-form
cra-tic-u-lar
cra-vat
Cra-ven-ette
crawl-er
cray-on
cra-zy
cream-er-y
creas-er
cre-at-ic
cre-a-tine
cre-at-i-nine

cre-a-tiv-i-ty
crea-ture
cre-den-tial
cre-den-za
cred-i-ble
cred-it-a-ble
cred-i-tor
cre-do
cre-du-li-ty
cred-u-lous
creed-ite
creep-er
cre-ma-to-ry
Cre-mo-na
cre-nate
cren-a-ture
cren-eled
cren-el-lat-ed
cre-nit-ic
cren-u-lat-ed
cre-oph-a-gous
cre-o-sol
cre-o-sote
crep-i-tant
cre-pus-cu-lar
cre-scen-do
cres-cen-tic
cre-sol
cre-sor-ci-nol
cre-sot-ic
cres-o-tine
cres-yl-ate
cres-yl-ic
cre-ta-ceous
cre-tin-ism
cre-tonne
cre-vasse
crev-ice
cre-vic-u-lar
crib-el-late
cri-bel-lum
cri-ce-tus
crick-et-er
cri-coid
Cri-me-an
crim-i-nal-i-ty
crim-i-no-log-ic
crim-i-nol-o-gy
crim-i-not-ic
cring-er
crin-kle
cri-noi-dal

crin-o-line
cri-nos-i-ty
crip-pling
cris-pate
crisp-er
cris-tate
cri-te-ri-a
crit-i-cal
crit-i-cism
cri-tique
croak-er
cro-ce-tin
cro-cheted
cro-chet-ing
cro-cid-o-lite
croc-o-dile
croc-o-ite
cro-con-ic
cro-ny-ism
cro-qui-gnole
cro-ta-lar-i-o-sis
crotch-et-y
cro-ton-ate
cro-ton-o-yl
crou-pi-er
croup-ous
crou-ton
cru-cial
cru-ci-ble
cru-ci-fix
cru-ci-form
cru-di-ty
cruis-er
crul-ler
crum-bling
crum-ple
cru-ral
cru-sad-er
crus-ta-ceous
crust-al
crus-tose
cry-o-gen-ics
cry-om-e-ter
cry-o-phil-ic
cry-oph-o-rus
cry-os-co-py
crypt-a-nal-y-sis
cryp-ta-rithm
cryp-ti-cal
cryp-to-gram-mic
cryp-tog-ra-pher
cryp-to-graph-ic

cryp-tom-e-ter
crys-taled
crys-tal-lin-i-ty
crys-tal-lite
crys-tal-li-za-tion
crys-tal-liz-er
crys-tal-log-ra-phy
crys-tal-loi-dal
cten-o-phore
cte-tol-o-gy
cu-bi-cal
cu-bic-u-lum
cub-ism
cub-ist
cu-bi-tal
cu-bi-tus
cu-boi-dal
cuck-old
cuck-oo
cudg-eled
cui-rass
cui-sine
cul-i-nar-y
cull-ing
cul-mi-na-tion
cu-lotte
cul-pa-ble
cul-prit
cult-ism
cul-ti-va-tor
cul-tur-al
cu-mal-de-hyde
cum-ber-some
cum-brous
cu-mene
cu-me-nyl
cu-mic
cu-mi-dine
cum-in
cu-min-o-in
cu-mi-nol
cu-mi-nyl
cu-mo-yl
cu-mu-la-tive
cu-mu-lene
cu-mu-lo-nim-bus
cu-mu-lus
cu-ne-ate
cu-ne-i-form
cu-no-ni-a-ceous
cu-pid-i-ty
cu-po-la

33

cu-pram-mo-ni-um
cu-pre-ine
cu-pre-ous
cu-pric
cu-prif-er-ous
cu-prite
cu-pro-cy-a-nide
cu-proid
cu-pro-ri-va-ite
cu-prous
cur-a-ble
Cu-ra-çao
cu-ra-re
cu-rate
cu-ra-tive
cu-ra-tor
cur-cu-min
cur-dle
cu-rette
cur-few
cu-rie
cu-rine
cu-ri-os-i-ty
cu-ri-o-so
cu-ri-ous
cu-rite
cu-ri-um
curl-i-cue
curl-i-ness
cur-mudg eon
cur-ric-u-lums
cur-sive
cur-so-ry
cur-tain
cur-te-sy
cur-va-ceous
cur-va-ture
cur-vet-ted
cur-vi-lin-e-ar
cur-vom-e-ter
cush-ioned
cus-pa-rine
cus-pi-dal
cus-pi-dor
cuss-ed-ness
cus-tard

dachs-hund
Da-cron
dac-tyl-ic
dac-tyl-o-graph
dac-ty-log-ra-phy

cus-to-di-an
cus-tom-ar-i-ly
cus-tom-ar-y
cus-tom-er
cu-ta-ne-ous
cu-ti-cle
cu-tic-u-lar
cy-an-a-mide
cy-a-nate
cy-an-e-ous
cy-an-ic
cy-a-ni-da-tion
cy-a-nide
cy-an-i-din
cy-a-nite
cy-an-o-gen
cy-a-no-ge-net-ic
cy-a-no-gua-ni-dine
cy-a-no-hy-drin
cy-a-nom-e-ter
cy-a-no-met-ric
cy-a-nope
cy-a-no-phy-cin
cy-a-no-sis
cy-a-nu-ric
cy-aph-e-nine
cy-ber-net-ics
cyc-la-mate
cy-cli-cal
cy-clic-i-ty
cy-cling
cy-clist
cy-cli-tis
cy-cli-za-tion
cy-clo-hex-i-mide
cy-clo-hex-yl-a-mine
cy-cloi-dal
cy-clol-y-sis
cy-clom-e-ter
cy-clon-ic
cy-clo-nite
Cy-clo-pe-an
cy-clo-ra-ma
cy-clo-ser-ine
cy-clot-o-my
cy-clo-tron

D

dac-ty-loid
dac-ty-lol-o-gy
dac-ty-los-co-py
dac-ty-lus
Dae-da-li-an

cyl-in-der
cyl-in-dra-ceous
cy-lin-dri-cal
cyl-in-dric-i-ty
cyl-in-drite
cy-mene
cy-mo-graph
cy-mose
cyn-i-cal
cyn-i-cism
cyn-o-don-tin
cy-no-sure
Cyn-thi-a
cy-press
Cyp-ri-an
Cyp-ri-ot (native of Cyprus)
Cy-prus
Cyr-e-na-ic
Cy-ril-lic
cys-tec-to-my
cys-te-ic
cys-teine
cys-tine
cys-ti-tis
cys-toid
cys-to-ma
cys-tom-e-ter
cys-to-scope
cys-tos-co-py
cy-tase
cyt-i-dine
cyt-i-dyl-ic
cyt-i-sine
cy-toc-i-dal
cy-to-ge-net-ics
cy-tog-e-nous
cy-tol-o-gy
cy-tol-y-sin
cy-tol-y-zate
cy-to-lyze
cy-tom-e-ter
cy-to-sine
czar-ism
Czech-o-slo-vak

daf-fo-dil
da-guerre-o-type
dahl-ia
Da-ho-me-an
dain-ti-ness

34

Dai-qui-ri	deb-it	dec-la-ma-tion
dair-y	deb-o-nair	de-clam-a-to-ry
dai-sy	de-bris	de-clar-ant
Da-kar	debt-or	dec-la-ra-tion
Da-kin	de-but	de-clar-a-tive
Dal-e-car-li-an	deb-u-tante	de-clar-a-to-ry
dal-li-ance	dec-ade	de-clin-a-ble
Dal-ma-tian	dec-a-dence	dec-li-na-tion
dam-a-scene	dec-a-dent	de-clin-a-to-ry
Da-mas-cus	dec-a-he-dral	dec-li-nom-e-ter
dam-ask	dec-a-lage	de-cli-vate
dam-na-ble	de-cal-co-ma-ni-a	de-cliv-i-ty
damn-ing	de-ca-les-cence	de-cli-vous
Dam-o-cles	Dec-a-lin	de-coct-i-ble
Da-mon	dec-a-li-ter	de-coc-tive
damp-en-er	dec-a-log	de-cod-er
damp-er	de-cam-e-ter (verse)	dec-o-ra-tive
damp-ish	de-ca-me-ter (measure)	dec-o-rous
dam-son	dec-a-me-tho-ni-um	de-co-rum
danc-ing	de-ca-nal (adj.)	dec-re-ment
dan-de-li-on	dec-a-nal (n.)	de-crem-e-ter
dan-druff	dec-ane	de-crep-i-tude
dan-ger-ous	dec-a-no-ic	de-cre-tive
dan-gling	dec-a-no-yl	dec-re-to-ry
Dan-ish	De-cap-o-da	dec-yl-ene
dan-seuse	de-cap-i-ta-tor	de-cyl-ic
dark-en	de-cant-er	ded-i-ca-to-ry
dar-ling	dec-are	de-duc-i-ble
da-sheen	de-cath-lon	de-duct-i-ble
das-tard	de-ce-dent	de-fal-ca-tion
da-sym-e-ter	de-ceiv-er	def-a-ma-tion
da-tive	de-cel-er-a-tor	de-fam-a-to-ry
da-tum	de-cel-er-om-e-ter	de-fat-i-ga-ble
da-tu-ric	de-cel-er-on	de-fea-si-ble
daub-er	De-cem-ber	def-e-ca-tor
daugh-ter	de-cen-cy	de-fec-ti-bil-i-ty
dau-phin	dec-ene	de-fec-tive
Da-vi-son-ite	de-cen-na-ry	de-fec-tor
da-vit	de-cen-ni-al	de-fend-ant
daw-dler	dec-e-nyl	de-fend-er
daz-zling	de-cep-tive	de-fen-si-ble
dea-con-ess	dec-i-bel	de-fen-sive
deaf-en-ing	de-cid-u-ous	de-fer
deal-er	dec-ile	def-er-ence
de-ba-cle	dec-i-mal	de-fer-ra-ble
de-bar-ka-tion	dec-i-ma-tion	de-fer-ves-cence
de-bat-a-ble	dec-i-me-ter	de-fi-bra-tor
deb-au-chee	de-ci-pher	de-fi-cient
de-bauch-er-y	de-ci-sion	def-i-cit
de-ben-ture	de-ci-sive	def-i-lade
deb-ile	deck-led	de-file
de-bil-i-tate		

de-fin-a-ble
def-i-ni-tion
de-fin-i-tive
def-la-gra-tion
de-fla-tion
de-flec-tive
de-flec-tom-e-ter
de-flec-tor
def-lo-ra-tion
def-lu-ent
de-fo-li-ate
de-form-a-ble
de-for-ma-tion
de-form-a-tive
de-for-me-ter
de-form-i-ty
de-frau-da-tion
de-frost-er
de-gen-er-a-tive
de-glu-ti-tion
deg-ra-da-tion
de-**grade**
de-guel-in
de-his-cent
de-hy-dra-tor
de-hy-dro-cho-late
de-hy-dro-cho-les-ter-ol
de-hy-dro-gen-ase
de-i-fi-ca-tion
de-is-tic
de-jeu-ner
Del-a-war-e-an
de-lec-ta-ble
del-e-gate
del-e-te-ri-ous
de-le-tion
de-lib-er-a-tive
del-i-ble
del-i-ca-cy
del-i-ca-tes-sen
de-li-cious
De-li-lah
de-lin-e-a-tor
de-lin-quen-cy
del-i-ques-cence
de-lir-i-ous
de-lir-i-um
de-lo-mor-phous
del-phi-nin
del-phin-i-um
Del-sar-ti-an
del-toi-dal

del-uge
de-lu-so-ry
dem-a-gog
dem-a-gog-ic
dem-a-gogu-er-y
de-mand-ant
de-mar-ca-tion
de-mean-or
de-men-tia
de-mer-it
de-**mesne**
dem-i-monde
de-mise
dem-i-tasse
de-mo-bi-li-za-tion
de-moc-ra-cy
dem-o-crat
de-moc-ra-tize
de-mog-ra-pher
de-mo-graph-ic
dem-oi-selle
de-mol-ish
dem-o-li-tion
de-mon-e-tize
de-mo-ni-a-cal
de-mon-ic
de-**mon-stra-ble**
dem-on-stra-tion
de-mon-stra-tive
dem-on-stra-tor
de-mor-al-ize
de-mul-cent
de-mur-rage
de-nar-i-us
de-na-ry
den-drit-ic
den-dro-lite
den-drol-o-gy
den-drom-e-ter
Den-eb
de-ner-vate
den-gue
de-ni-er (one who de-
   nies)
de-nier (coin; silk)
den-i-gra-to-ry
den-im
den-i-zen
de-nom-i-**na**-tive
de-nom-i-na-tor
de-noue-ment
den-sim-e-ter

den-si-tom-e-ter
den-si-ty
den-tal
den-ti-cle
den-tic-u-lar
den-ti-frice
den-tig-er-ous
den-tist-ry
de-nu-da-tion
de-nun-ci-a-tive
de-nun-ci-a-to-ry
de-o-dor-ant
de-o-dor-iz-er
de-ox-y-ri-bose
de-part-men-tal-ize
de-par-ture
de-pend-a-ble
de-pend-en-cy
de-pend-ent
de-perm-ing
de-phleg-ma-to-ry
dep-i-late
de-pil-a-to-ry
de-plor-a-ble
dep-lo-ra-tion
de-po-nent
de-por-ta-tion
de-port-ee
de-pos-al
de-pos-er
de-pos-i-tar-y
de-pos-it-ed
dep-o-si-tion
de-pos-i-to-ry
de-pot
dep-ra-va-tion
de-prav-i-ty
dep-re-ca-to-ry
de-pre-ci-ate
dep-re-da-tion
de-pre-da-to-ry
de-pres-sant
de-press-i-ble
de-pres-sor
de-priv-al
dep-ri-va-tion
depth-om-e-ter
dep-u-ra-tor
dep-u-tize
de-rac-i-nate
de-re-cho
der-e-lict

de ri-gueur
de-ri-sive
der-i-va-tion
de-riv-a-tive
der-ma-ti-tis
der-mat-o-graph
der-ma-tol-o-gy
der-ma-to-sis
der-moi-dal
der-nier
der-o-gate
de-rog-a-to-ry
der-vish
des-cant
de-scend-ant
de-scend-er
de-scend-i-ble
de-scrib-a-ble
de-scrip-tive
des-cry
des-e-crat-er
des-e-de-ri-um
Des-er-et
de-sert (n., that which is deserved)
des-ert (n., adj., barren tract)
de-sert (v.)
de-sert-er
des-ic-cate
des-ic-ca-tor
de-sid-er-a-tum
de-sig-na-ble
des-ig-nat-a-ble
des-ig-na-tive
des-ig-na-tor
de-sign-ed-ly
des-ig-nee
de-sign-er
de-sip-i-ent
de-sir-a-ble
de-sist-ance
des-mo-di-um
des-mo-lase
des-mol-y-sis
des-mo-trop-ic
des-mot-ro-pism
des-o-la-tion
des-ox-y-cho-lic
des-ox-y-ri-bo-nu-cle-ase
de-spair
des-per-a-do

des-per-ate
des-pi-ca-ble
de-spis-a-ble
de-spis-er
de-spite
de-spoil
de-spo-li-a-tion
de-spond-ence
de-spond-ent
des-pot-i-cal
des-pot-ism
des-pu-ma-tion
des-qua-ma-tion
des-sert
des-ti-na-tion
des-ti-ny
des-ti-tute
de-stroy-er
de-struct-i-ble
de-struc-tive
de-struc-tor
des-ue-tude
des-ul-to-ry
des-yl
de-syn-ap-sis
de-tect-a-ble
de-tec-tive
de-tec-tor
de-ten-tive
de-ter-gent
de-te-ri-o-ra-tive
de-ter-mi-na-ble
de-ter-mi-nant
de-ter-min-er
de-ter-rence
de-test-a-ble
det-o-nant
det-o-na-tor
de-trac-tor
det-ri-men-tal
de-tri-tal
de-tri-tus
deu-ter-ide
deu-te-ri-um
deu-ter-on
Deu-ter-o-nom-ic
Deu-ter-on-o-my
deut-sche
dev-as-ta-tor
de-vel-op-men-tal
de-vi-a-tor
de-vice

dev-il-ish
dev-il-try
de-vi-ous
dev-i-see
de-vis-er
dev-i-sor (legal)
De-vo-ni-an
dev-o-tee
Dew-ar
dex-ter-i-ty
dex-tral-i-ty
dex-trin-ate
dex-trin-o-gen-ic
dex-tro-car-di-a
dex-tro-pi-mar-ic
dex-trorse
dex-trose
dex-trous
di-a-ban-tite
di-a-be-tes
di-a-bet-ic
di-a-bol-i-cal
di-ab-o-lism
di-ac-e-tyl
di-a-dem
di-ag-no-sis
di-ag-nos-ti-cian
di-ag-o-nal
di-a-gramed
di-a-gram-mat-i-cal
di-a-lec-tic
di-a-lec-tol-o-gy
di-a-log
di-a-lu-ric
di-al-y-sis
di-a-lyt-ic
di-a-lyz-er
di-a-man-tine
di-am-e-ter
di-a-met-ri-cal
di-am-i-no-gen
di-a-mond
Di-an-a
di-a-nite
di-a-pa-son
di-a-per
di-aph-a-nom-e-ter
di-aph-a-nous
di-a-phon-ic
di-aph-o-re-sis
di-a-phragm
di-a-phrag-mat-ic

37

di-ar-rhe-a
di-a-ry
di-as-po-ra
di-a-spore
di-a-stase
di-a-sta-sis
di-a-stat-ic
di-a-stim-e-ter
di-as-to-le
di-a-stol-ic
di-a-sto-mat-ic
di-as-tro-phe
di-a-stroph-ic
di-ath-e-sis
di-a-ther-my
di-a-thet-ic
di-a-tom
di-a-to-ma-ceous
di-at-o-mite
di-at-ro-pism
di-a-zine
di-a-zo-ic
di-az-o-im-ide
di-a-zole
di-az-o-meth-ane
di-a-zo-ni-um
di-az-o-tize
di-az-o-type
di-ba-sic
di-bro-mo-a-ce-tic
di-bu-caine
di-ce-tyl
di-chlone
di-chlo-ro-di-flu-o-ro-
    meth-ane
di-cho-tom-ic
di-chot-o-mous
di-chot-o-my
di-chro-mat-ic
di-con-dyl-ic
di-cot-y-le-don
di-cou-ma-rol
di-crot-ic
Dic-ta-phone
dic-ta-tor
dic-ta-to-ri-al
dic-tion-ar-y
Dic-to-graph
di-dac-tic
di-dym-i-um
di-er-e-sis
di-e-ret-ic

die-sel-ize
di-e-tar-y
di-e-tet-ic
di-e-ti-tian
dif-fer-en-tial
dif-fi-dence
dif-flu-ent
dif-frac-tion
dif-frac-tom-e-ter
dif-fran-gi-ble
dif-fus-er
dif-fus-i-ble
dif-fu-sive
di-gest-er
di-gest-i-ble
di-ges-tive
dig-i-tal
dig-i-tal-is
dig-i-tal-i-za-tion
dig-i-tal-ose
dig-i-ti-ner-vate
dig-it-iz-er
dig-i-to-gen-in
dig-i-to-nin
dig-ni-tar-y
di-he-dral
di-hy-dro-er-go-cor-nine
di-hy-dro-er-got-a-mine
di-hy-drox-y-a-ce-tic
di-lap-i-dat-ed
di-lat-ant
dil-a-ta-tion
di-la-tion
dil-a-tom-e-ter
di-la-tor
dil-a-to-ry
di-lem-ma
dil-et-tan-te
dil-u-ent
di-lut-ant
di-lut-er
di-me-don
di-men-hy-dri-nate
di-men-si-ble
di-mer-cap-rol
di-mer-ic
di-meth-yl
di-mid-i-ate
di-min-ish
dim-i-nu-tion
di-min-u-tive
dim-i-ty

di-mor-phous
din-ghy
di-ni-tro-tol-u-ene
di-no-saur
di-oc-e-san
di-o-cese
Di-og-e-nes
di-op-side
di-op-ter
di-op-tom-e-ter
di-o-ra-ma
di-o-ram-ic
di-o-rite
di-par-tite
di-phen-yl
diph-the-ri-a
diph-the-rit-ic
diph-the-roid
diph-thong-al
di-pic-o-lin-ic
di-ple-gi-a
di-plex-er
dip-loi-dal
dip-loid-ize
di-plo-ma-cy
dip-lo-mat
di-plo-ma-tist
di-plo-sis
dip-o-dy
dip-so-ma-ni-a
dip-ter-al
di-rec-tiv-i-ty
di-rec-tor-ate
di-rec-to-ri-al
dir-i-gi-ble
dirn-dl
dirt-i-ness
dis-ap-peared
dis-ap-point-ed
dis-as-ter
dis-as-trous
dis-az-o
dis-burs-al
dis-burs-er
dis-cern-i-ble
dis-cerp-ti-ble
dis-ci-ple
dis-ci-pli-nar-i-an
dis-ci-pli-nar-y
dis-ci-plin-er
dis-clo-sure
dis-coi-dal

dis-com-fi-ture
dis-con-so-late
dis-cord-ant
dis-co-theque
dis-cour-sive
dis-crep-an-cy
dis-crete
dis-cre-tion-ar-y
dis-crim-i-na-ble
dis-crim-i-na-tor
dis-cur-sive
dis-cus
dis-cuss-ant
dis-cuss-i-ble
dis-cus-sion
dis-eas-es
di-seuse
dis-ha-bille
di-shev-eled
dis-in-fect-ant
dis-in-te-grate
dis-man-tle
dis-mis-sal
dis-par-ag-er
dis-par-ate
dis-par-i-ty
dis-patch-er
dis-pen-sa-ble
dis-pen-sa-ry
dis-pens-er
dis-per-sal
dis-pers-ant
dis-pers-er
dis-pers-i-ble
dis-per-sive
dis-per-soid
dis-pir-it
dis-pos-al
dis-put-a-ble
dis-pu-tant
dis-pu-ta-tious
dis-pu-ta-tive
dis-put-er
dis-qui-si-tion
dis-quis-i-tive
dis-rep-u-ta-ble
dis-re-pute
dis-rupt-er
dis-sat-is-fied
dis-sect-i-ble
dis-sec-tor
dis-sem-i-na-tive

dis-sen-sion
dis-sent-er
dis-sim-i-la-tive
dis-si-pat-er
dis-sol-u-ble
dis-so-lute
dis-solv-a-ble
dis-sol-vent
dis-so-nance
dis-suad-er
dis-sua-sive
dis-sym-me-try
dis-taff
dis-tant
dis-tem-per
dis-ten-si-ble
dis-ten-tion
dis-til-la-tion
dis-tilled
dis-till-er-y
dis-till-ing
dis-tinc-tive
dis-tin-guished
dis-to-ma-ta
di-sto-ma-to-sis
di-stom-a-tous
dis-tor-tive
dis-tract-er
dis-tract-i-ble
dis-trac-tive
dis-tress-ing
dis-trib-ut-a-ble
dis-trib-u-tar-y
dis-trib-ute
dis-trib-u-tec
dis-tri-bu-tion
dis-trib-u-tive
dis-trib-u-tor
dis-turb-ance
dis-turb-er
di-thi-o-nate
di-thi-o-nous
di-thi-zone
dith-y-ram-bic
di-tol-yl
di-u-re-sis
di-u-ret-ic
di-ur-nal
di-va-ga-tion
di-van
div-er
di-ver-gent

di-vers (several)
di-ver-si-ty
di-vert-er
di-vert-i-ble
di-ver-tic-u-lec-to-my
di-ver-tic-u-lo-sis
di-ver-tic-u-lum
di-ver-tise-ment
di-ver-tisse-ment
di-ver-tive
di-ver-tor (electricity)
di-vest-i-ble
di-ves-ti-ture
di-vid-ed
div-i-dend
di-vid-er
div-i-na-tion
di-vin-a-to-ry
di-vin-i-ty
di-vis-i-ble
di-vi-sion
di-vi-so-ry
di-vor-cee
di-vul-gence
do-blon
do-cent
doc-i-ble
doc-ile
do-cil-i-ty
dock-et
doc-o-sane
doc-tor-al
doc-tor-ate
doc-tri-naire
doc-tri-nal
doc-u-ment-a-ble
doc-u-men-ta-ry
do-de-cane
do-dec-a-no-ic
Do-dec-a-nese
do-dec-ant
do-de-cyl-ene
dodg-er
dog-ger-el
dog-mat-ic
dog-ma-tism
dog-ma-tize
dol-drum
dol-er-ite
dol-i-cho-ce-phal-ic
do-lo-mite

39

do-lo-rous
dol-phin
do-main
do-mes-ti-cate
do-mes-tic-i-ty
dom-i-cil-i-ar-y
dom-i-nant
dom-i-na-tor
dom-i-neer
Dom-i-ni-ca
do-min-i-cal
Do-min-i-can
dom-i-nie
do-min-ion
dom-i-no
do-na-ble
do-nee
don-keys
do-nor
doo-dle
Dopp-ler
Do-ri-an
Dor-ic
Dor-is
dor-mant
dor-mer
dor-mi-to-ry
Dor-o-the-a
dor-sal
dor-sa-lis
dos-age
do-sim-e-ter
do-sim-e-try
dos-sier
dot-age
dot-ard
dot-ing
dot-ish
dou-ble
dou-blet
dou-bling
dou-bloon
dou-bly
dough-ty
dou-rine
dow-a-ger
dow-eled
down-i-ness
dox-o-log-i-cal
dox-ol-o-gy
doy-en
doz-en

drag-on
dra-goon
drain-age
dra-ma
Dram-a-mine
dra-mat-ic
dra-ma-tis per-so-nae
dram-a-tize
drap-er-y
dream-i-ness
drear-i-ness
dredg-er
dredg-ing
dress-er
dri-er
drift-age
drift-er
drill-ing
drink-om-e-ter
driv-el-er
driv-en
driv-er
droll-er-y
drom-e-dar-y
drop-si-cal
drop-sonde
dro-som-e-ter
dro-ver
drows-i-ness
drudg-er-y
drunk-ard
drunk-en-ness
dru-pa-ceous
du-al-ism
du-ar-chy
du-bi-e-ty
du-bi-ous
du-bi-ta-ble
du-cal
duc-at
duch-ess
du-chesse
duc-ti-ble
duc-tile
dudg-eon
duf-fel-bag
duff-er
du-fre-nite
dul-ci-mer
dul-ci-tol
dul-lard
dull-er

dum-found
dump-er
dump-ling
dump-y
dun-ga-ree
Dun-ge-ness
dun-geon
du-nite
Dun-kard
Dun-stan
du-o-dec-i-mos
du-o-de-nal
du-o-de-ni-tis
du-o-de-nos-co-py
du-o-de-num
du-op-o-ly
du-op-so-ny
du-plex-er
du-pli-ca-tive
du-pli-ca-tor
du-plic-i-ty
du-ra-bil-i-ty
du-ral-u-min
dur-ance
du-ra-tion
du-rene
du-ress
du-rom-e-ter
dur-yl
dusk-i-ness
dust-er
du-te-ous
du-ti-ful
du-ve-tyn
dwarf-ish
dwell-ing
dwin-dling
Dy-cril
dy-nam-e-ter
dy-nam-i-cal
dy-nam-ics
dy-na-mit-er
dy-na-mi-za-tion
dy-na-mom-e-ter
dy-na-mo-met-ric
dy-na-mom-e-try
dy-na-mos
dy-na-mo-tor
Dy-na-Soar
dy-nas-tic
dy-na-tron
Dy-nel

40

dy-node
dys-cra-site
dys-en-ter-y

dys-pep-si-a
dys-pho-ri-a

dysp-ne-a
dys-pro-si-um

E

ea-ger
ea-glet
ear-li-er
earn-er
ear-nest
earth-en-ware
ea-sel
eas-i-ly
Eas-ter
east-er (storm)
east-ern-er
eb-on-ite
eb-on-y
e-bul-lient
e-bul-li-om-e-ter
e-bul-li-o-scop-ic
e-bul-li-os-co-py
eb-ul-li-tion
ec-cen-tric-i-ty
ec-cle-si-as-ti-cal
ec-dys-i-al
ec-go-nine
ech-e-lon
e-chi-noid
e-chi-nus
ech-o-me-ter
ec-lamp-si-a
ec-lec-ti-cal
e-clip-tic
e-clo-sion
ec-o-log-i-cal
e-col-o-gy
e-con-o-met-ric (adj.)
e-con-o-me-trics (n.)
ec-o-nom-i-cal
ec-o-nom-ics
e-con-o-mist
e-con-o-mize
ec-o-sphere
ec-sta-sy
ec-stat-ic
ec-to-der-moi-dal
ec-tog-e-nous
ec-to-pi-a
ec-top-ic
ec-to-plasm
ec-typ-al

Ec-ua-dor-an
ec-u-men-i-cal
ec-ze-ma
ec-zem-a-tous
e-del-weiss
e-de-ma
e-dem-a-tous
ed-i-ble
ed-i-fi-ca-tion
ed-i-fice
e-di-tion
ed-i-to-ri-al-ize
ed-u-ca-ble
ed-u-ca-tor
e-duc-i-ble
e-duc-tor
ee-ri-ly
ef-fac-ing
ef-fect-i-ble
ef-fec-tive
ef-fec-tu-al
ef-fem-i-nate
ef-fer-ves-cence
ef-fer-ves-ci-ble
ef-fi-ca-cious
ef-fi-ca-cy
ef-fi-cien-cy
ef-fi-cient
ef-fi-gy
ef-flo-res-cence
ef-flu-vi-um
ef-fron-ter-y
ef-ful-gence
ef-fu-si-om-e-ter
ef-fu-sive
e-gal-i-tar-i-an
e-go-cen-trism
e-go-ism
e-go-is-ti-cal
e-go-tism
e-go-tis-ti-cal
e-gre-gious
E-gyp-tol-o-gy
el-co-sane
ei-der
ei-gen
eight-een

eight-i-eth
ei-ko-nom-e-ter
ein-stein-i-um
eis-e-ge-sis
Ei-sen-how-er
ei-ther
e-jac-u-la-to-ry
e-jec-tive
e-jec-tor
e-lab-o-ra-tive
e-las-tic-i-ty
e-las-to-mer
e-las-tom-e-ter
e-las-to-sis
e-lat-er-in
el-a-te-ri-um
el-der
el-e-cam-pane
e-lec-tion-eer
e-lec-tive
e-lec-tor-al
e-lec-tor-ate
e-lec-tri-cal
e-lec-tric-i-ty
e-lec-tri-fi-ca-tion
e-lec-tro-car-di-o-gram
e-lec-tro-cute
e-lec-trode
e-lec-tro-graph-ic
e-lec-trog-ra-phy
e-lec-trol-y-sis
e-lec-tro-lyte
e-lec-tro-lyt-i-cal
e-lec-trom-e-ter
e-lec-tron-i-cal-ly
e-lec-tron-ics
e-lec-troph-o-rus
e-lec-trot-o-nus
el-ee-mos-y-nar-y
el-e-gant
el-e-gi-ac
el-e-gy
el-e-men-tar-i-ly
el-e-men-ta-ry
el-e-phan-ti-a-sis
el-e-va-tor

e-lev-enth
el-e-von
elf-in
e-lic-it
el-i-gi-ble
e-lim-i-nant
e-lim-i-na-tor
e-lix-ir
E-liz-a-be-than
el-lip-soi-dal
el-lip-som-e-ter
el-lip-ti-cal
el-lip-tic-i-ty
e-lo-gi-um
e-lon-ga-tion
el-o-quent
e-lu-ci-date
e-lud-i-ble
e-lu-so-ry
e-lu-tri-ate
e-lu-vi-um
E-lyr-i-a
E-ly-sian
E-ly-si-um
e-ma-ci-ate
em-a-nate
e-man-ci-pate
em-a-nom-e-ter
e-mar-gi-nate
e-mas-cu-late
em-ba-cle
em-bar-go
em-bar-ka-tion
em-bar-ras (n.)
em-bar-rass (v.)
em-bed-ded
em-bla-zon
em-blem-at-i-cal
em-bod-i-ment
em-bold-en
em-bol-ic
em-bo-lism
em-bo-lus
em-boss-er
em-bou-chure
em-brac-er
em-bra-sure
em-broi-der-y
em-bry-ol-o-gy
em-bry-on-ic
e-mend-a-ble
e-men-da-tion

e-mend-a-to-ry
em-er-al-dine
e-mer-gen-cy
e-mer-i-tus
e-mer-sion
em-er-y
e-met-ic
em-e-tine
em-i-grant
em-i-gree
em-i-nence
em-is-sar-y
e-mis-siv-i-ty
e-mit-ter
em-o-din
e-mol-lient
e-mol-u-ment
e-mot-er
e-mo-tion-al-ize
em-path-ic
em-pa-thy
em-pen-nage
em-per-or
em-pha-sis
em-phat-ic
em-phy-se-ma
em-pir-i-cal
em-pi-ris-tic
em-ploy-ee
em-po-ri-um
em-press
emp-ti-ness
em-py-e-ma
em-py-re-an
em-py-reu-ma
em-u-la-tive
em-u-la-to-ry
em-u-lous
e-mul-si-fi-er
e-mul-sive
e-mul-soi-dal
en-a-bling
en-am-el-er
en-am-o-ra-to
en-am-ored
e-nan-thic
en-ar-gite
en-ar-thro-sis
en-cap-su-late
en-caus-tic
en-ceinte
en-ce-phal-ic

en-ceph-a-li-tis
en-ceph-a-lo-cele
en-ceph-a-lo-gram
en-ceph-a-lo-graph
en-ceph-a-log-ra-p..
en-ceph-a-loid
en-chi-la-da
en-chym-a-tous
en-clos-er
en-clo-sure
en-coi-gnure
en-co-mi-ast
en-co-mi-um
en-coun-ter
en-cour-age
en-cri-nal
en-crin-ic
en-cum-ber
en-cum-brance
en-cyc-li-cal
en-cy-clo-pe-di-a
en-cys-ta-tion
end-ar-te-ri-tis
en-deav-ored
en-de-mi-al
en-dem-i-cal-ly
en-de-mic-i-ty
en-de-mi-ol-o-gy
En-der-by
end-er-gon-ic
en-dive
en-do-car-di-tis
en-do-cri-nal
en-do-crine
en-do-cri-no-log-ic
en-do-cri-nol-o-gy
en-do-crin-o-path-i.
en-do-cri-nop-a-thy
en-doc-ri-nous
en-do-ge-net-ic
en-do-ge-nic-i-ty
en-dog-e-nous
en-do-me-tri-tis
en-do-plas-ma
en-dors-a-ble
en-dors-ee
en-dors-er
en-dos-co-py
en-drin
en-dur-a-ble
en-dur-ance
ene-di-ol

en-e-ma
en-er-get-i-cal-ly
en-er-giz-er
en-er-vate
en-fi-lade
en-force-a-ble
en-fran-chise
en-gen-der
en-gi-neer-ing
en-gine-ry
Eng-land
Eng-lish
en-grav-er
e-nig-mat-ic
e-nig-ma-tize
en-join-der
en-liv-en
en-mi-ty
en-nui
e-nor-mi-ty
e-nor-mous
en-rolled
en-roll-ee
en-sem-ble
en-sign
en-si-lage
en-ter-ic
en-ter-i-tis
en-ter-o-cri-nin
en-ter-os-to-my
en-thal-py
en-thu-si-asm
en-thu-si-as-tic
en-tire-ty
en-ti-ty
en-to-mo-log-i-cal
en-to-mol-o-gy
en-tou-rage
en-trails
en-trance
en-tree
en-tre-pre-neur-i-al
en-tro-py
e-nu-cle-ate
e-nu-mer-ate
e-nun-ci-a-tive
en-vel-op (v.)
en-ve-lope (n.)
en-vel-op-ment
en-vi-a-ble
en-vi-ous
en-vi-ron

en-vis-age
en-zy-mat-ic
en-zy-mol-o-gy
e-o-sin-o-phil
e-os-pho-rite
ep-a-go-ge
ep-au-let
ep-en-dy-ma
e-phed-rine
e-phem-er-al
e-phem-er-is
E-phra-im
Eph-ra-ta
ep-i-cal
ep-i-cu-re-an
ep-i-dem-i-cal
ep-i-de-mi-o-log-i-cal
ep-i-de-mi-ol-o-gy
ep-i-der-mis
ep-i-der-moi-dal
ep-i-dote
ep-i-du-ral
ep-i-ge-al
e-pig-e-nous
ep-i-glot-tis
e-pig-ra-pher
ep-i-la-tor
ep-i-lep-tic
ep-i-log
ep-i-mer-i-za-tion
ep-i-neph-rine
Ep-i-nine
E-piph-a-ny
e-piph-y-sis
ep-i-pter-ic
E-pi-rus
E-pis-co-pa-lian
ep-i-sco-tis-ter
ep-i-sod-ic
e-pis-ta-sis
ep-i-stat-ic
e-pis-te-mol-o-gy
e-pis-tle
e-pis-to-lar-y
ep-i-stome
ep-i-taph
ep-i-the-li-um
e-pith-e-sis
ep-i-thet
e-pit-o-me
ep-i-tom-i-cal
e-pit-ro-phy

ep-och-al
ep-ox-y
ep-si-lon
eq-ua-ble
e-qualed
e-qual-iz-er
e-qua-nim-i-ty
e-quat-ive
e-qua-to-ri-al
eq-uer-ry
e-ques-tri-an
e-qui-dis-tant
e-qui-lat-er-al
eq-ui-len-in
e-quil-i-bra-tion
e-qui-lib-rist
e-qui-lib-ri-stat
e-qui-lib-ri-um
e-qui-noc-tial
e-qui-nox
eq-ui-page
eq-ui-poise
e-quipped
eq-ui-ta-ble
eq-ui-ty
e-quiv-a-lent
e-quiv-o-cal
e-quiv-o-ca-tor
e-rad-i-ca-tor
e-ras-er
e-ra-sure
er-bi-um
Er-e-bus
e-rec-tile
e-rec-tor
er-e-ma-cau-sis
er-ga-tive
er-god-ic
er-go-gen-ic
er-gom-e-ter
er-go-no-vine
er-gos-ter-ol
er-got
er-got-a-mine
er-got-ic
er-go-tize
e-rin-e-um
er-in-ite
er-i-nose
er-i-o-dic-ty-ol
er-i-om-e-ter
Er-len-mey-er

43

er-mine
e-rod-i-ble
e-ro-sive
e-rot-i-cism
err-a-bil-i-ty
er-ra-ta
er-rat-ic
er-ro-ne-ous
er-u-bes-cent
e-ru-cic
e-ruc-ta-tion
er-u-di-tion
e-rup-tiv-i-ty
er-y-sip-e-las
er-y-the-ma
er-y-them-a-tous
er-y-thrine
er-y-thrite
e-ryth-ri-tol
e-ryth-ro-cyte
e-ryth-ro-cy-tom-e-ter
er-y-thro-i-dine
er-y-thro-pi-a
e-ryth-ro-scope
er-y-throse
e-ryth-ro-sin
er-y-thro-sis
e-ryth-ru-lose
es-ca-drille
es-ca-la-tor
es-cal-loped
es-cap-a-ble
es-ca-pade
es-cap-ee
es-cap-ism
es-cap-ist
es-ca-role
es-carp-ment
es-cha-tol-o-gy
es-chy-nite
es-cri-toire
es-crow
es-cu-dos
es-cu-lent
es-cutch-eon
es-er-o-line
Es-ki-mos
e-soph-a-ge-al
e-soph-a-gi-tis
e-soph-a-go-scope
e-soph-a-gos-co-pist
e-soph-a-gus

es-o-ter-ic
es-pal-ier
es-pe-cial
Es-pe-ran-to
es-pi-o-nage
es-pla-nade
es-pous-al
es-pous-er
es-tab-lish
es-ter-ase
es-ter-ize
es-thet-ic
es-ti-ma-ble
es-ti-ma-tor
es-ti-va-tor
Es-to-nian
es-top-pel
es-to-vers
es-tra-di-ol
es-trange
es-tro-gen-ic
es-tu-a-rine
es-tu-ar-y
e-ter-ni-ty
eth-ane
eth-a-nol-a-mine
eth-a-nol-y-sis
eth-e-nyl
e-the-re-al
e-the-re-ous
e-ther-ize
eth-i-cal
eth-i-on-ic
e-thi-o-nine
E-thi-o-pi-an
eth-moi-dal
eth-moid-i-tis
eth-ni-cal
eth-nog-e-ny
eth-no-graph-ic
eth-nog-ra-phy
eth-no-log-i-cal
eth-nol-o-gy
eth-ox-y-line
eth-yl-a-mine
eth-yl-ate
eth-yl-ene-di-a-mine
eth-yl-e-nic
eth-yl-e-phed-rine
eth-yl-i-dine
eth-y-nyl-a-tion

e-ti-o-late
e-ti-o-log-i-cal
e-ti-ol-o-gy
e-ti-o-phyl-lin
et-i-quette
et-y-mo-log-i-cal
et-y-mol-o-gy
eu-ca-lyp-tus
Eu-cha-rist
eu-chred
eu-chro-ite
eu-clase
Eu-clid-e-an
eu-da-lene
eu-di-om-e-ter
Eu-ge-nia
eu-gen-ic
eu-gen-ist
eu-ge-nol
eu-lo-gis-ti-cal
eu-lo-gize
eu-lo-gy
eu-nuch
eu-pa-to-rin
eu-pav-er-ine
eu-phe-mism
eu-pho-ni-um
eu-pho-ny
eu-pho-ri-a
Eur-a-sian
eu-re-ka
Eu-ro-pe-an
eu-ro-pi-um
eu-ryth-mics
Eu-sta-chi-an
eu-tha-na-si-a
eu-then-ics
eux-e-nite
e-vac-u-ate
e-vag-i-nate
ev-a-nes-cence
e-van-gel-i-cal
e-van-ge-list
e-van-ge-lize
e-vap-o-ra-tor
e-vap-o-rim-e-ter
e-va-si-ble
e-va-sive
e-ven-ing (making l
eve-ning (close of d
e-ven-tu-al-i-ty
e-ver-si-ble

ev-er-y
e-vic-tor
ev-i-denc-ing
ev-i-den-tial
e-vinc-i-ble
e-vis-cer-a-tor
ev-i-ta-ble
e-voc-a-to-ry
ev-o-lu-tion-ar-y
ev-o-lu-tion-ist
ex-ac-er-bat-ing
ex-ac-ti-tude
ex-ag-ger-ate
ex-al-ta-tion
ex-am-i-na-tion
ex-am-in-er
ex-as-per-ate
ex-ca-va-tor
ex-cel-len-cy
ex-cel-si-or
ex-cept-a-ble
ex-cerpt-er
ex-cerpt-i-ble
ex-ces-sive
ex-cheq-uer
ex-cip-i-ent
ex-cit-a-ble
ex-cit-ant
ex-cit-a-tive
ex-cit-er
ex-cla-ma-tion
ex-clam-a-to-ry
ex-clud-a-ble
ex-clu-so-ry
ex-co-ri-a-tion
ex-cre-ment
ex-cres-cence
ex-cre-to-ry
ex-cru-ci-ate
ex-cul-pa-to-ry
ex-cus-a-ble
ex-e-cra-to-ry
ex-ec-u-tant
ex-e-cut-ed
ex-ec-u-tive
ex-ec-u-to-ry
ex-e-ge-sis
ex-e-get-ic
ex-em-pla-ry
ex-empt-i-ble
ex-emp-tive
ex-e-qua-tur

ex-er-cis-er
ex-er-e-sis
ex-ert-ive
ex-hal-ant
ex-ha-la-tion
ex-haust-ed
ex-haust-i-ble
ex-haus-tive
ex-hib-it
ex-hi-bi-tion
ex-hib-i-tive
ex-hib-i-to-ry
ex-hil-a-ra-tive
ex-hor-ta-tion
ex-hort-a-to-ry
ex-hu-ma-tion
ex-i-gen-cy
ex-i-gi-ble
ex-i-gu-i-ty
ex-ig-u-ous
ex-ist-ence
ex li-bris
ex-o-don-ti-a
ex-o-dus
ex-og-e-nous
ex-on-er-ate
ex-o-pep-ti-dase
ex-or-bi-tant
ex-or-di-um
ex-o-ter-ic
ex-o-ther-mic-i-ty
ex-ot-ic
ex-pand-a-ble
ex-pand-er
ex-pan-si-ble
ex-pan-sive
ex-pa-ti-ate
ex-pa-tri-ate
ex-pect-an-cy
ex-pect-ant
ex-pec-ta-tion
ex-pect-a-tive
ex-pec-to-ra-tor
ex-pe-di-en-cy
ex-pe-dit-er
ex-pe-di-tious
ex-pel-lee
ex-pel-ling
ex-pend-i-ture
ex-pen-sive
ex-pe-ri-ence

ex-per-i-men-tal
ex-per-i-ment-er
ex-per-tise (n.)
ex-pert-ize (v.)
ex-pi-a-to-ry
ex-pi-ra-tion
ex-pir-a-to-ry
ex-pla-na-tion
ex-plan-a-to-ry
ex-ple-tive
ex-pli-ca-ble
ex-pli-ca-tive
ex-pli-ca-tor
ex-plic-a-to-ry
ex-plic-it-ly
ex-plod-er
ex-ploi-ta-tion
ex-ploit-a-tive
ex-ploit-er
ex-plo-ra-tion
ex-plor-a-to-ry
ex-plo-si-ble
ex-plo-sim-e-ter
ex-plo-sive
ex-po-nen-tial
ex-port-a-ble
ex-por-ta-tion
ex-pose (v.)
ex-po-sé (n.)
ex-po-si-tion
ex-pos-i-to-ry
ex-pos-tu-late
ex-po-sure
ex-press-age
ex-press-er
ex-press-i-ble
ex-pres-sive
ex-pres-sor
ex-pug-na-to-ry
ex-pul-sive
ex-pur-ga-to-ry
ex-quis-ite
ex-sic-cate
ex-tem-po-ra-ne-i-ty
ex-tem-po-re
ex-tem-po-rize
ex-tend-a-ble
ex-tend-er
ex-ten-si-ble
ex-ten-som-e-ter
ex-ten-sor
ex-ten-u-a-tor

ex-te-ri-or-ize
ex-ter-mi-na-tor
ex-ter-nal-i-ty
ex-tinc-tive
ex-tin-guish-er
ex-tir-pa-tor
ex-tract-a-ble
ex-tract-ant
ex-trac-tive
ex-trac-tor
ex-tra-dit-a-ble
ex-tral-i-ty

ex-tra-ne-ous
ex-traor-di-nar-i-ly
ex-trap-o-lat-ed
ex-trap-o-la-to-ry
ex-tra-sen-so-ry
ex-trav-a-gance
ex-trav-a-sa-tion
ex-tre-mism
ex-trem-ist
ex-trem-i-ty
ex-tri-cate
ex-trin-sic

ex-tro-vert-ish
ex-tro-ver-tive
ex-trud-er
ex-tru-si-ble
ex-tu-ber-ance
ex-u-ber-ant
ex-u-da-tion
ex-ult-ant
ex-ul-ta-tion
ex-ur-bi-a
eye-le-teer
ey-ing

F

fa-ba-ceous
Fa-bi-an
fa-bled
fab-ri-ca-tor
Fab-ri-koid
fab-u-lous
fa-cade
face-a-ble
fac-er
fac-et-ed
fa-ce-tious
fa-cial
fa-cient
fa-ci-es
fac-ile
fa-cil-i-ty
fac-ing
fa-con-ne
fac-sim-i-le
fac-tic-i-ty
fac-tious
fac-ti-tious
fac-tor
fac-to-ri-al
fac-to-ry
fac-to-tum
fac-u-la
fac-ul-ty
fa-cun-di-ty
fade-om-e-ter
fad-er
fa-gine
fag-ot
Fahr-en-heit
fa-ience
fail-ure
fai-naigue
fair-y-like

fak-er (one who fakes)
fa-kir (dervish)
Fa-lan-gist
fal-cip-a-rum
fal-con-er
fa-la-cious
fal-la-cy
fall-en
fal-li-bil-i-ty
Fal-lo-pi-an
fal-set-tos
fal-si-fi-ca-tion
fal-si-ty
Fal-staff-i-an
fal-ter
fa-mil-iar
fa-mil-i-ar-i-ty
fa-mil-iar-ize
fam-i-ly
fam-ish
fa-mous
fam-u-lus
fa-nat-i-cal
fa-nat-i-cism
fan-ci-er
fan-ci-ful
Fan-euil
fan-gled
fan-ta-sia
fan-ta-size
fan-tas-tic
fan-ta-sy
far-ad
Far-a-day
fa-rad-ic
far-a-dism
far-ci-cal
fa-ri-na

far-i-na-ceous
far-i-nose
farm-er
far-ther
far-thing
far-thin-gale
fas-ces
fas-ci-cle
fas-cic-u-lar
fas-ci-na-tor
fas-ci-o-li-a-sis
fas-cism
Fas-cist
Fa-scis-ti
fash-ion-a-ble
fas-ten-er
fas-tid-i-ous
fas-tig-i-um
fa-tal-ism
fa-tal-i-ty
fa-ther
fath-om-a-ble
Fa-thom-e-ter
fat-i-ga-ble
fa-tigue
fa-tigu-ing-ly
Fat-i-ma
fa-tu-i-tous
fat-u-ous
fau-cal-ize
fau-cet
fau-nal
fau-vism
fa-ve-o-lus
fa-vism
fa-vor-ite
fa-vor-it-ism
fa-vrile

fa-yal-ite
fe-al-ty
fea-sance
fea-si-bil-i-ty
feath-er-ing
fea-tured
fe-bric-i-ty
fe-bric-u-la
fe-brif-ic
fe-brif-u-gal
feb-ri-fuge
fe-brif-u-gine
feb-rile
fe-bril-i-ty
Feb-ru-ar-y
fe-cal
fec-u-lent
fe-cund
fec-un-date
fe-cun-da-tive
fe-cun-di-ty
fed-er-a-cy
fed-er-al-ese
fed-er-a-tive
fee-ble
Feh-ling
feld-spath-ic
feld-spath-oi-dal
fe-li-cide
fe-lic-i-tate
fe-lic-i-tous
fe-line
fe-lin-i-ty
fel-on
fe-lo-ni-ous
fel-o-ny
felt-er
Felt-ham
fe-luc-ca
fem-i-ne-i-ty
fem-i-nin-i-ty
fem-i-nism
fem-o-ral
fe-mur
fen-chene
fen-chone
fen-chyl
fen-ci-ble
fend-er
fe-nes-tra
fen-es-tra-tion
Fe-ni-an

fe-ra-cious
Fer-di-nand
fer-ment-a-ble
fer-men-ta-tion
fer-ment-a-tive
fer-ment-er
fer-men-tive
fer-mi-um
fe-ro-cious
fe-roc-i-ty
fer-rif-er-ous
fer-ri-na-trite
fer-rit-ic
fer-ri-tin
fer-ro-cene
fer-ro-cy-a-nide
fer-rom-e-ter
fer-ru-gi-nous
fer-rule
fer-til-i-ty
fer-til-iz-a-ble
fer-til-iz-er
fe-ru-lic
fer-va-nite
fer-ven-cy
fer-vor
fes-ter
fes-ti-val
fes-tiv-i-ty
fes-toon
fe-tal
fet-e-ri-ta
fe-ti-cide
fet-id
fe-tid-i-ty
fet-ish-ism
fe-tus
feu-dal-ism
feud-ist
feuil-le-ton
fe-ver-ous
fi-an-ce
Fi-ber-glas
fi-ber-ize
fi-bril-la-tion
fi-brin-o-gen-ic
fi-bri-nog-e-nous
fi-broid
fi-bro-in
fi-bro-sis
fi-bro-si-tis
fi-brous

fib-u-la
fick-le
fic-tile
fic-ti-tious
fid-dler
fi-del-i-ty
fidg-et-y
fi-du-ci-ar-y
field-er
fiend-ish
fi-er-y
fi-es-ta
fight-er
fig-ur-al
fig-u-ra-tion
fig-u-ra-tive
fig-u-rine
fil-a-men-tous
fi-lar-i-al
fil-a-ri-a-sis
fil-bert
fil-i-al
fil-i-bus-ter
fil-i-gree
Fil-i-pi-no
fill-er (filled)
fil-ler (money unit)
fil-let
fil-o-selle
fil-ter-er
filth-i-ness
fil-tra-ble
fil-tra-tion
fin-a-ble
fi-na-gle
fi-nal-e
fi-nal-i-ty
fi-nan-cial
fin-an-cier
fi-nanc-ing
find-er
fin-er-y
fi-nesse
fin-ger
fin-i-cal
fin-ick-y
fi-nis
fin-ished
fi-nite
fin-i-tude
Finn-ish
fir-ing

47

fir-kin
fir-ma-ment
firm-er
fis-cal
fisch-er-ite
fish-er-y
fis-sion
fis-sip-a-rous
fis-sure
fist-i-cuff
fis-tu-la
fis-tu-lous
fix-a-tive
flac-cid-i-ty
flag-el-lant
flag-el-la-tor
flag-eo-let
fla-gi-tious
flag-on
fla-grant
flam-beau
flam-boy-ant
fla-min-go
flam-ma-ble
flang-er
flank-er
flap-er-on
flar-ing
flat-u-lence
flau-tist
flav-a-none
fla-van-throne
fla-ves-cence
fla-vi-an-ic
fla-vin
fla-vo-nol
fla-vo-pur-pu-rin
fla-vor
fledg-ling
fletch-er-ize
flex-i-bi-lize
flex-om-e-ter
flex-or
flex-ur-al
flick-er-y
flin-ders
flir-ta-tious
float-er
floc-cu-lant (n.)
floc-cu-la-tor
floc-cu-lent (adj.)
flood-om-e-ter

flo-ral
Flor-ence
flor-enc-ite
Flor-en-tine
flo-res-cence
flo-ret
flo-ri-cul-tur-al
Flor-i-da
Flo-rid-i-an
flor-id-ness
flo-rif-er-ous
flo-ri-gen
flor-in
flo-rist
flo-riv-o-rous
flor-u-lent
flo-tage
flo-ta-tion
flo-til-la
flot-sam
floun-der
flour-ish
fluc-tu-ate
flu-en-cy
fluff-i-ness
flu-id-i-ty
flu-mer-in
flu-o-bo-rate
flu-o-bo-rite
flu-o-ran-thene
flu-or-ap-a-tite
flu-o-rene
flu-o-re-nyl
flu-o-res-ce-in
flu-o-res-cence
flu-o-ri-date
flu-o-ride
flu-o-ri-dize
flu-o-ri-nate
flu-o-rine
flu-o-rite
flu-o-ro-a-ce-tic
flu-o-ro-graph-ic
flu-o-rog-ra-phy
flu-o-rom-e-ter
flu-o-ro-scope
flu-o-ros-co-py
flu-o-ro-sis
flu-o-sil-i-cate
flu-o-si-lic-ic
flus-ter
flut-ist

flu-vi-al
flu-vi-ol-o-gy
flux-i-ble
flux-ion-al
flux-me-ter
Foam-ite
fo-cal-ize
fo-com-e-ter
fo-cus-er
fo-cus-ing
foi-ble
fol-de-rol
fo-li-a-ceous
fo-li-age
fo-lic
fo-lin-ic
fo-li-o-late
fol-lic-u-lar
fol-lic-u-li-tis
fo-men-ta-tion
fon-dant
fond-ling
fool-er-y
fool-ish
foo-zle
for-age
fo-ra-men
fo-ram-i-na
Fo-ram-i-nif-er-a
fo-ram-i-nif-er-ous
fo-ram-i-nous
for-ay
for-bear-ance
for-ceps
forc-er
forc-i-ble
forc-ing
fore-clo-sure
for-eign-er
fo-ren-si-cal
fore-see-a-ble
for-est-a-tion
for-est-er \
for-est-ry
for-feit-er
for-feit-ure
forg-er
for-ger-y
fo-rint
for-mal
form-al-de-hyde
For-ma-lin

48

for-mal-ist
for-mal-i-ty
for-mal-ize
form-am-ide
form-am-i-dine
form-ant
for-mate
for-ma-tion
form-a-tive
form-a-zan
form-er (one who forms)
for-mer (previous)
for-mic
For-mi-ca
for-mi-cide
for-mi-da-ble
for-mol-ize
For-mo-san
for-mu-la
for-mu-la-ri-za-ble
for-mu-lar-i-za-tion
for-mu-lar-y
for-mu-la-tor
for-myl-ate
for-ni-ca-tion
for-syth-i-a
for-ti-eth
for-ti-fi-ca-tion
for-ti-fy
for-tis-si-mo
for-ti-tude
for-tress
for-tu-i-tous
for-tu-i-ty
for-tu-nate
for-ty
fo-rum
fos-sil-if-er-ous
fos-sil-ize
fos-so-ri-al
fos-ter
fou-lard
foun-da-tion
found-er (n.)
foun-der (v.; also as n.,
  act of foundering)
found-ling
found-ry
foun-tain
Four-drin-i-er
Fou-ri-er
four-ra-gere

fo-ve-o-late
Fow-ler
fowl-er
fra-cas
frac-tion-ate
frac-tious
frac-tog-ra-phy
frac-tur-al
frag-ile
fra-gil-i-ty
frag-men-tal
frag-men-tar-y
frag-ment-ize
fra-grance
frail-ty
fram-er
fran-chise
fran-ci-um
fran-gi-ble
fran-gi-pan-i
frank-furt-er
fran-kin-cense
fran-ti-cal-ly
fra-ter-nal
fra-ter-ni-ty
frat-er-nize
frat-ri-ci-dal
fraud-u-lent
frau-lein
freck-led
free-dom
freez-er
freight-er
fre-net-ic
fren-zied
fre-quen-cy
fre-quen-ta-tion
fresh-et
Freud-i-an
fric-an-deau
fric-as-see
frig-ate
fright-ened
frig-id
Frig-i-daire
fri-gid-i-ty
frig-o-rim-e-ter
fris-ket
frisk-i-ly
fri-vol-i-ty
friv-o-lous
frizz-ing

frol-icked
fron-des-cence
front-age
fron-tal
fron-ta-lis
fron-tier
fron-tis-piece
fron-to-gen-e-sis
front-o-ly-sis
fron-to-pa-ri-e-tal
frost-i-ness
froth-i-ly
frow-zy
fro-zen
fruc-tif-er-ous
fruc-ti-fy
fruc-tose
fru-gal-i-ty
fruit-age
fru-i-tion
frump-ish
frus-trate
frus-tum
fru-tes-cence
fu-ca-ceous
fuch-sia
fuch-sin-o-phil
fu-coi-dal
fu-cos-ter-ol
fu-el-er
fu-ga-cious
fu-gac-i-ty
fu-gi-tive
ful-crum
ful-fill-ing
ful-gen-ic
ful-gide
ful-gu-rant
ful-gu-ra-tion
ful-gu-rite
fu-lig-i-nous
full-ness
ful-mi-nate
ful-min-ic
ful-min-u-ric
fu-ma-rase
fu-mar-ic
fu-mar-o-yl
fum-bler
fu-mig-a-cin
fu-mi-ga-tor
fu-mu-lus

49

fu-nam-bu-list
fun-da-men-tal
fun-dus-co-py
fu-ner-al
fu-ne-re-al
fun-gi-ble
fun-gi-ci-dal
fun-giv-o-rous
fun-goid
fun-gous (adj.)
fun-gus (n.)
fu-ni-cle
fu-nic-u-lar
fun-neled
fu-ra-nose
fu-ran-o-side
fur-be-low
fur-bish

fur-fu-ra-ceous
fur-fu-ral
fur-fu-ryl-i-dene
fu-ri-ous
fur-long
fur-lough
fur-nace
fur-nish-er
fur-ni-ture
fu-ro-ic
fu-ror
fur-ring
fur-ther
fur-thest
fur-tive
fu-run-cle
fu-run-cu-lo-sis
fu-ryl

fu-sar-i-um
fu-see
fu-sel
fu-se-lage
fu-si-ble
fu-si-lier
fu-sil-lade
fu-sion
fu-so-spi-ro-chete
fus-tian
fu-tile
fu-til-i-ty
fu-tu-ram-ic
fu-tur-ist
fu-tu-ri-ty
fuzz-i-ness

G

gab-ar-dine (fabric)
ga-ba-rit
gab-er-dine (gown)
ga-bi-on
ga-bling
Ga-bon
Gab-o-nese
Ga-bri-el
gadg-et-eer
gadg-et-ry
gad-o-le-ic
gad-o-lin-i-um
Gael-ic
gaf-fer
gag-er
gai-ner (diving)
gain-er (one who gains)
Gains-bor-ough
gait-er (harness)
gai-ter (overshoe)
ga-lac-ta-gogue
ga-lac-tic
ga-lac-to-lip-id
gal-ac-tom-e-ter
gal-ac-ton-ic
ga-lac-to-poi-e-sis
ga-lac-tos-a-mine
ga-lac-to-sid-ase
gal-ac-to-sis
ga-lac-tu-ron-ic
Ga-la-pa-gos
gal-a-te-a
ga-lax-i-al

gal-ax-y
ga-le-gine
ga-le-na
ga-le-nic (mineral)
ga-len-ic (medicinal)
ga-le-no-bis-mu-tite
Ga-li-cian
Gal-i-le-an
gal-lant-ry
gal-le-in
gal-ler-y
gal-li-na-ceous
gal-li-nule
Gal-lip-o-li
gal-li-vant
gal-lo-cy-a-nine
gal-lop
gal-op
ga-lore
ga-losh
gal-van-ic
gal-va-nism
gal-va-ni-za-tion
gal-va-nom-e-ter
gal-va-no-met-ric
gal-van-o-scope
Gam-bi-an
gam-bling
gam-boled
game-ster
ga-mete
ga-met-ic
ga-me-to-cide
gam-e-toid

gam-in
gam-ing
gam-ut
gan-der
Gan-dha-ra
Gan-dhi
gan-gling
gan-gli-on-at-ed
gan-gli-on-ic
gan-gli-o-side
gan-gre-nous
gang-ster
gan-is-ter
ga-nom-a-lite
gant-let (track)
Gan-tri-sin
gan-try
gap-er
ga-rage
gar-an-cine
Ga-rand
gar-bage
gar-bling
gar-den-er
gar-de-nia
Gar-di-nol
gar-gan-tu-an
gar-gling
gar-goyle
gar-ish
gar-land
gar-lick-y
gar-ner

gar-ni-er-ite
gar-nish-ee
gar-ni-ture
gar-ru-li-ty
gas-con-ade
gas-e-ous
gas-i-fy
gas-ket
gas-o-line
gas-om-e-ter
gas-o-met-ric
gas-sing
gas-ter-o-sto-ma-ta
gas-tral-gi-a
gas-tra-li-um
gas-trec-to-my
gas-tric
gas-tri-tis
gas-tro-cne-mi-us
gas-tro-en-ter-os-to-my
gas-tro-in-tes-ti-nal
gas-trol-o-ger
gas-tro-nom-ic
gas-tron-o-my
gas-tro-pod
Gas-trop-o-da
gas-tros-co-py
gas-tros-to-my
gath-er-ing
Ga-tun
gau-che-rie
gau-chos
gaud-i-ness
gau-lei-ter
Gaull-ist
gaunt-let
ga-vage
gav-el-er
ga-votte
gawk-i-ness
ga-zelle
gaz-er
ga-zette
gaz-et-teer
Gei-ger
gei-sha
gel-a-tin-ase
ge-lat-i-nate
ge-lat-i-ni-za-tion
ge-lat-i-niz-er
ge-lat-i-no-chlo-ride
ge-lat-i-nous

ge-la-tion
geld-ing
ge-lid-i-ty
gel-ig-nite
gel-ling
gel-ose
gel-se-mic
gem-i-na-tive
Gem-i-ni
gem-mif-er-ous
gen-dar-mer-y
gen-der
gen-e-al-o-gist
gen-e-al-o-gy
gen-er-a-lis-si-mo
gen-er-al-i-ty
gen-er-al-ize
gen-er-a-tor
ge-ner-i-cal
gen-er-os-i-ty
gen-e-sis
gen-et
ge-net-i-cal
Ge-ne-va
ge-nial
ge-ni-al-i-ty
gen-ic
ge-nic-u-late
ge-nie
gen-in
ge-ni-o-plas-ty
ge-nis-te-in
gen-i-tal
gen-i-tive
gen-i-to-u-ri-nar-y
ge-nius
Gen-o-a
gen-o-ci-dal
ge-nome
ge-no-mere
gen-o-type
genth-ite
gen-tian-in
gen-tian-ose
gen-til-i-ty
gen-ti-o-bi-ose
gen-tis-ic
gen-ti-sin
gent-ly
gen-try
gen-u-flec-to-ry
gen-u-ine

ge-nus
ge-o-ce-rite
ge-oc-ro-nite
ge-o-des-ic
ge-od-e-sy
ge-o-det-i-cal
ge-od-ic
ge-o-dim-e-ter
ge-og-e-nous
ge-og-nos-tic
ge-og-o-ny
ge-og-ra-pher
ge-o-graph-ic
ge-og-ra-phy
ge-oi-dal
ge-o-log-i-cal
ge-ol-o-gist
ge-ol-o-gy
ge-om-a-lism
ge-om-e-ter
ge-o-met-ri-cal
ge-om-e-triz-er
ge-om-e-try
ge-o-pon-ics
geor-gette
Geor-gian
ge-os-co-py
ge-ot-ri-cho-sis
ge-o-trop-ic
ge-ot-ro-pism
ge-ran-ic
ge-ra-ni-ol
ge-ra-ni-um
ge-ra-nyl
Ge-rard
ge-rat-ic
ger-a-tol-o-gy
ge-rent
ger-i-a-tri-cian
ger-i-at-rics
ger-mane
ger-ma-nite
ger-ma-ni-um
ger-mi-ci-dal
ger-mi-nal
ger-mi-na-tor
Ge-ron-i-mo
ger-on-toc-ra-cy
ge-ron-to-log-i-cal
ger-on-tol-o-gy
Ger-trude
ger-und

51

ger-un-di-val
ge-run-dive
ge-sell-schaft
Ge-stalt
Ge-sta-po
ges-ta-tion
ges-tic-u-late
ges-ture
Geth-sem-a-ne
gey-ser
Gha-na-ian
gher-kin
ghoul-ish
gibbs-ite
Gi-bral-tar
gi-gan-tic
gi-gan-tism
gild-er
gil-son-ite
gim-baled
gin-ger
ging-ham
gin-gi-val
gin-gi-vi-tis
gink-go
gin-seng
gi-raffe
Gi-rard
gird-er
gir-dling
girl-ish
gi-tal-in
gi-tox-i-gen-in
giv-en
gla-bres-cent
gla-brous
gla-cial
gla-ci-a-tion
gla-cier
gla-ci-ol-o-gy
gla-ci-om-e-ter
glad-i-a-tor
glad-i-o-lus
glam-or-ous
glam-our
glan-ders
glan-du-lar
glar-ing
glass-ine
glass-i-ness
glau-ber-ite
glau-co-cer-i-nite

glau-co-ma
glau-co-ma-tous
glau-co-nite
glau-cous
glaz-er
gla-zier
glis-ten
gloam-ing
glob-al-ism
glo-bal-i-ty
glo-boid
glob-u-lar
glob-ule
glob-u-lif-er-ous
glob-u-lin
glo-mer-u-lar
gloom-i-ly
glo-ri-fy
glo-ri-ous
glos-sa-ry
gloss-i-ness
gloss-me-ter
Glouces-ter
glov-er
glu-ca-mine
glu-car-ic
glu-cin-i-um
glu-ci-tol
glu-ci-tyl
glu-co-nate
glu-con-ic
glu-co-py-ran-o-side
glu-co-sa-mine
glu-cose
glu-co-si-dase
glu-co-side
glu-cu-ron-ic
glu-cu-ron-i-dase
glu-cu-ro-nide
glu-ey-ness
glu-ing
glut-a-con-ic
glu-ta-mate
glu-tam-ic
glu-ta-min-ase
glu-ta-mine
glu-ta-min-ic
glu-tam-o-yl
glu-ta-thi-one
glu-te-al
glu-ten
glu-te-nin

glu-ten-ous
glu-ti-nous
glyc-er-ate
gly-ce-mi-a
gly-ce-mic
glyc-er-al-de-hyde
gly-cer-ic
glyc-er-ide
glyc-er-in
glyc-er-ol
glyc-er-o-phos-phor-ic
glyc-er-yl
glyc-ide
gly-cid-ic
glyc-i-dol
gly-cine
gly-co-cy-a-mine
gly-co-gen
gly-co-gen-ol-y-sis
gly-co-gen-o-lyt-ic
gly-col-y-sis
gly-co-lyt-ic
gly-co-si-dase
glyc-u-re-sis
gly-cyl
gly-ox-yl-ic
glyp-tol-o-gy
gnath-ism
gneiss-oid
gnom-ish
gno-se-ol-o-gy
gno-sis
gnos-tic
goa-tee
gob-ble-dy-gook
gob-bler
Go-be-lin
gob-lin
Goe-thals
goi-ter
goi-tro-gen-ic
goi-tro-ge-nic-i-ty
goi-trous
gold-en
Go-li-ath
go-nad-ec-to-my
go-nad-o-tro-phin
gon-do-la
gon-fa-lon
go-nid-i-al
go-nid-i-um
go-ni-om-e-ter

go-ni-o-met-ric
gon-o-coc-ci
gon-or-rhe-al
goo-gol-plex
go-pher
gor-geous
go-ril-la
gor-lic
Go-shen
gos-pel-er
gos-sa-mer
gos-syp-i-trin
Goth-am-ite
Goth-ic
gour-man-diz-er
gov-ern-ess
gov-ern-men-tal
gov-er-nor
goy-a-zite
Graaf-i-an
grac-ile
gra-cious
gra-da-tion
grad-a-to-ry
grad-er
gra-di-ent
gra-di-om-e-ter
grad-u-al
grad-u-ate
graft-er
gra-ham
grai-ning (fish)
grain-ing (of grain)
gram-i-cid-in
gram-i-na-les
gram-ine
gra-min-e-ous
gram-mar-i-an
gram-mat-i-cal
gra-na-ry
gran-dam
gran-deur
gran-dil-o-quent
gran-di-ose
grang-er
gran-ite
gra-nit-ic
gran-o-blas-tic
gran-o-di-o-rite
grant-ee
grant-er
Grant-ham

grant-or
gran-u-lar-i-ty
gran-u-late
gran-ule
gran-u-lo-ma-to-sis
gran-u-lous
graph-eme
gra phe-mic
graph-i-cal
graph-ite
gra-phit-ic
gra-phol-o-gy
graph-o-met-ric
grap-pling
grasp-er
grat-er
grat-i-cule
grat-i-fy
grat-in
gra-tis
grat-i-tude
gra-tu-i-tous
gra-va-men
grav-eled
grav-el-ly
grav-en
grav-id
gra-vid-i-ty
grav-i-me-ter
grav-i-met-ri-cal-ly
gra-vim-e-try
grav-i-sphere
grav-i-tat-er
grav-i-tom-e-ter
grav-i-ty
gra-vure
graz-er
greas-er
greas-i-ness
Gre-cian
greed-i-ness
green-sward
gre-gar-i-ous
Gre-go-ri-an
grei-sen
gre-nade
gren-a-dier
gren-a-dine
Gresh-am
grid-i-ron
griev-ance
griev-ous

Gri-gnard
gril-lage
grim-ace
gri-mal-kin
grind-er
grin-gos
griph-ite
gris-e-o-ful-vin
gris-tly
griz-zly
gro-cer-y
gro-per (fish)
grop-er
gro-schen
gros-grain
gro-tesque
gro-tes-que-rie
ground-ling
grou-per (fish)
group-er
grou-ser (timber; cleats)
grous-er
grout-er
grov-el-er
growl-er
grum-bler
gru-mose
grun-ion
Gru-yere
guai-ac
guai-a-col
Gua-ma-ni-an
gua-na-mine
gua-ni-dine
gua-nif-er-ous
gua-nine
gua-nyl-ic
gua-ra-ni
guar-an-tee (n., v.)
guar-an-ty (n.) (legal)
guard-i-an
Gua-te-ma-la
gua-va
gua-yu-le
gu-ber-na-to-ri-al
gudg-eon
guer-don
Guern-sey
guer-ril-la
guid-ance
gui-don
guil-lo-tine

53

guilt-i-ly
Guin-ea
gui-pure
gui-tar
gul-den
gul-li-ble
gu-lose
Gun-ite
gur-gi-ta-tion
gur-gling

gur-nard
gush-er
gus-set
gus-ta-to-ry
Gu-ten-berg
gut-tur-al
Guy-a-nese
gym-na-si-um
gym-nas-tic
gym-no-sto-ma-ta

gym-no-stom-a-tous
gyn-e-coc-ra-cy
gyn-e-col-o-gy
gyp-se-ous
gyp-sif-er-ous
gy-ra-to-ry
gy-roi-dal
gy-ro-scop-ic

H

ha-be-as
ha-ben-dum
hab-er-dash-er-y
ha-bil-i-ment
hab-it-a-ble
hab-i-ta-tion
ha-bit-u-al
ha-bit-u-e
ha-chure
ha-ci-en-da
hack-ler
Ha-des
haf-ni-um
Ha-ga-nah
hag-i-ol-o-gy
Hai-fa
hai-kwan
Hai-tian
ha-la-tion
hal-a-zone
hal-berd-ier
hal-cy-on
hal-i-but
ha-lide
hal-i-dom
hal-i-eu-tics
hal-i-ste-re-sis
ha-lite
hal-i-to-sis
hal-le-lu-jah
Hal-low-een
hal-lu-ci-na-tion
ha-lo
hal-o-gen-a-tion
ha-log-e-nous
hal-o-hy-drin
ha-lom-e-ter
ha-lot-ri-chite
halt-er (one who halts)
hal-ter (other meanings)

ham-burg-er
Ham-mar-skjold
ham-per
ham-ster
hand-i-cap
hand-i-craft
hand-i-ly
hand-i-work
han-dle-a-ble
han-dler
han-dling
hand-som-est
hang-ar
hang-er
han-ker
Han-o-ver
Ha-nuk-kah
hap-pi-ness
har-a-kir-i
ha-rangued
ha-rangu-er
har-assed
har-bin-ger
har-bor
hard-en-er
har-di-ness
Har-ding
har-dy
ha-rem
har-i-cot
hark-en
har-le-quin
har-ma-line
har-mon-i-al
har-mon-i-ca
har-mo-ni-ous
har-mo-nize
har-ness
harp-ist
har-poon

harp-si-chord
har-te-beest
Hart-ley
har-um-scar-um
har-vest-er
hash-ish
has-sled
has-tate
has-ten
hast-i-ly
Hast-ings
hatch-er-y
hatch-et
ha-tred
haugh-ti-ness
hau-teur
Ha-va-na
ha-ven
hav-er-sack
hav-oc
Ha-wai-ian
haw-ser
haz-ard-ous
ha-zel
haz-ing
head-quar-ters
health-i-est
heart-i-ly
heat-er
hea-then
heath-er
heav-en
heav-i-ly
Heav-i-side
heb-dom-a-dal
He-bra-ic
He-brew
Heb-ri-des
Hec-a-te
hec-a-tomb

54

heck-ler
hec-o-gen-in
hec-tare
hec-to-li-ter
hec-to-me-ter
hed-er-in
he-don-ics
he-do-nism
he-do-nis-tic
he-do-nom-e-ter
he-dral
heg-e-mon-ic
he-gem-o-ny
he-gi-ra
heif-er
hei-li-gen-schein
hei-nous
Hel-e-na
hel-e-nin
he-li-a-cal
he-li-an-the-mum
he-li-an-thus
hel-i-cal
hel-i-ces
hel-i-coi-dal
Hel-i-con
hel-i-cop-ter
he-li-o-graph
he-li-og-ra-phy
he-li-om-e-ter
he-li-o-met-ric
he-li-om-e-try
he-li-o-pho-bic
he-li-o-trope
he-li-ot-ro-pism
hel-i-port
he-li-um
he-lix
he-lix-om-e-ter
Hel-len-ic
Hel-le-nism
Hel-les-pont
hel-min-thic
hel-min-tho-spo-rin
hel-ot-ism
hel-ter-skel-ter
hel-vite
hel-vol-ic
he-ma-cy-tom-e-ter
he-ma-fi-brite
he-mag-glu-ti-nin
he-mal-bu-men

he-man-gi-o-ma-to-sis
he-ma-poi-e-sis
he-mar-thro-sis
he-ma-tal
he-ma-te-in
he-mat-ic
hem-a-tin-om-e-ter
hem-a-tite
hem-a-tit-ic
hem-a-to-cele
hem-a-to-crit
hem-a-tog-e-nous
hem-a-to-lite
he-ma-tol-o-gy
he-ma-to-ma
he-ma-tom-e-ter
hem-a-to-por-phy-rin
he-ma-to-sis
he-ma-tox-y-lin
hem-i-ac-e-tal
hem-i-cy-clic
hem-i-he-dral
hem-i-kar-y-on
he-min
he-mip-ter-oid
hem-i-spher-ic
hem-i-stich-al
he-mo-chro-mo-gen
he-mo-chro-mom-e-ter
he-mo-co-ni-o-sis
he-mo-cy-a-nin
he-mo-cyte
he-mo-cy-tol-y-sis
he-mo-glo-bin
he-mo-glo-bi-nom-e-ter
he-mol-y-sin
he-mol-y-sis
he-mo-lyt-ic
he-mom-e-ter
hem-or-rhag-ic
hem-or-rhoi-dal
he-mo-sid-er-in
he-mo-sid-er-o-sis
he-mo-stat-ic
hemp-en
hen-e-quen
hep-a-rin
he-pat-i-ca
hep-a-ti-tis
hep-a-to-cu-pre-in
hep-a-to-fla-vin
hep-a-tos-co-py
hep-ta-dec-yl

hep-tag-o-nal
hep-tam-e-ter
hep-tar-chy
hep-tu-lose
hep-tyl-ene
her-ald
he-ral-dic
her-ba-ceous
herb-age
her-bar-i-um
her-bi-ci-dal
her-biv-o-rous
Her-cu-les
her-e-dit-a-ment
he-red-i-tar-y
Her-e-ford
her-e-sy
her-e-tic
he-ret-i-cal
her-it-age
her-maph-ro-dite
her-me-neu-tics
her-met-i-cal
her-mit-age
her-ne-ar-in
her-ni-a
her-ni-ot-o-my
he-ro-ic
her-o-ine
her-o-ism
her-on
her-pes
her-pe-tol-o-gy
Hertz-i-an
hes-i-tan-cy
hes-i-tat-er
hes-i-ta-tion
hes-per-i-din
Hes-per-is
Hes-sian
hess-ite
het-er-o-aux-in
het-er-o-cy-clic
het-er-o-dox-y
het-er-o-ge-ne-ous
het-er-og-e-nous
het-er-o-ki-ne-sis
het-er-ol-o-gy
het-er-ol-y-sis
het-er-o-ou-si-a
het-er-o-pol-y
het-er-os-co-py

hex-a-chlo-ro-eth-ane
hex-a-gon
hex-ag-o-nal
hex-a-he-dral
hex-am-e-ter
hex-a-no-yl
hex-es-trol
hex-os-a-mine
hex-u-lose
hex-u-ron-ic
hex-yl-ene
hi-a-tus
hi-ber-na-tor
hick-o-ry
hid-e-ous
hi-dro-sis
hi-drot-ic
hi-er-ar-chy
hi-er-o-glyph-ic
high-fa-lu-tin
hi-lar-i-ous
hill-ocked
hi-lus
Hi-ma-la-yan
hin-der (v.)
hind-er (adj.)
hin-drance
Hin-du-stan-i
hint-er
hin-ter-land
Hip-po-crat-ic
hip-po-pot-a-mus
hip-pu-ric
Hir-o-shi-ma
hir-su-tal
His-pa-ni-a
His-pan-ic
his-pa-ni-dad
his-tam-i-nase
his-ta-mine
his-ti-dine
his-to-log-i-cal
his-tol-o-gy
his-tol-y-sis
his-to-ri-an
his-tor-i-cal
his-to-ric-i-ty
his-to-ry
his-tri-on-ic
hith-er-to
hock-ey

hod-o-graph
Hoh-en-zol-lern
hoist-er
hold-er
hol-i-day
ho-li-ness
hol-lan-daise
Hol-land-er
hol-mi-um
hol-o-caust
hol-o-graph
hol-o-he-dral
hol-o-pho-tal
ho-loph-ra-sis
hol-ster
Hol-yoke
hom-age
ho-me-ol-o-gy
ho-me-o-path-ic
ho-me-op-a-thy
ho-me-o-sta-sis
hom-i-ci-dal
hom-i-let-ics
hom-i-ly
hom-ish
hom-o-cys-teine
ho-mog-a-my
ho-mo-ge-ne-i-ty
ho-mo-ge-ne-ous
ho-mog-e-ni-za-tion
ho-mog-e-niz-er
ho-mog-e-nous
hom-o-log
ho-mol-o-gous
ho-mol-y-sis
hom-o-nym-ic
ho-mo-thet-ic
Hon-du-ran
hon-ey
Hon-i-ton
Hon-o-lu-lu
hon-or-a-ble
hon-o-rar-i-um
hon-or-ar-y
hon-or-if-ic
Hoo-ver
ho-ra-ry
ho-ri-zon
hor-i-zon-tal
hor-mo-nal
hor-mon-ic
ho-rol-o-gy
hor-o-scope

ho-ros-co-py
hor-ren-dous
hor-rif-ic
hor-ta-to-ry
hor-ti-cul-tur-al
ho-san-na
ho-sier-y
hos-pi-ta-ble
hos-pi-tal-i-za-tion
hos-tage
host-al
hos-tel-ry
host-ess
hos-til-i-ty
hos-tler
Hou-dry
hous-ing
hov-el
hov-er
how-it-zer
howl-er
how-lite
hua-ra-che
huck-ster
Hue-ne-me
Hu-gue-not
hul-la-ba-loo
hu-man-i-tar-i-an
hu-man-ize
hum-bling
hu-mec-tant
hu-mer-us
hu-mid-i-ty
hu-mil-i-a-tion
hu-min
hum-ite
hu-mi-ture
hu-mor-ous
hu-mous (adj.)
hu-mu-lene
hu-mus (n.)
hun-dred
Hun-gar-i-an
hun-ger
hun-gry
hunt-er
hur-dler
hurl-er
Hu-ron
hur-ried-ly
hur-ter (bumper)
hurt-er

56

hur-tling
hus-band-ry
husk-i-ness
hus-ting
hus-tler
hy-a-cin-thine
Hy-a-des
hy-a-les-cence
hy-a-lin-i-za-tion
hy-a-li-no-sis
hy-al-o-gen
hy-al-o-phane
hy-a-lu-ro-nate
hy-a-lu-ron-i-dase
hy-brid-ize
hy-dan-to-in-ate
hy-da-tid-o-sis
hy-da-to-gen-ic
hy-drac-ry-late
hy-dra-cryl-ic
hy-dral-a-zine
hy-dra-mat-ic
hy-dra-mine
hy-dran-ge-a
hy-drar-gil-lite
hy-dras-ti-nine
hy-dra-tor
hy-drau-lic
hy-dra-zide
hy-draz-i-dine
hy-dra-zine
hy-dra-zin-i-um
hy-dra-zo-ate
hy-dra-zone
hy-dre-mi-a
hy-dri-od-ic
hy-dri-o-dide
hy-dro-ab-i-et-yl
hy-dro-cal-u-mite
hy-dro-cele
hy-dro-ce-phal-ic

hy-dro-ceph-a-lous (adj.)
hy-dro-ceph-a-lus (n.)
hy-dro-chlo-ric
hy-dro-flu-or-ide
hy-dro-form-ate
hy-dro-gen-a-tion
hy-dro-gen-a-tor
hy-drog-e-nous
hy-drog-no-sy
hy-drog-ra-pher
hy-dro-graph-ic
hy-dro-lase
hy-drol-o-gy
hy-drol-y-sate
hy-drol-y-sis
hy-drol-yze
hy-drom-e-ter
hy-dro-met-ric
hy-dro-ni-um
hy-drop-a-thy
hy-dro-pho-bi-a
hy-dro-pon-ics
hy-drox-ide
hy-drox-im-i-no
hy-drox-y-am-i-no
hy-drox-y-bu-tyr-ic
hy-drox-yl-a-mine
hy-drox-yl-ate
hy-drox-y-zine
hy-e-tom-e-ter
hy-gi-en-ic
hy-gien-ist
hy-grom-e-ter
hy-gro-met-ric
hy-gro-scop-ic
hy-me-ne-al
hy-me-no-cal-lis
hy-per-bo-la
hy-per-bo-le
hy-per-bol-i-cal
hy-per-bo-loi-dal

hy-per-crit-i-cal
hy-per-e-mi-a
hy-per-go-lic-i-ty
hy-per-i-cin
hy-per-in
hy-per-o-pi-a
hy-per-sthene
hy-per-ten-sive
hy-per-troph-ic
hy-per-tro-phy
hy-phen-ate
hyp-no-sis
hyp-not-ic
hyp-no-tism
hy-po-bro-mous
hy-po-chlo-rous
hy-po-chon-dri-a
hy-poc-ri-sy
hyp-o-crite
hy-po-der-mic
hy-poid
hy-po-i-o-dous
hy-po-mor-pho-sis
hy-pos-ta-sis
hy-pot-e-nuse
hy-poth-e-cate
hy-poth-e-sis
hy-po-thet-i-cal
hy-pox-e-mi-a
hy-pox-i-a
hyp-som-e-ter
hys-taz-a-rin
hys-ter-ec-to-my
hys-ter-e-sis
hys-ter-i-a
hys-ter-i-cal
hys-ter-or-rha-phy
hys-ter-os-co-py
hys-ter-ot-o-my
hy-ther-graph

I

i-at-ro-gen-ic
i-at-ro-ge-nic-i-ty
I-be-ri-an
Ice-land-er
Ice-lan-dic
ich-neu-mon
ich-nog-ra-phy
Ich-thy-ol
ich-thy-o-sis
i-ci-cle

ic-ing
i-con-o-clast
i-co-nog-ra-phy
i-co-nol-a-try
i-co-nom-e-ter
i-con-o-scope
ic-ter-ic
I-da-ho-an
i-de-al-ism
i-de-al-ist

hy-per-crit-i-cal
i-de-al-i-za-tion
i-den-ti-cal
i-den-ti-fi-a-ble
i-de-oc-ra-cy
i-de-og-ra-phy
i-de-o-log-i-cal
i-de-ol-o-gy
id-i-o-cy
i-di-o-gram-mat-ic
id-i-om

57

id-i-o-mat-ic
id-i-om-e-ter
id-i-o-path-ic
id-i-op-a-thy
id-i-o-syn-cra-sy
id-i-ot-i-cal
id-i-tol
i-dol-a-ter
i-dol-a-trous
i-dol-ize
i-dyl-lic
i-dyll-ist
ig-loo
ig-ne-ous
ig-nit-a-ble
ig-nit-er
ig-ni-tron
ig-no-min-i-ous
ig-no-min-y
ig-no-ra-mus
ig-no-rance
Ig-o-rot
il-e-i-tis
il-e-os-to-my
il-e-um
il-leg-i-ble
il-lic-it
il-lim-it-a-ble
Il-li-nois-an
il-lu-mi-nant
il-lu-mi-na-tor
il-lu-min-er
il-lu-mi-nom-e-ter
il-lu-sive
il-lu-so-ry
il-lus-tra-tive
il-lu-vi-al
il-men-ite
I-lo-i-lo
im-age-ry
i-mag-i-na-ble
i-mag-i-nar-y
i-mag-i-na-tive
i-ma-go
im-be-cil-i-ty
im-bri-cate
im-bro-glio
im-id-az-ole
im-id-az-o-line
im-ide
im-i-do
im-in-az-ole

im-i-no
im-i-ta-tive
im-mac-u-late
im-ma-nence
im-mar-gin-ate
im-me-di-a-cy
im-mem-o-ra-ble
im-me-mo-ri-al
im-men-si-ty
im-men-su-ra-ble
im-mers-i-ble
im-mers-ing
im-mer-sion
im-mi-gra-tion
im-mi-nent
im-mis-ci-ble
im-mo-late
im-mu-ni-ty
im-mu-ni-za-tion
Im-mu-no-gen
im-mu-nol-o-gy
im-mu-ta-ble
im-pac-tive
im-pal-pa-ble
im-par-ta-tion
im-part-i-ble
im-pass-a-ble
im-pas-si-ble
im-pas-sive
im-pa-tience
im-pe-cu-ni-ous
im-ped-ance
im-ped-i-ble
im-ped-i-men-tal
im-pe-dom-e-ter
im-pe-dor
im-pel-ling
im-per-a-tive
im-pe-ra-tor
im-per-cep-ti-ble
im-per-fo-rate
im-pe-ri-al
im-per-iled
im-pe-ri-ous
im-per-scrip-ti-ble
im-per-son-a-tor
im-per-sua-si-ble
im-per-turb-a-ble
im-per-vi-ous
im-pe-ti-go

im-pet-u-os-i-ty
im-pe-tus
im-ping-er
im-ping-ing
im-pi-ous
imp-ish
im-plac-a-ble
im-plan-ta-tion
im-plau-si-ble
im-ple-men-tal
im-pli-cate
im-plic-it-ly
im-plo-sion
im-pol-i-tic
im-por-tance
im-por-tant
im-port-er
im-por-tu-nate
im-post-er
im-pos-tor (deceiv)
im-pos-ture
im-po-tence
im-pov-er-ish
im-prec-a-to-ry
im-preg-na-tor
im-pre-sar-i-o
im-pre-scrip-ti-ble
im-press-a-ble
im-press-i-ble
im-pres-sive
im-pri-ma-tur
im-promp-tu
im-prov-i-dent
im-prov-i-sa-tion
im-pro-vise
im-pu-dence
im-pul-sive
im-pu-ni-ty
im-pu-ri-ty
im-put-a-ble
im-pu-ta-tion
in-ad-vert-ent
in-am-o-ra-ta
in-an-i-mate
in-a-ni-tion
in-an-i-ty
in-au-gu-ra-tion
in-cal-cu-la-ble
in-ca-les-cent
in-can-des-cent
in-ca-pac-i-tate
in-car-cer-ate

in-car-nate
in-cen-di-ar-y
in-cen-tive
in-cep-tive
in-ces-tu-ous
in-cho-ate
in-ci-den-tal
in-cin-er-a-tor
in-cip-i-ent
in-ci-sive
in-ci-sor
in-cit-ant
in-ci-ta-tion
in-cit-er
in-clem-ent
in-clin-a-ble
in-cli-na-tion
in-cli-na-to-ry
in-cli-nom-e-ter
in-clud-a-ble
in-clu-sive
in-cog-ni-to
in-com-pa-ra-ble
in-com-pat-i-ble
in-con-cus-si-ble
in-con-gru-ous
in-cor-po-ra-tor
in-cor-ri-gi-ble
in-creas-er
in-cred-i-ble
in-cre-du-li-ty
in-cred-u-lous
in-cre-ment
in-crim-i-nate
in-crus-ta-tion
in-cu-ba-tor
in-cu-bous (adj.)
in-cu-bus (n.)
in-cum-bent
in-cu-nab-u-lum
in-cur-a-ble
in-cur-ra-ble
in-cur-sive
in-da-mine
in-da-zole
in-de-fat-i-ga-ble
in-dem-ni-fi-ca-tion
in-dene
in-den-ta-tion
in-dent-er
in-den-ture
in-de-pend-ent

in-de-struct-i-ble
In-di-an
In-di-an-a
In-di-an-ap-o-lis
In-di-an-i-an
in-di-can
in-di-ca-tion
in-dic-a-tive
in-di-ca-tor
in-di-ci-a
in-dic-o-lite
in-dict-a-ble
in-dict-er
In-dies
in-dig-e-nous
in-di-gent
in-di-gest-i-ble
in-di-go
in-dig-o-lite
In-di-go-sol
in-dig-o-tin
in-di-ru-bin
in-dis-pen-sa-ble
in-dis-pu-ta-ble
in-dis-sol-u-ble
in-di-um
in-di-vid-u-al-ize
in-di-vis-i-ble
in-doc-tri-nate
in-dole-a-ce-tic
in-do-lent
in-do-line
in-do-lyl
in-dom-i-ta-ble
In-do-ne-sian
in-do-phe-nin
in-dox-yl
in-du-bi-ta-ble
in-duc-er
in-duc-i-ble
in-duct-ance
in-duct-ee
in-duc-tive
in-duc-tom-e-ter
in-duc-tor
in-duc-to-ri-um
in-dul-gence
in-du-line
in-du-ra-tive
in-dus-tri-al-i-za-tion
in-e-bri-ate
in-ef-fa-ble

in-ef-face-a-ble
in-e-luc-ta-ble
in-ep-ti-tude
in-ert-ance
in-er-tial
in-ev-i-ta-ble
in-ex-o-ra-ble
in-ex-press-i-ble
in-ex-pres-sive
in-ex-pung-i-ble
in-ex-tir-pa-ble
in-ex-tri-ca-ble
in-fa-mous
in-fan-ti-cide
in-fan-tile
in-fan-try
in-fat-u-ate
in-fect-ant
in-fect-i-ble
in-fec-tious
in-fec-tive
in-fe-lic-i-tous
in-fer-a-ble
in-fer-ence
in-fe-ri-or-i-ty
in-fer-nal
in-fest-ant
in-fes-ta-tion
in-fil-tra-tor
in-fil-trom-e-ter
in-fi-nite
in-fin-i-tes-i-mal
in-fin-i-ti-val
in-fin-i-ty
in-fir-ma-ry
in-fir-mi-ty
in-flat-a-ble
in-flect-i-ble
in-flict-er
in-flo-res-cence
in-flu-en-tial
in-for-mal-i-ty
in-for-ma-lize
in-form-ant
in-for-ma-tion
in-form-a-tive
in-form-er
in-fract-i-ble
in-fran-gi-ble
in-fring-er
in-fun-dib-u-lum
in-fu-ri-ate

in-fu-si-ble
in-fu-so-ri-al
in-ge-nious
in-ge-nue
in-ge-nu-i-ty
in-gen-u-ous
in-ges-tant
in-got
in-gra-ti-ate
in-grat-i-tude
in-gra-ves-cence
in-grav-i-date
in-gre-di-ent
in-gui-nal
in-gur-gi-tate
in-hab-it-a-bil-i-ty
in-hab-it-ant
in-hab-it-er
in-hal-ant
in-ha-la-tion
in-ha-la-tor
in-her-ent
in-her-it-a-ble
in-her-it-ance
in-her-it-er
in-hib-it-er
in-hi-bi-tion
in-hib-i-tor (chem.)
in-hib-i-to-ry
in-hos-pit-a-ble
in-im-i-cal
in-im-i-ta-ble
in-iq-ui-tous
i-ni-tial
i-ni-ti-a-tive
in-jec-tor
in-junc-tive
in-ju-ri-ous
in-kling
in me-mo-ri-am
in-nas-ci-ble
in-noc-u-ous
in-no-va-to-ry
in-nu-en-do
in-nu-mer-a-ble
in-oc-u-late
in-or-di-nate
i-no-si-tol
in per-so-nam
in-quir-er
in-quir-y
in-qui-si-tion
in-quis-i-tive

in-sa-tia-ble
in-scrib-a-ble
in-scrib-er
in-scru-ta-ble
in-sec-ti-ci-dal
in-sec-tiv-o-ra
in-sec-tiv-o-rous
in-sec-tol-o-gy
in-sem-i-na-tion
in-sen-sate
in-ser-tive
in-sid-i-ous
in-sig-ne
in-sig-ni-a
in-sig-nif-i-cant
in-sip-id
in-si-pid-i-ty
in-sist-ence
in-sist-er
in-so-lence
in-sol-u-ble
in-sol-vent
in-sou-ci-ance
in-sou-ci-ant
in-spec-tor
In-spec-to-scope
in-spir-a-ble
in-spi-ra-tion
in-spir-a-tive
in-stal-la-tion
in-stalled
in-stan-ta-ne-ous
in-sti-ga-tor
in-stinc-tive
in-sti-tu-tor
in-struct-i-ble
in-struc-tive
in-struc-tor
in-stru-men-tal-i-ty
in-su-lar
in-su-la-tor
in-su-lin
in-su-per-a-ble
in-sur-ance
in-sur-er
in-sur-gen-cy
in-tagl-io
in-tan-gi-ble
in-te-ger
in-te-gral
in-te-gra-tor
in-teg-ri-ty

in-teg-u-men-tal
in-tel-lec-tu-al
in-tel-li-gen-tsi-a
in-tend-ant
in-ten-si-fy
in-ten-si-tom-e-ter
in-ten-si-ty
in-ten-sive
in-ter-ca-lar-y
in-ter-cede
in-ter-cep-tor
in-ter-cos-tal
in-ter-est
in-ter-fer-ence
in-ter-fer-om-e-ter
in-ter-im
in-te-ri-or
in-ter-jec-tor
in-ter-jec-tur-al
in-ter-lin-gua
in-ter-loc-u-to-ry
in-ter-lop-er
in-ter-me-di-ate
in-ter-mi-na-ble
in-tern
in-ter-nal
in-ter-ne-cine
in-ter-nist
in-ter-po-lat-er
in-ter-pret-a-ble
in-ter-pre-ta-tive
in-ter-pret-er
in-ter-pre-tive
in-ter-ro-gate
in-ter-rog-a-to-ry
in-ter-rupt-ed
in-ter-rupt-er
in-ter-rupt-i-ble
in-ter-rupt-ing
in-ter-stic-es
in-ter-sti-tial
in-ter-ven-er
in-ter-ve-nor (law)
in-tes-tate
in-tes-ti-nal
in-ti-ma-cy
in-ti-mat-er
in-tim-i-da-tor
in-to-nate
In-tox-im-e-ter
in-trac-ta-ble
in-tran-si-gent (n.,

in-trav-a-sa-tion
in-tra-ve-nous
in-trep-id
in-tre-pid-i-ty
in-tri-ca-cy
in-trigu-er
in-trigu-ing
in-trin-si-cal
in-tro-duc-to-ry
in-tro-spec-tive
in-tro-ver-si-ble
in-trud-er
in-tru-sive
in-tu-i-tive
in-tu-mes-cence
in-u-lase
in-un da-tor
in-vad-er
in-va-lid (n., v., adj., not well)
in-val-id (adj., not valid)
in-val-i-date
in-va-lid-i-ty
in-var-i-a-ble
in-vec-tive
in-vei-gle
in-vent-a-ble
in-ven-tor
in-ven-to-ry
in-vert-ase
in-ver-te-brate
in-vert-er
in-vert-i-ble
in-ver-tor (muscle)
in-ves-ti-ga-tor
in-ves-ti-ture
in-ves-tor
in-vet-er-ate
in-vid-i-ous
in-vig-o-rate
in-vin-ci-ble
in-vi-o-la-ble
in-vis-i-ble
in-vi-ta-tion
in-vit-er
in-vo-ca-tion
in-voc-a-tive
in-vo-lu-cre

i-o-di-nate
i-o-dine
i-o-din-oph-i-lous
i-o-do-a-ce-tic
i-o-do-form
i-o-do-hy-drin
i-o-dom-e-try
i-o-do-ni-um
i-o-do-phthal-ein
i-o-do-pyr-a-cet
i-o-dox-y-ben-zene
i-od-y-rite
I-o-ni-an
I-on-ic
i-o-ni-um
i-on-i-za-tion
i-o-nom-e-ter
i-o-none
i-on-o-spher-ic
I-o-wan
ip-e-cac
I-ra-ni-an
i-ras-ci-ble
ir-i-dec-to-my
i-rid-ic
i-rid-i-um
i-ron-i-cal
i-ron-y (of iron)
i-ro-ny (sarcasm)
Ir-o-quois
ir-ra-di-ate
ir-rad-i-ca-ble
ir-rec-on-cil-a-ble
ir-re-duc-i-ble
ir-ref-ra-ga-ble
ir-ref-u-ta-ble
ir-re-me-di-a-ble
ir-rep-a-ra-ble
ir-re-press-i-ble
ir-re-sist-i-ble
ir-re-spon-si-ble
ir-re-vers-i-ble
ir-rev-o-ca-ble
ir-ri-ga-ble
ir-ri-tant
i-sa-go-ge
i-sa-gog-ics

I-sa-iah
i-sa-tin-ic
is-che-mi-a
i-sin-glass
Is-lam-ic
is-land-er
is-let
i-so-am-yl-ene
i-so-bar-ic
i-so-bath-y-therm
i-soch-ro-nal
i-so-chrone
i-soch-ro-nism
i-so-cla-site
i-so-cli-nal
i-so-drin
i-sog-a-mous
i-so-gly-co-sa-mine
i-sog-o-nal
i-so-gon-ic
i-so-lat-a-ble
i-so-leu-cine
i-so-mer-ic
i-som-er-ize
i-so-met-ri-cal-ly
i-som-e-try
i-so-ni-a-zid
i-so-phthal-ic
i-so-pre-noid
i-so-pro-pe-nyl
i-so-pro-pyl
i-sos-ce-les
i-sos-ta-sy
i-so-ther-mal
i-so-top-ic
i-so-to-py
i-so-tron
Is-rae-li
Is-ra-el-ite
Is-tan-bul
isth-mus
it-a-con-ic
I-tal-ian
i-tal-i-cize
i-tem-ize
it-er-ate
i-tin-er-ar-y
i-vo-ry

J

ja-bot
jack-al

jack-a-napes
jack-et

Ja-cob
Jac-o-be-an

61

Ja-co-bi-an
Jac-o-bin
Jac-o-net
Jac-quard
Jacque-mi-not
jag-uar
jal-ap
ja-lop-y
jal-ou-sie
Ja-mai-can
jam-bo-ree
jan-gling
jan-i-tor
Jan-u-ar-y
Ja-nus
Ja-pan
Jap-a-nese
ja-panned
ja-pon-i-ca
jar-di-niere
jar-gon-ize
jar-ring
jas-mine
jas-per
jaun-dice
jaunt-i-ly
jav-a-nese
jav-e-lin
jeal-ous-y
Jef-fer-so-ni-an
Je-ho-vah
je-ju-nos-to-my
je-ju-num
Je-kyll
jeop-ard-ize
jeop-ard-y
Je-ru-sa-lem
jes-sa-mine
Jes-u-it

Je-sus
jew-eled
Jez-e-bel
jin-gling
jin-rik-i-sha
jock-ey
jo-cos-i-ty
joc-u-lar
joc-und
jo-cun-di-ty
jodh-pur
joh-nin
John-ston
join-der
joint-er
join-ture
jok-er
joke-ster
Jo-nah
jon-quil
Jor-da-ni-an
jo-se-ite
Jo-seph
Jo-se-phine
Josh-u-a
jos-tled
jos-tling
jour-nal-ist
jour-ney
jo-vi-al-i-ty
ju-bi-lant
ju-bi-la-tion
Ju-da-ism
judg-ment
ju-di-ca-to-ry
ju-di-ca-ture
ju-di-cial
ju-di-ci-ar-y
ju-di-cious

ju-gal
jug-gler
jug-gling
jug-u-lar
ju-jit-su
ju-jube
Ju-lian
ju-li-enne
Ju-li-et
Ju-lius
jum-bled
jump-er
junc-tur-al
Ju-neau
jun-ior
ju-nior-i-ty
ju-ni-per
Jun-ius
Jun-ker
junk-er
jun-ket-eer
Ju-pi-ter
Ju-ras-sic
ju-rat
ju-rid-i-cal
ju-ri-di-cial (obs.)
ju-ris-dic-tion
ju-ris-pru-dence
ju-ris-tic
ju-ror
jus-tice
jus-ti-ci-a-ble
jus-ti-fi-ca-tion
jus-tif-i-ca-to-ry
ju-ve-nes-cence
ju-ve-nile
ju-ve-nil-i-ty
jux-ta-po-si-tion

K

Kad-iak
Kaf-fir
kai-nite
kai-nos-ite
kai-ser
ka-lei-do-scop-ic
kal-i-bo-rite
ka-lic-i-nite
ka-lig-e-nous
Kal-i-spell
ka-mi-ka-ze

kan-ga-roo
Kan-san
ka-o-lin-ic
ka-o-lin-ite
ka-pok
Ka-rā-chi
kar-y-o-gam-ic
kar-y-og-a-my
kar-y-o-ki-ne-sis
kar-y-ol-o-gy
kar-y-ol-y-sis

kar-y-o-mi-to-sis
kar-y-o-some
ka-tab-a-sis
kat-a-bat-ic
Ka-tan-gan
Kath-a-rine
ka-ty-did
kay-ak
keep-er
ken-o-tron
Ken-tuck-i-an

Ken-yan
ker-a-tin
ke-rat-i-nous
ker-a-ti-tis
Ker-a-tol
ker-a-tol-y-sis
ker-a-to-sis
ker-chiefed
ker-mes-ite
ker-neled
ker-o-gen
ker-o-sene
ker-sey
ke-ta-zine
Ketch-i-can
ke-tene
ke-ti-mine
ke-to-gen-e-sis
ke-to-glu-tar-ic
ke-tol-y-sis
ke-to-lyt-ic
ke-tone
ke-to-side
ke-to-sis
Keynes-i-an
kha-ki
Khar-toum
khe-dive
Khru-shchev
kib-itz
ki-bosh
kid-nap-er
kie-sel-guhr
kill-er

kil-o-cy-cle
kil-o-me-ter
kil-o-ton
kil-o-watt
ki-mo-no
ki-nase
kin-der-gar-ten
kin-der-gart-ner
kind-li-ness
kin-dling
kin-dred
kin-e-mat-ics
kin-e-scope
ki-ne-si-at-rics
ki-ne-sics
kin-e-sim-e-ter
ki-ne-si-o-log-ic
ki-ne-si-ol-o-gy
kin-es-the-si-a
ki-net-ic
ki-ne-to-phone
ki-ne-to-scope
kin-e-to-sis
Kings-ton
Kirch-hoff
Kirsch-ner
kitch-en-ette
Kjel-dahl
Klam-ath (river, etc.)
Klee-nex
klep-to-ma-ni-a
klys-tron
knav-ish

knick-er-bock-er
knock-er
knowl-edge-a-ble
knuck-led
ko-gas-in
Koh-i-noor
kohl-ra-bi
ko-jic
kok-sa-ghyz
ko-lin-sky
kol-khoz
Kom-man-da-tu-ra
ko-nim-e-ter
ko-ni-ol-o-gy
Koo-te-nay
ko-peck
Ko-ran
Ko-re-an
ko-ru-na
ko-sher
kreu-zer
kro-nen
kro-ner
kryp-ton
ku-lak
Kuo-min-tang
kur-to-sis
Ku-wait
Ku-wai-ti
Kwaj-a-lein
kwa-shi-or-kor
ky-mo-graph
ky-mog-ra-phy
kyn-u-ren-ine

L

lab-a-rum
lab-e-fac-tion
la-beled
la-bel-er
la-bi-al
la-bile
la-bi-lize
la-bi-um
lab-o-ra-to-ry
la-bor-er
la-bo-ri-ous
lab-ra-dor-ite
la-bur-num
lab-y-rin-thine
lac-er-ate
lach-es

lach-ry-mose
lack-a-dai-si-cal
la-con-ic
lac-o-nism
lac-quer
lac-ri-mal
la-crosse
lac-tal-bu-min
lac-tase
lac-te-al
lac-tes-cent
lac-tif-er-ous
lac-to-fla-vin
lac-tom-e-ter
lac-tose
la-cu-na

la-cus-trine
lad-en-ing
lad-ing
la-di-no
la-dler
la-drone
La-fay-ette
la-ger
la-gniappe
la-goon-al
la-gu-na
lai-tance
la-lop-a-thy
la-ma-ser-y
lam-bent
lam-bre-quin

63

la-mel-lar
lam-el-late
la-mel-lose
la-ment
lam-en-ta-ble
lam-en-ta-tion
lam-i-na-graph
lam-i-nag-ra-phy
lam-i-nal
lam-i-nar-in
lam-i-nate
lam-i-na-tor
lam-i-ni-tis
lam-poon
lam-prey
la-nat-o-side
Lan-ce-lot
lan-ce-o-lar
lanc-er
lan-cet
lan-ci-nate
lan-dau-let
Lang-shan
lan-guage
lan-guish
lan-guor-ous
lan-o-ce-ric
lan-o-lin
la-nos-ter-ol
Lan-ston
lan-tern
lan-tha-nide
lan-tha-num
lan-thi-o-nine
lap-a-rot-o-my
la-pel-er
lap-i-dar-y
la-pis
lap-is la-zu-li
La-o-tian
Lar-a-mie
lar-ce-nous
lar-da-ceous
lar-der
larg-er
lar-gess
larg-est
lar-i-at
lar-va
lar-vi-cid-al
lar-vic-o-lous
lar-viv-o-rous

la-ryn-ge-al
lar-yn-gec-to-my
lar-yn-git-ic
lar-yn-gi-tis
la-ryn-go-log-i-cal
lar-yn-gol-o-gy
la-ryn-go-scope
lar-yn-gos-co-py
lar-yn-got-o-my
lar-ynx
las-civ-i-ous
las-si-tude
Lat-a-ki-a
la-teen
la-ten-cy
lat-er
lat-er-al
lat-er-ite
la-tes-cent
lat-est
la-tex
lath-er-ing
lat-i-cif-er-ous
Lat-in-ize
la-tite
lat-i-tu-di-nous
la-trine
laud-a-ble
lau-dan-i-dine
lau-da-nine
lau-dan-o-sine
lau-da-num
laud-a-to-ry
launch-er
laun-der
Laun-der-om-e-ter
laun-dress
Laun-dro-mat
lau-rate
lau-re-ate
lau-reled
Lau-rence
Lau-ren-tian
lau-ric
lau-ro-len-ic
lau-ryl
la-vage
lav-a-liere
lav-a-to-ry
lav-en-der
lav-ish
Law-rence

law-renc-ite
lay-ette
Laz-a-rus
la-zi-ly
laz-u-rite
lead-er
lea-guer
leak-age
learn-ed (adj.)
leath-er-ine
leav-en
Leb-a-nese
le-bens-raum
lech-er-ous
lec-i-thin-ase
lec-tern
lec-tur-er
ledg-er
le-dol
leg-a-cy
le-gal-i-ty
le-gal-ize
leg-ate (n.)
le-gate (v.)
leg-a-tee
le-ga-tion
leg-end-ar-y
leg-er-de-main
le-ger-i-ty
leg-i-ble
le-gion-naire
leg-is-la-tive
leg-is-la-tor
leg-is-la-to-ri-al
le-git-i-ma-cy
leg-ume
le-gu-mi-nous
Leices-ter
leish-ma-ni-a-sis
lei-sure
lem-on-ade
lend-er
length-en
le-ni-en-cy
len-i-ty
Lent-en
len-ti-cel
len-tic-u-lar
len-ti-go
len-til
Leom-in-ster
Leon-ard

Le-o-nar-desque
le-o-nine
leop-ard
lep-er
lep-i-do-cro-cite
le-pid-o-lite
Lep-i-dop-ter-a
lep-i-do-sis
lep-rol-o-gy
lep-ro-sar-i-um
le-pro-sis
lep-ro-sy
lep-rous
lep-to-ceph-a-lus
lep-to-mat-ic
lep-to-spi-ro-sis
le-sion
Le-so-tho
les-pe-de-za
les-see
less-en
less-er
les-son
les-sor
le-thal
leth-ane
le-thar-gic
leth-ar-gy
leu-cite
leu-con-ic
leu-cop-te-rin
leu-co-sin
leu-co-sphe-nite
leu-cot-o-my
leu-cov-o-rin
leu-ke-mi-a
leu-ke-mic
leu-ker-gy
leu-ko-cyte
leu-ko-cyt-ic
leu-ko-cy-to-sis
leu-ko-poi-e-sis
leu-ko-poi-et-ic
leu-kor-rhe-a
leu-ko-sis
lev-an
Le-vant
Le-vant-er
Le-van-tine
le-va-tor
le-vee (reception)
lev-ee (dam)

lev-el-er
le-ver
le-ver-age
le-vi-a-than
lev-i-ga-tor
lev-i-tat-ing
lev-i-ty
le-vo-glu-co-san
lev-u-li-nate
lev-u-lin-ic
lev-u-lose
lev-y-ing
lew-is-ite
lex-i-cog-ra-pher
lex-i-co-graph-ic
lex-i-cog-ra-phy
lex-ig-ra-phy
li-ai-son
li-bel-ant
li-beled
li-bel-ous
lib-er-al-i-ty
lib-er-a-tor
lib-er-tar-i-an
lib-er-tine
lib-er-ty
li-bid-i-nous
li-bi-do
Li-bra
li-brar-i-an
li-bra-to-ry
li-bret-to
Lib-y-an
li-can-ic
li-cens-a-ble
li-censed
li-cens-ee
li-cens-er
li-cen-sor
li-cen-tious
li-chen-in
lic-o-rice
lid-o-caine
Lie-der-kranz
lien-ee
lien-or
lieu-ten-an-cy
lift-er
lig-a-men-tous
li-ga-tion
lig-a-ture
light-ened

light-en-ing (brighten ing)
light-er-age
light-ning (a flash)
lig-ne-ous
lig-nes-cent
lig-nite
lig-num vi-tae
lig-ro-in
lig-u-lar
lik-a-ble
lik-en
li-la-ceous
lil-li-pu-tian
lim-ber
Lim-burg-er
lime-ade
li-mic-o-lous
lim-i-ta-tion
lim-it-ed
li-miv-o-rous
lim-ner
lim-nim-e-ter
lim-nol-o-gy
Li-moges
lim-o-nene
li-mo-nite
lim-ou-sine
lim-pid-i-ty
lin-a-ble
lin-age
lin-al-o-ol
lin-a-mar-in
Lin-coln
lin-dane
lin-e-age
lin-e-al
lin-e-a-ment
lin-e-ar-i-ty
lin-en
lin-e-o-late
lin-er
lin-ger
lin-ge-rie
lin-gual
lin-guis-tics
lin-guist-ry
link-age
Lin-nae-us
li-no-le-ate
lin-o-le-ic
li-no-le-in

65

lin-o-le-nic
li-no-le-um
Li-no-type
li-nox-yn
lin-tel
lint-er
li-on-ess
li-on-ize
lip-a-rid
li-pe-mi-a
lip-ide
lip-i-do-sis
lip-o-chon-dri-on
lip-o-fus-cin
li-pog-e-nous
li-po-ic
lip-oi-do-sis
li-pol-y-sis
lip-o-lyt-ic
li-po-ma-to-sis
li-po-si-tol
lip-o-trop-ic
li-qua-tion
liq-ue-fa-cient
liq-ue-fy
li-ques-cent
li-queur
liq-uid
liq-ui-da-tor
li-quid-i-ty
liq-uid-us
liq-uor
li-roc-o-nite
lis-e-ran
lisp-er
lis-ten-er
lis-ter-el-lo-sis
lis-te-ri-a
lis-ter-ize
lit-a-ny
li-tchi
li-ter
lit-er-al-ly
lit-e-ra-ti
lit-e-ra-tim
lit-er-a-ture
lith-arge
li-the-mi-a
lith-i-a
li-thi-a-sis
li-thid-i-o-nite
lith-i-um

lith-o-cho-lic
lith-o-graph
li-thog-ra-pher
lith-o-graph-ic
li-thog-ra-phy
lith-ol-a-pax-y
lith-o-log-ic
li-thol-o-gy
lith-o-pone
lith-o-sol
li-thot-o-my
li-thot-ri-ty
Lith-u-a-ni-an
li-thu-ri-a
lit-i-ga-ble
lit-i-ga-tor
li-ti-gious
lit-ter-a-teur
lit-to-ral
li-tur-gi-cal
lit-ur-gy
liv-a-ble
live-li-hood
liv-er-y
liv-id
Liv-ing-ston
Li-vo-ni-an
lix-iv-i-ate
liz-ard
lla-ma
load-er
load-om-e-ter
loaf-er
loath-er
lo-bar
lo-bate
lob-bied
lo-bec-to-my
lo-be-li-a
lo-be-line
lo-bot-o-my
lob-u-lar
lob-u-lose
lo-cale
lo-cal-i-ty
lo-cal-iz-er
lo-cant
lo-cat-er
loc-a-tive
lo-ca-tor
lock-age
lock-er

lo-co-mo-tive
loc-u-late
lo-cust
lodg-er
lo-ga-nin
log-a-rith-mic
log-i-cal
lo-gi-cian
lo-gis-ti-cian
lo-gis-tics
log-o-gram-mat-ic
log-o-pe-dic
log-o-type
loi-ter
lol-li-pop
Lom-bar-dy
lone-li-ness
long-er
lon-ger (cask)
lon-ge-ron
long-est
lon-gev-i-ty
lon-gi-fo-lene
lon-gi-tu-di-nal
loos-en
loot-er
lo-phine
lop-sid-ed
lo-qua-cious
lo-quac-i-ty
lo-ran
lor-gnette
Los An-ge-les
los-er
los-ing
loss-er
Lo-thar-i-o
Lou-i-si-an-i-an
lous-i-ness
lou-ver
lov-a-ble
lox-o-drom-ic
loy-al-ist
loz-enge
lu-bri-ca-tor
lu-bric-i-ty
lu-cid-i-ty
Lu-ci-fer
lu-cif-er-ase
lu-cite
lu-cra-tive

lu-cu-brate
lu-di-crous
lu-gu-bri-ous
lum-bar
lu-men
lu-miere
lu-mi-fla-vin
lu-mi-naire
lu-mi-nar-y
lu-mi-nes-cence
lu-mi-nif-er-ous
lu-mi-nom-e-ter
lu-mi-nos-i-ty
lu-mi-nous
lu-mis-ter-ol
lu-na-cy
lu-nar-i-an
lu-na-tic
lunch-eon

lu-nette
lu-nik
lu-nu-late
lu-pet-i-dine
lu-pin-ine
lu-pu-lone
lu-rid
lus-cious
Lu-si-ta-ni-a
lus-ter (shine)
lust-er (n.) (one that
    lusts)
lus-trous
lu-te-in-ize
lu-te-o-lin
lu-te-o-vi-res-cent
lu-te-ti-um
Lu-ther-an
lu-ti-din-ic
Lux-em-bourg-er

lux-u-ri-ant
lux-u-ri-ous
ly-ce-um
ly-co-pene
lydd-ite
lymph-ad-e-ni-tis
lymph-ad-e-nop-a-thy
lym-phan-gi-al
lym-phat-ic
lym-pho-cyte
lymph-oid
lym-pho-ra-to-sis
ly-o-phil-ic
ly-oph-i-lize
lyr-i-cal
ly-ser-gic
ly-sim-e-ter
ly-sine
ly-so-gen-ic

M

ma-ca-bre
mac-ad-am-ize
mac-a-ro-ni
mac-a-ron-ic
mac-a-roon
Ma-cas-sar
ma-caw
Mac-ca-be-an
Mac-e-do-ni-an
mac-er-a-tor
ma-che-te
Mach-i-a-vel-li-an
ma-chi-nal
mach-i-na-tion
ma-chin-er-y
ma-chin-ist
mack-er-el
mack-in-tosh
mac-ro-bi-o-sis
mac-ro-cosm
mac-ro-cy-clic
mac-ro-cy-to-sis
mac-ro-mol-e-cule
ma-cron
ma-crop-si-a
mac-ro-scop-ic
mac-u-la-ture
mad-am
ma-dame
Ma-dei-ra

ma-de-moi-selle
ma-don-na
Ma-dras
Ma-drid
mad-ri-gal
mael-strom
mae-stro
Ma-fi-a
maf-ic
mag-a-zine
Mag-da-len
Mag-de-burg
ma-gen-ta
mag-i-cal
ma-gi-cian
Ma-gi-not
ma-gis-ter
mag-is-te-ri-al
mag-is-tra-cy
mag-na-nim-i-ty
mag-nan-i-mous
mag-ne-sia
mag-ne-si-o-chro-mite
mag-ne-site
mag-ne-si-um
mag-ne-syn
mag-net-i-cal-ly
mag-net-ism
mag-net-ite
mag-net-ize

mag-ne-to-graph
mag-ne-tom-e-ter
mag-ne-to-met-ric
mag-ne-tom-e-try
mag-ne-tos
mag-ne-tron
mag-ni-fi-ca-tion
mag-nif-i-cence
mag-ni-fy
mag-nil-o-quent
mag-ni-tude
mag-no-lia
ma-guey
mah-jong
ma-hog-a-ny
Ma-hom-et
maid-en
mail-er
Main-er
main-te-nance
mai-so-nette
mai-tre d'ho-tel
ma-jes-tic
maj-es-ty
ma-jol-i-ca
ma-jor-i-ty
maj-us-cule
ma-jus-cu-lar
mak-er
mal-a-chite

67

mal-a-dy
Mal-a-ga
Mal-a-gas-y
mal-a-gue-na
mal-aise
ma-lar
ma-lar-i-al
ma-lar-i-om-e-try
mal-a-thi-on
Ma-la-wi
Ma-lay-an
Ma-lay-sian
ma-le-ate
mal-e-dic-tion
mal-e-fac-tor
ma-lef-i-cent
ma-le-ic
ma-lev-o-lent
mal-fea-sance
Ma-li-an
mal-ic
mal-ice
ma-li-cious
ma-lif-er-ous
ma-lign
ma-lig-nant
ma-lin-ger
mal-le-a-ble
mal-o-nate
ma-lo-nic
malt-ase
Mal-tese
mal-tha
Mal-thu-sian
malt-ose
mam-ma-li-an
mam-ma-lif-er-ous
mam-mal-o-gy
mam-ma-ry
mam-mif-er-ous
man-a-cle
man-age-a-ble
man-ag-er
man-a-ge-ri-al
Ma-na-gua
ma-ña-na
man-a-tee
Man-chu-ri-an
man-da-mus
man-da-rin-ate
man-da-to-ry
man-del-ate

man-di-ble
man-dib-u-lar
man-do-lin-ist
man-drake
man-drel
ma-nege
ma-neu-ver
man-ga-nate
man-ga-nese
man-gan-ic
man-ga-nif-er-ous
man-ga-nin
man-ga-nite
man-ga-no-site
man-ga-nous
man-ger
man-gler
man-gy
ma-ni-ac
ma-ni-a-cal
ma-ni-co-ba
man-i-cur-ist
man-i-fes-tant
man-i-fes-ta-tion
man-i-fold-er
man-i-kin
Ma-nil-a
ma-nil-la
man-i-oc
ma-nip-u-la-tor
man-nu-ron-ic
ma-nom-e-ter
man-o-met-ric
ma-nom-e-try
man-or
ma-no-ri-al
man-o-stat
man-sard
man-tel (arch)
man-tle (garment)
man-tling
man-u-al
man-u-duc-to-ry
man-u-fac-tur-er
ma-nure
ma-quette
ma-quis
mar-a-bou
ma-rac-a
mar-a-schi-no
ma-ras-mus
ma-raud-er

mar-bled
mar-ble-ize
mar-ca-site
mar-che-se
mar-chion-ess
mar-ga-rate
Mar-ga-ret
mar-gar-ic
mar-ga-rin
mar-ga-rite
mar-ga-ro-san-ite
mar-gin-al
mar-gi-na-li-a
mar-gin-ate
mar-gue-rite
Mar-i-an
Mar-i-co-pa
mar-i-gold
mar-i-hua-na
ma-rim-ba
ma-ri-na
ma-rine
mar-i-ner
Ma-ri-nist (of Ma
ma-ri-nist (sea)
ma-ri-no-ra-ma
mar-i-o-nette
mar-i-tal
ma-rit-i-cide
mar-i-time
mar-jo-ram
Mar-jo-ry
mark-er
mar-ket-er
mar-la-ceous
marl-ite
mar-ma-lade
mar-mo-ra-ceous
mar-mo-re-al
mar-mo-set
ma-roon
mar-que-try
mar-quis
mar-qui-sette
mar-riage-a-ble
Mar-seil-laise
Mar-seilles
mar-shaled
mar-shal-er
mar-su-pi-al-ize
mar-tens-ite
mar-tial

mar-ti-net
mar-tin-gale
Mar-ti-ni
mar-tite
mar-tyr-ize
mar-vel-ous
Mar-y-land-er
Ma-sa-ryk
mas-cu-lin-i-ty
mask-er
mas-och-ism
mas-och-is-tic
Ma-son-ite
ma-son-ry
masqu-er
mas-quer-ade
Mas-sa-chu-setts-an
mas-sa-cred
mas-sag-er
mas-sive
mast-er (with masts)
mas-ter (owner, etc.)
mas-tic
mas-ti-cate
mas-tiff
mas-tit-ic
mas-ti-tis
mas-to-don
mas-toi-dal
mas-toid-i-tis
mas-toid-ot-o-my
ma-su-ri-um
mat-a-dor
mat-er
ma-te-ri-al-ize
ma-te-ri-a med-i-ca
ma-te-ri-el
ma-ter-ni-ty
math-e-mat-i-cal
math-e-ma-ti-cian
math-e-mat-ics
ma-thet-ic
mat-in-al
mat-i-nee
ma-tri-ar-chal
mat-ri-ces
ma-tri-ci-dal
ma-tric-u-late
mat-ri-mo-ni-al
ma-trix
ma-tron
mat-ro-nym-ic

mat-u-ra-tion
mat-u-ra-tive
ma-tu-ri-ty
ma-tu-ti-nal
mat-zoth
maud-lin
maul-er
maun-der
Mau-re-ta-ni-an
Mau-rice
Mau-ri-ti-us (island)
Mau-ser
mau-so-le-um
mau-vine
mav-er-ick
mawk-ish
max-i-miz-er
max-i-mum
may-on-naise
may-or-al-ty
maz-a-rine
ma-zur-ka
mea-con-ing
mead-ow
mea-ger
meal-y-mouthed
me-an-der
mea-sles
mea-sly
meas-ur-a-ble
meas-ured
me-a-tus
me-cap-rine
me-chan-i-cal
mech-a-ni-cian
mech-a-nism
mech-a-ni-za-tion
mech-a-no-mor-phic
me-com-e-ter
me-con-ic
mec-o-nin
me-co-ni-um
med-al-ist
me-dal-lion
med-dler
me-di-an
me-di-as-ti-ni-tis
me-di-as-ti-num
me-di-a-tor
me-di-ca-ble
med-ic-aid
med-i-cal

me-dic-a-ment
med-i-care
Med-i-ci
me-dic-i-nal
med-i-cine
me-di-e-val
Me-di-na
me-di-o-cre
me-di-oc-ri-ty
med-i-ta-tive
Med-i-ter-ra-ne-an
me-di-um
me-dul-la
med-ul-lar-y
meer-schaum
meg-a-lo-ma-ni-a
meg-a-lop-o-lis
meg-a-lo-pol-i-tan
meg-a-phone
meg-a-ton
meg-ohm-me-ter
me-grim
mei-o-nite
mei-ot-ic
mei-ster
me-lac-o-nite
mel-a-mine
mel-an-cho-li-a
mel-an-chol-y
me-lange
me-lan-ger
me-lan-ic
mel-a-nin
mel-a-no-ma-to-sis
mel-a-no-sis
mel-a-no-stib-i-an
me-lan-ter-ite
me-lee
me-lez-i-tose
mel-i-bi-ose
mel-i-lite
me-lio-ra-tive
Me-lis-sa
mel-i-tose
mel-lif-lu-ous
mel-li-tate
mel-lit-ic
me-lod-ic
me-lo-di-on
me-lo-di-ous
mel-o-dra-ma
mel-o-dy

mel-o-ma-ni-a
mel-o-nite
mel-o-plas-ty
melt-er
mem-bra-nate
mem-bra-nous
me-men-tos
mem-oir
mem-o-ra-ble
mem-o-ran-dums
me-mo-ri-al-iz-ing
mem-o-riz-er
men-ace
men-a-di-one
me-nag-er-ie
me-naph-thone
men-da-cious
men-dac-i-ty
men-de-le-vi-um
Men-de-li-an
men-de-lye-ev-ite
mend-er
men-di-cant
men-dic-i-ty
men-ha-den
me-ni-al
Me-ni-ere
men-i-lite
me-nin-ge-al
me-nin-gi-o-ma
men-in-git-ic
men-in-gi-tis
me-nin-go-cele
me-nin-go-coc-cus
me-nin-go-my-e-li-tis
me-nis-cus
Men-non-ite
Me-nom-i-nee
men-o-pau-sal
me-no-rah
men-ses
men-stru-al
men-su-ra-ble
men-su-ral
men-su-ra-tion
men-tal-i-ty
men-tha-di-ene
men-thane
men-tha-nol
men-the-none
men-tho-lat-ed
men-thyl

men-ti-cide
me-per-i-dine
me-phen-e-sin
Meph-is-to-phe-li-an
me-phit-ic
me-phi-tis
me-pro-ba-mate
mer-al-lu-ride
mer-can-tile
mer-cap-to
mer-cap-tom-er-in
mer-cap-tu-ric
Mer-ca-tor
mer-ce-nar-y
mer-cer-ize
mer-chan-dise
mer-chant-a-ble
mer-cu-rate
mer-cu-ri-al
mer-cu-ric
mer-cu-rous
me-ren-gue
me-re-ol-o-gy
mer-e-tri-cious
mer-gan-ser
mer-gence
Mer-gen-tha-ler
merg-er
me-rid-i-an
me-rid-i-o-nal
me-ringue
me-ri-nos
mer-it-ed
mer-i-to-ri-ous
mer-o-crine
mer-o-gon-ic
me-rog-o-ny
mer-o-he-dral
Mer-o-pe
me-ro-pi-a
me-rot-o-mize
me-rox-ene
mer-sal-yl
Mer-thi-o-late
mes-al-liance
mes-ar-te-ri-tis
mes-en-ce-phal-ic
mes-en-ceph-a-lon
mes-en-chy-ma
mes-en-chym-a-tous
mes-en-chyme
mes-en-ter-ic

mes-en-ter-i-tis
me-sic
mes-i-dine
mes-i-tyl
me-sit-y-lene
mes-mer-ism
mes-o-blast
mes-o-car-di-a
mes-o-ce-phal-ic
mes-o-derm
mes-o-lite
mes-o-mer-ic
me-som-er-ism
mes-on
mes-o-phyll
mes-o-sphere
mes-ox-al-ic
mes-ox-a-lyl
Mes-o-zo-ic
mes-quite
mes-sage
mes-sen-ger
mes-si-an-ic
mes-ti-zos
mes-yl
me-tab-a-sis
met-a-bi-o-sis
met-a-bi-ot-ic
met-a-bol-ic
me-tab-o-lism
me-tab-o-liz-a-ble
met-a-bo-rate
met-a-car-pus
me-tag-ra-phy
met-al-de-hyde
me-tal-lic
met-al-lif-er-ous
met-al-lize
met-al-log-ra-phy
met-al-lur-gi-cal
met-al-os-co-py
met-a-mer-ic
met-am-er-ism
met-a-mor-phism
met-a-mor-pho-sis
met-a-phor-i-cal
met-a-phys-ics
met-ar-te-ri-ole
met-a-so-ma-to-sis
met-a-sta-ble
me-tas-ta-sis
me-tath-e-sis

me-tem-psy-cho-sis
me-te-or-ic
me-te-or-ite
me-te-or-it-ics
me-te-or-o-graph
me-te-or-og-ra-phy
me-te-or-oid
me-te-or-o-log-i-cal
me-te-or-ol-o-gist
me-te-or-ol-o-gy
me-te-or-om-e-ter
me-te-or-o-scope
me-te-or-os-co-py
me-ter
meth-ac-ry-late
meth-a-cryl-ic
meth-a-done
meth-al-lyl
meth-ane
meth-a-nol
meth-a-no-lic
meth-a-nol-y-sis
meth-a-nom-e-ter
meth-an-the-line
me-the-na-mine
meth-ene
meth-ide
meth-i-on-ic
me-thi-o-nine
me-thi-um
meth-od
me-thod-i-cal
Meth-od-ist
meth-od-ize
meth-od-ol-o-gy
me-tho-ni-um
meth-ox-ide
me-thox-y-car-bon-yl
meth-ox-yl
Me-thu-se-lah
meth-yl-a-mine
meth-yl-ate
meth-yl-ene
meth-yl-en-i-mine
meth-yl-eth-yl-pyr-i-
dine
me-thyl-i-dyne
meth-yl-naph-tha-lene
meth-yl-ol-u-re-a
me-**tic**-u-lous
me-tier
me-ton-y-my

me-top-ic
met-o-pon
met-o-pos-co-py
Met-ra-zol
met-ric
met-ri-cal
me-tri-tis
me-trol-o-gy
met-ro-nome
me-tro-nym-ic
met-ro-pole
me-trop-o-lis
met-ro-pol-i-tan
mev-a-lon-ic
mez-za-nine
mho-me-ter
mi-ar-gy-rite
mi-ca-ceous
mi-cel-lar
mi-celle
Mi-chael
Mich-ael-mas
Mich-i-gan-ite
mi-cri-nite
mi-cro-bi-al
mi-cro-cosm
mi-crog-ra-phy
mi-cro-lite
mi-cro-me-rit-ics
mi-crom-e-ter
mi-cro-met-ri-cal
mi-crom-e-try
mi-cro-mho
mi-cron-ize
mi-cro-phon-ic
mi-crop-si-a
mi-cro-scop-ic
mi-cros-co-py
mi-crot-o-my
mid-dling
midg-et
mi-gnon-ette
mi-graine
mi-grain-oid
mi-grant
mi-gra-tet-ics
mi-gra-to-ry
mi-ka-do
Mi-lan
Mil-a-nese
mil-i-a-ri-a
mil-i-ar-y

mi-lieu
mil-i-tant
mil-i-ta-rism
mil-i-tate
mi-li-tia
milk-er
mil-le-nar-y
mil-len-ni-um
mill-er
mil-les-i-mal
mil-let
mil-li-am-me-ter
mil-li-ner-y
mil-lion-aire
Mim-e-o-graph
mi-met-ic
mim-e-tite
mim-ick-er
mim-ic-ry
mi-mo-sa
mi-mo-sine
min-a-ble
min-a-ret
minc-ing
mi-nen-wer-fer
min-er
min-er-ag-ra-phy
min-er-al-iz-er
min-er-al-og-i-cal
min-er-al-o-gy
Mi-ner-va
min-e-stro-ne
mi-nette
min-gling
min-i-a-ceous
min-i-a-ture
Min-ie
min-i-**mize**
min-i-**mum**
min-ion
min-is-te-ri-al
min-is-try
min-i-track
Min-ne-so-tan
mi-nom-e-ter
mi-nor-i-ty
min-strel
mint-age
mint-er
min-u-et
mi-nus-cu-lar
min-us-cule

71

min-ute (time)
mi-nute (small)
min-ute-ly (every min-
ute)
mi-nute-ly (precisely)
mi-nu-ti-a
mi-o-sis
mi-ot-ic
mi-rab-i-lite
mir-a-cle
mi-rac-u-lous
mi-rage
mis-an-throp-ic
mis-an-thro-py
mis-ceg-e-na-tion
mis-cel-la-ne-ous
mis-cel-la-ny
mis-chie-vous
mis-ci-bil-i-ty
mis-cre-ant
mis-de-mean-or
mis-er-a-ble
Mis-e-re-re
mi-ser-ly
mis-er-y
mis-fea-sance
mis-no-mer
mi-sog-y-nist
mis-pri-sion
mis-sil-eer
mis-sile-ry
Mis-sis-sip-pi-an
mis-sive
Mis-sou-ri-an
mis-spelled
mis-tak-a-ble
mis-tak-en
mis-ter
mis-tle-toe
mis-tral
mis-tress
mi-ter
mit-i-ga-tor
mi-to-chon-dri-a
mi-to-sis
mi-tot-ic
mi-trail-leuse
mi-tral
mix-ture
mne-mon-ic
mo-bile
mo-bil-i-ty

mo-bi-li-za-tion
mo-bil-om-e-ter
mob-oc-ra-cy
moc-ca-sin
mo-cha
mock-er-y
mod-al-ism
mod-al-i-ty
mod-eled
mod-er-a-tor
mod-ern-is-tic
mod-ern-ize
mod-es-ty
mod-i-fy
mod-i-fy
mod-ish
mo-diste
mod-u-la-bil-i-ty
mod-u-lar
mod-u-la-tor
mod-u-lus
mo-dus op-e-ran-di
Mo-ham-med-an
Mo-ha-ve
moi-e-ty
moi-re
moist-en-er
mois-ture
mo-lar-i-ty
mo-la-ry
mo-las-ses
mold-er
mo-lec-u-lar
mol-e-cule
mo-les-ta-tion
mol-ten
molt-er
mo-lyb-date
mo-lyb-de-num
mo-lyb-do-me-nite
mol-y-site
mo-men-tar-i-ly
mo-men-tar-y
mo-men-tous
mo-men-tum
mom-ism
Mon-a-can
mo-nad
mo-nad-ic
mo-nan-dry
mo-nar-chal
mo-nar-chi-cal

mon-ar-chist
mon-as-te-ri-al
mon-as-ter-y
mo-nas-tic
mon-a-tom-ic
mon-a-zite
mo-nel
mo-ne-sia
mon-e-tar-y
mon-e-tite
mon-e-tize
mon-eys
mon-ger
Mon-go-li-an
Mon-gol-oid
mon-grel
mon-i-ker
mo-nim-o-lite
mon-ism
mo-nis-tic
mon-i-to-ry
mon-keys
monk-ish
mon-o-ac-e-tin
mon-o-ac-id
mon-o-a-cid-ic
mon-o-am-ide
mon-o-a-mine
mon-o-chro-mous
mo-noch-ro-nous
mon-o-cle
mon-o-coque
mo-noc-ra-cy
mon-o-crot-ic
mo-noc-u-lar
mo-nog-a-my
mo-nog-o-ny
mon-o-gramed
mon-o-gram-mat-ic
mo-nog-ra-pher
mon-o-graph-ic
mo-nog-y-ny
mon-o-lith-ic
mon-o-log
mo-nol-o-gist
mo-nom-a-chy
mon-o-ma-ni-a
mon-o-mer
mon-o-nom-e-ter
mo-no-mi-al
mon-o-nu-cle-o-sis
mon-o-plane

mo-nop-o-lize
mo-nop-so-ny
mon-o-rail
mon-o-the-ism
mon-o-tone
mo-not-o-nous
mo-not-ro-py
mon-ox-ide
mon-sei-gneur
mon-sieur
mon-si-gnor
mon-ster
mon-stros-i-ty
mon-strous
mon-tage
Mon-tan-an
Mon-te-ne-grin
Mon-tes-so-ri
mon-tic-u-lous
mont-mo-ril-lon-ite
Mon-tre-al
mon-troy-dite
mon-u-men-tal
mon-zo-nite
Moor-ish
mo-quette
mo-raine
mor-al
mo-rale
mor-al-ist
mo-ral-i-ty
mor-al-ize
mo-rass-ic
mor-a-to-ri-um
Mo-ra-vi-an
mo-ra-vite
mor-bid-i-ty
mor-bose
mor-da-cious
mor-dac-i-ty
mor-dant
mo-reen
mo-rel-lo
mo-ren-cite
mo-res
mor-ga-nat-ic
mor-i-bund
mo-rin-done
mo-rin-ite
Mor-mon-ite
morn-ing
Mo-roc-co

mo-ron-ic
mo-ros-i-ty
mor-pheme
mor-phe-mics
Mor-pheus
mor-phine
mor-phog-ra-phy
mor-pho-line
mor-pho-log-i-cal
mor-phol-o-gy
mor-phom-e-try
mor-pho-sis
mor-phot-o-my
mor-tal-i-ty
mort-ga-gee
mort-ga-gor
mor-ti-cian
mor-ti-fi-ca-tion
mor-tis-er
mor-tu-ar-y
mo-sa-i-cism
mo-ses-ite
mos-qui-toes
mo-tel
moth-er
mo-til-i-ty
mo-ti-vate
mo-tor
mo-to-ri-al
mou-lage
mou-lin
moun-tain-eer
moun-te-bank
mount-er
mourn-er
mous-er
mous-que-taire
mousse-line
mov-a-ble
mov-ant
mov-er
mov-ie
mu-ce-dine
mu-ced-i-nous
mu-cic
mu-cif-er-ous
mu-ci-lage
mu-ci-lag-i-nous
mu-cin-o-gen
mu-cin-oid
mu-ci-no-lyt-ic
mu-coi-dal

mu-co-i-tin
mu-co-lyt-ic
mu-con-ic
mu-co-sa
mu-cos-i-ty
mu-cous (adj.)
mu-cus (n.)
mud-dled
muf-fler
Muh-len-berg
mu-lat-toes
mulch-er
mu-le-teer
mul-ish
mul-li-ga-taw-ny
mull-ite
mul-ti-far-i-ous
mul-tif-er-ous
Mul-ti-graph
Mul-ti-lith
mul-til-o-quent
mul-tim-e-ter
mul-tim-e-try
mul-tip-a-rous
mul-ti-par-tite
mul-ti-ple
mul-ti-plic-a-ble
mul-ti-pli-ca-tion
mul-ti-plic-i-ty
mul-ti-tu-di-nous
mul-ti-va-lent
mum-bling
Mun-chau-sen
mun-dane
Mu-nich
mu-nic-i-pal
mu-nif-i-cent
mu-ni-tion
mu-ral
mu-rar-i-um
mur-der-ous
mu-ri-at-ic
mu-rine
mu-ri-um
mur-mur-ous
mus-ca-dine
mus-ca-rine
mus-ca-tel
mus-cle
Mus-co-vite
mus-cu-lar
mus-cu-la-ture

mus-cu-lo-trop-ic
mu-se-ol-o-gy
mu-se-um
mu-si-cal
mu-si-col-o-gy
mus-ing
mus-ket-eer
mus-tache
mus-tard
mu-ta-bil-i-ty
mu-ta-gen-ic
mu-tant
mu-tase
mu-ta-tive
mu-ti-late
mu-ti-nous
mut-ism
mu-tu-al-ism
mu-zhik
muz-zling
my-al-gi-a
My-an-e-sin
my-as-the-ni-a

my-as-then-ic
my-ce-li-um
my-ce-to-ma
my-co-my-cin
my-co-sis
myc-ter-ic
my-dri-a-sine
my-dri-a-sis
myd-ri-at-ic
my-e-li-tis
my-e-lo-cyte
my-e-loid
my-e-lo-ma-to-sis
my-e-lom-a-tous
my-e-lop-a-thy
my-e-lo-sis
my-o-car-di-tis
my-op-a-thy
my-o-pi-a
my-op-ic
my-o-sin
my-o-si-tis
my-os-mine

my-ot-o-my
myr-i-ad
myr-i-am-e-ter
my-ric-e-tin
my-ric-i-trin
myr-i-cyl
myr-in-gi-tis
myr-in-got-o-my
my-ris-tate
myr-mi-don
myrrh-ic
myr-tle
mys-te-ri-ous
mys-ter-y
mys-ti-cal
mys-ti-fi-ca-tion
mys-tique
myth-i-cal
myth-o-log-i-cal
my-thol-o-gy
myx-o-bac-te-ri-al
myx-o-ma-to-sis

N

na-bob
na-celle
na-cre-ous
na-crite
na-dir
nad-or-ite
Na-ga-sa-ki
nah-co-lite
nail-er
nain-sook
na-ive
na-ive-te
na-ked
nam-a-ble
na-no-gram
na-palm
na-per-y
na-phaz-o-line
naph-tha
naph-tha-lene
naph-tha-len-ic
naph-thal-ic
naph-thene
naph-the-nic
naph-thi-o-nate
naph-thi-on-ic
naph-thol-ate

naph-tho-res-or-cin-ol
naphth-ox-y-a-ce-tic
naph-tho-yl
naph-thyl-a-mine
naph-thy-lene
Na-ples
Na-po-le-on
na-prap-a-thy
nar-cis-sism
nar-co-lep-sy
nar-co-sis
nar-cot-ic
nar-co-tol-ine
na-res
nar-in-gen-in
nar-rin-gin
Nar-ra-gan-sett
nar-rat-a-ble
nar-ra-tor
na-sa-lis
na-sal-i-ty
nas-cent
na-so-scope
nas-ti-ly
nas-tur-tium
na-tal

my-ot-o-my
na-tant
na-ta-to-ri-al
na-ta-to-ri-um
Natch-ez
Na-than-iel
na-tion-al-ist
na-tiv-is-tic
na-tiv-i-ty
na-tri-um
na-tro-lite
na-troph-i-lite
nat-u-ral-ist
nat-u-ral-ize
na-ture
na-tur-o-path
na-tur-op-a-thy
naugh-ti-ness
nau-pli-us
nau-se-ate
nau-seous
nau-ti-cal
nau-ti-lus
nau-to-phone
Nav-a-ho
na-val
nav-ar
na-vel

WORDFINDER

na-vic-u-lar
nav-i-ga-ble
nav-i-ga-tor
na-vite
Naz-a-rene
na-zism
Ne-an-der-thal
Ne-a-pol-i-tan
near-est
ne-ar-thro-sis
Ne-bras-kan
neb-u-lar
ne-bu-li-um
neb-u-los-i-ty
neb-u-lous
nec-es-sar-i-ly
ne-ces-si-tate
ne-ces-si-tous
nec-ro-bi-o-sis
nec-ro-log-i-cal
ne-crol-o-gy
nec-ro-man-cy
ne-crop-o-lis
ne-crop-sy
ne-cros-co-py
nec-ro-sin
ne-cro-sis
ne-crot-ic
ne-crot-o-my
nec-tar-ine
nec-ta-ry
nee-dler
ne-far-i-ous
ne-ga-tion
neg-a-tive
neg-a-to-ry
neg-a-tron
ne-glect-er
neg-li-gee
neg-li-gence
neg-li-gi-ble
ne-go-ti-a-ble
ne-go-ti-a-tor
Ne-gress
Ne-grit-ic
Ne-gro
Ne-groid
Ne-gus
neigh-bor
nei-ther
ne-mat-ic
nem-a-to-ci-dal

nem-a-tode
nem-a-to-di-a-sis
nem-a-tol-o-gy
Nem-bu-tal
ne-mes-ic
nem-e-sis
ne-moph-i-ly
nem-o-ral
Ne-o-ant-er-gan
ne-o-ars-phen-a-mine
ne-o-dym-i-um
ne-og-a-my
ne-o-lith-ic
ne-o-log-i-cal
ne-ol-o-gy
ne-o-my-cin
ne-on-tol-o-gy
ne-o-phyte
ne-o-pla-si-a
ne-o-prene
ne-o-stig-mine
Ne-o-sy-neph-rine
ne-o-ter-ic
ne-ot-o-cite
Ne-pal
Nep-a-lese
ne-pen-the
neph-e-lin-ite
neph-e-lite
neph-e-lom-e-ter
neph-e-lo-scope
neph-ew
ne-phol-o-gy
neph-o-scope
ne-phrec-to-my
neph-ric
ne-phrid-i-al
neph-rite
ne-phrit-ic
ne-phri-tis
ne-phrol-o-gy
neph-rop-to-sis
ne-phro-sis
ne-phrot-ic
ne-phrot-o-my
nep-i-on-ic
ne-pot-ic
nep-o-tism
nep-tu-ni-um
ne-rit-ic
ne-rol-i-dol
nerv-ate

nerv-ine
ner-von-ic
nerv-ous
ner-vule
ne-science
nest-ling (n.)
nes-tling (v.)
Nes-tor
neth-er
Ne-trop-sin
net-tled
Neuf-châ-tel
neu-ral-gia
neur-as-the-ni-a
neur-as-then-ic
neu-rec-to-my
neu-rine
neu-rit-ic
neu-ri-tis
neu-ro-blas-to-ma
neu-ro-crine
neu-ro-gen-ic
neu-rog-ra-phy
neu-roid
neu-ro-log-i-cal
neu-rol-o-gy
neu-rol-y-sis
neu-ro-path-ic
neu-rop-a-thy
neu-ro-sis
neu-rot-ic
neu-rot-i-cism
neu-rot-o-my
neu-ro-trop-ic
neu-rot-ro-pism
neu-ter
neu-tral-i-ty
neu-tral-iz-er
neu-tri-no
neu-tro-dyne
neu-tron
Ne-vad-an
ne-vus
new-com-er
New-to-ni-an
New Zea-land-er
nex-us
ni-a-cin-a-mide
Ni-ag-a-ra
nib-b'ing
Nic-a-ra-guan
ni-ce-ty

75

nick-el-if-er-ous
nick-el-ine
nick-el-o-de-on
nic-o-tin-a-mide
nic-o-tin-ate
nic-o-tin-ic
nic-o-ti-no-yl
nic-o-tin-u-ric
ni-dic-o-lous
nid-i-fi-cate
ni-dol-o-gy
Nietz-sche-ism
Ni-ger
Ni-ge-ri-a
ni-ger-ite
night-in-gale
ni-gres-cence
ni-grine
ni-grom-e-ter
ni-gro-sine
ni-grous
ni-hi-list
ni-lom-e-ter
nim-bly
nim-bo-stra-tus
ni-mi-e-ty
Nin-hy-drin
Ni-o-be
ni-o-bic
ni-o-bi-um
nip-e-cot-ic
Nip-pon-ese
Nir-va-na
Ni-sei
ni-sin
ni-ter
ni-tra-mine
ni-trate
ni-tra-tor
ni-tric
ni-trid-ize
ni-tri-fi-ca-tion
ni-trite
ni-tro-an-i-line
ni-tro-fu-ra-zone
ni-tro-gen-ate
ni-tro-gen-ize
ni-trog-e-nous
ni-tro-lic
ni-trom-e-ter
ni-tro-ni-um
ni-tros-a-mine

ni-tro-sate
ni-tro-so
ni-tro-tol-u-ene
ni-tro-tol-u-ol
ni-trous
ni-trox-yl-ene
ni-tryl
No-bel
no-bel-i-um
no-bil-i-ty
no-blesse
no-bly
no-car-di-o-sis
no-cer-ite
no-ci-cep-tor
noc-tam-bu-list
noc-ti-lu-cine
noc-tiv-a-gant
noc-tur-nal
noc-turne
noc-u-ous
nod-al
no-dal-i-ty
nod-u-lar
nod-ule
no-e-ma-ta-chom-e-ter
nois-i-ly
noi-some
no-lo con-ten-de-re
no-mad-ic
no-men-cla-ture
no-mi-al
nom-i-nal-ize
nom-i-nat-ed
nom-i-na-tion
nom-i-na-tive
no-moc-ra-cy
nom-o-gram
nom-o-graph-ic
no-mog-ra-phy
non-a-co-sane
non-a-dec-ane
non-a-ge-nar-i-an
no-nane
non-a-no-ic
no-na-nol
non-cha-lance
non-de-script
no-nene
non-en-ti-ty
no-no-ic
non-pa-reil

non-plused
non pro-se-qui-tur
non se-qui-tur
non-yl-ene
no-nyl-ic
noo-dle
no-ol-o-gy
no-pi-nene
Nor-dic
nor-di-hy-dro-guai-a-
ret-ic
nor-mal-i-ty
nor-mal-iz-er
nor-ma-tive
North-amp-ton
north-ern
North-um-ber-land
Nor-we-gian
no-se-lite
no-sog-ra-phy
no-sol-o-gist
nos-tal-gi-a
nos-tril
nos-trum
nos-y
no-ta-ble
no-tam
no-tar-i-al
no-ta-ry
notch-er
noth-ing
no-tice-a-ble
no-ti-fi-ca-tion
no-to-ri-e-ty
no-to-ri-ous
nou-gat
nour-ish
nou-veau
nov-el-ette
nov-el-ist
no-vel-la
nov-el-ty
No-vem-ber
no-ve-na
nov-ice
no-vi-ti-ate
no-vo-cain
nox-ious
Nu-bi-an
nu-cle-ar
nu-cle-ate
nu-cle-in-a-tion

nu-cle-og-o-ny
nu-cle-o-his-tone
nu-cle-o-lar
nu-cle-ol-y-sis
nu-cle-om-e-ter
nu-cle-on-ics
nu-cle-o-tid-ase
nu-cle-us
nu-clide
nu-clid-ic
nudg-er
nud-ism
nu-di-ty
nu-ga-to-ry
nui-sance

nul-li-ty
num-bered
nu-mer-al
nu-mer-a-tive
nu-mer-a-tor
nu-mer-i-cal
nu-mer-ol-o-gy
nu-mis-mat-ics
nu-mis-ma-tist
num-skull
nun-ci-a-ture
nup-tial
nup-ti-al-i-ty
Nur-em-berg

nurs-er
nurs-er-y
nur-tur-al
nu-tri-a
nu-tri-ent
nu-tri-lite
nu-tri-tious
nu-tri-tive
nyc-ta-lo-pi-a
ny-lon
nym-pha
nymph-al
nys-tag-mus
nys-ta-tin
ny-tril

O

oak-en
oa-kum
o-a-sis
ob-bli-ga-to
ob-du-ra-cy
ob-du-rate
o-be-di-ence
o-bei-sance
o-be-li-al
ob-e-lisk
o-be-si-ty
ob-fus-ca-to-ry
o-bit-u-ar-y
ob-jec-tee
ob-jec-tiv-ism
ob-jec-tiv-i-ty
ob-jec-tor
ob-ju-ra-tion
ob-jur-gate
ob-last
ob-la-to-ry
ob-li-ga-tor
o-blig-a-to-ry
ob-li-gee
o-blig-ing
ob-li-gor
o-blique
ob-liq-ui-ty
ob-lit-er-ate
ob-li-ves-cence
ob-liv-i-on
ob-liv-i-ous
ob-long-at-ed
ob-lo-quy
ob-mu-tes-cence

ob-nox-ious
ob-nu-bi-la-tion
ob-o-lus
ob-scen-i-ty
ob-scu-ran-tism
ob-scu-ri-ty
ob-se-qui-ous
ob-seq-ui-ty
ob-se-quy
ob-serv-ance
ob-serv-ant
ob-ser-va-tion
ob-serv-a-to-ry
ob-serv-er
ob-ses-sion
ob-sid-i-an
ob-so-les-cence
ob-so-lete
ob-sta-cle
ob-ste-tri-cian
ob-stet-rics
ob-sti-na-cy
ob-strep-er-ous
ob-struc-tive
ob-struc-tor
ob-tru-sive
ob-tund-ent
ob-tu-ra-tor
ob-tu-si-ty
ob-ver-tend
oc-a-ri-na
oc-ca-sion
oc-ci-den-tal
oc-cip-i-ta-lis

oc-cip-i-to-pa-ri-e-tal
oc-ci-put
oc-clu-sal
oc-clu-sion
oc-cul-ta-tion
oc-cult-ism
oc-cu-pan-cy
oc-cu-pa-tive
oc-curred
oc-cur-rence
o-cea-nar-i-um
o-ce-an-ic
o-cean-o-graph-ic
o-cean-og-ra-phy
oc-el-late
o-ce-lot
o-cher-ous
och-loc-ra-cy
o-chro-no-sis
oc-ta-co-sane
oc-ta-dec-a-di-e-no-ic
oc-ta-dec-ane
oc-ta-dec-a-no-ic
oc-ta-dec-yl
oc-ta-gon
oc-tag-o-nal
oc-ta-he-dron
oc-ta-mer
oc-tam-er-ous
oc-tam-e-ter
oc-tane
oc-tan-gu-lar
oc-ta-no-ate
oc-ta-nol
oc-ta-no-yl

oc-ta-vos
Oc-to-ber
oc-to-ge-nar-i-an
oc-tog-e-nar-y
oc-to-ic
Oc-top-o-da
oc-to-pus
oc-to-roon
oc-tose
oc-tu-ple
oc-tup-let
oc-tyl-ene
oc-u-lar
oc-u-list
oc-u-lo-gy-ric
o-da-lisque
odd-i-ty
o-dif-er-ous
o-di-om-e-ter
o-di-ous
od-ist
o-di-um
o-dom-e-ter
o-don-ti-tis
o-don-to-gen-ic
o-don-tol-o-gy
o-don-tom-e-ter
o-don-tot-o-my
o-dor-ant
o-dor-if-er-ous
o-dor-om-e-ter
o-dor-ous
Od-ys-sey
oed-i-pal
oe-nan-thic
oer-sted
of-fal
of-fend-er
of-fen-sive
of-fer-to-ry
of-fi-cer
of-fi-cial
of-fi-ci-ate
of-fic-i-nal
of-fi-cious
off-ing
of-ten
o-gi-val
o-gre-ish
O-hi-o-an
ohm-ic
ohm-me-ter

oil-er
oi-ti-ci-ca
o-ken-ite
O-ki-na-wan
O-kla-ho-man
ok-o-nite
o-kra
old-en
old-ster
o-le-ag-i-nous
o-le-an-der
o-le-an-drin
o-lec-ra-non
o-le-fin-ic
o-le-ic
o-le-in-ic
o-le-og-ra-phy
o-le-o-mar-ga-rine
o-le-om-e-ter
o-le-o-res-in
o-le-o-yl
ol-fac-tom-e-ter
ol-fac-to-ry
ol-i-gar-chi-cal
ol-i-gar-chy
ol-i-ge-mi-a
ol-i-go-chro-ne-mi-a
ol-i-go-clase
ol-i-go-dy-nam-ic
ol-i-go-nite
ol-i-gop-o-ly
ol-i-gop-so-ny
ol-i-va-ceous
ol-i-var-y
o-liv-en-ite
ol-i-ves-cence
ol-i-vine
O-lym-pi-an
O-ma-ha
om-bro-graph
om-brom-e-ter
om-buds-man
o-me-ga
om-e-let
o-men-ol-o-gy
om-i-cron
om-i-nous
o-mis-si-ble
o-mis-sion
o-mit-ted
om-ni-bus
om-nif-i-cence

om-nim-e-ter
om-nip-o-tence
om-ni science
om-niv-o-rous
om-pha-li-tis
on-a-ger
on-co-gen-ic
on-cog-e-ny
on-col-o-gy
on-col-y-sis
on-com-e-ter
on-cot-o-my
on-dom-e-ter
on-du-le
O-nei-da
on-er-ous
on-ion
on-o-ma-si-ol-o-gy
on-o-mat-o-poe-ia
On-on-da-ga
On-tar-i-an
on-tog-e-ny
on-to-log-i-cal
on-tol-o-gy
on-y-chol-y-sis
on-y-cho-my-co-sis
on-y-choph-a-gy
on-y-cho-sis
o-ol-o-gy
o-pa-cim-e-ter
o-pac-i-ty
o-pal-es-cent
o-pal-ine
o-paqu-er
o-paqu-ing
o-pei-do-scope
op-er-a
op-er-a-ble
op-er-and
op-er-ate
op-er-at-ic
op-er-a-tive
op-er-a-tor
o-per-cu-lar
oph-i-cleide
o-phid-i-an
o-phi-ol-o-gy
o-phit-ic
oph-thal-mi-a
oph-thal-mic
oph-thal-mo-log-ic
oph-thal-mol-o-gy

oph-thal-mom-e-ter
oph-thal-mo-met-ric
oph-thal-mo-scope
oph-thal-mos-co-py
o-pi-an-ic
o-pi-ate
o-pin-ion-at-ed
o-pin-ion-a-tor
op-i-som-e-ter
o-pis-tho-gas-tric
o-pi-um
o-pos-sum
op-po-nent
op-por-tun-ism
op-por-tun-ist
op-por-tu-ni-ty
op-pos-al
op-po-site
op-press-i-ble
op-pres-sive
op-pres-sor
op-pro-bri-um
op-ti-cal
op-ti-cian
op-ti-mal-ize
op-ti-me
op-tim-e-ter
op-ti-mism
op-ti-mis-tic
op-ti-mum
op-tom-e-ter
op-to-met-ric
op-tom-e-try
op-u-lent
or-a-cle
o-rac-u-lar
o-ral-ly
or-ange
o-ran-ge-lo
or-ange-ry
o-rang-u-tan
o-ra-tion
or-a-tor
or-a-tor-l-cal
or-a-to-ri-o
or-bic-u-lar
or-bit-al
or-bit-ed
or-bit-er
or-bit-ing
or-chard
or-ches-tra

or-chi-da-ceous
or-chid-ol-o-gy
or-cin-ol
or-deal
or-dered
or-di-nal
or-di-nance
or-di-nar-i-ly
or-di-nar-y
ord-nance
Or-do-vi-cian
Or-e-go-ni-an
or-gan-dy
or-gan-ic
or-ga-nism
or-gan-ist
or-ga-niz-a-ble
or-ga-ni-za-tion
or-ga-niz-er
or-gan-o-gel
or-ga-no-gen-ic
or-ga-nog-e-ny
or-ga-nog-ra-phy
or-ga-nos-co-py
or-gan-o-sol
or-gi-as-tic
o-ri-el
O-ri-ent
o-ri-en-tal
o-ri-en-ta-lia
o-ri-en-ta-tor
o-ri-en-tite
or-i-fi-cial
or-i-flamme
or-i-gin
o-rig-i-nal-i-ty
o-rig-i-nat-ing
o-rig-i-na-tive
o-ri-ole
O-ri-on
or-is-mol-o-gy
or-i-son
Or-lan-do
Or-le-ans
Or-lon
or-mo-lu
or-na-men-tal
or-ner-y
or-ni-thine
or-ni-tho-log-i-cal
or-ni-thol-o-gy
or-ni-thop-ter

or-ni-tho-rhyn-chus
or-ni-tho-sis
or-ni-thot-o-my
or-nith-u-ric
o-rog-e-ny
o-rog-ra-phy
o-ro-ide
o-rol-o-gy
o-rom-e-ter
or-o-met-ric
o-ro-tun-di-ty
or-phan-age
or-pi-ment
or-ris
or-sel-lin-ic
or-tha-nil-ic
or-thi-con
or-tho-ar-se-nate
or-tho-ben-zo-qui-none
or-tho-clase
or-tho-don-ti-a
or-tho-don-tist
or-tho-dox-y
or-tho-e-py
or-tho-for-mic
or-thog-o-nal
or-thog-ra-phy
or-thom-e-try
or-tho-pe-dic
or-tho-pe-dist
or-thop-ne-a
Or-thop-ter-a
or-thop-tics
or-tho-sis
or-tho-typ-ic
or-to-lan
o-ryc-tol-o-gy
o-ryc-tog-no-sy
o-sa-zone
Os-car
os-cil-la-tor
os-cil-la-to-ry
os-cil-lom-e-ter
os-cil-lo-scope
os-ci-tant
os-cu-la-to-ry
os-cu-lom-e-ter
O-si-ris
os-mi-dro-sis
os-mi-rid-i-um
os-mi-um
os-mom-e-ter

os-mo-met-ric
os-mom-e-try
os-mo-sis
os-mot-ic
os-phre-sis
os-prey
os-se-ous
os-si-cle
os-sic-u-lar
os-si-cu-lec-to-my
os-sif-i-ca-to-ry
os-si-fy
os-te-al
os-te-it-ic
os-te-i-tis
os-ten-si-ble
os-ten-ta-tious
os-te-o-chon-dro-sis
os-te-ol-o-gy
os-te-ol-y-sis
os-te-o-ma
os-te-o-ma-tous
os-te-om-e-try
os-te-o-my-e-li-tis
os-te-o-path
os-te-op-a-thy
os-te-ot-o-my
os-tra-cism
os-tra-cize
os-trich
o-tal-gi-a
o-the-o-scope
oth-er
o-ti-ose
o-ti-os-i-ty
o-ti-tis me-di-a
o-tog-e-nous
o-to-lar-yn-go-log-i-cal
o-to-lar-yn-gol-o-gy

o-tos-co-py
o-to-sis
oua-ba-in
ou-bli-ette
ou-ri-cu-ry
oust-er
out-er
out-land-ish
out-law-ry
out-ra-geous
out-rag-er
ou-trance
out-rid-er
out-sid-er
o-val-i-form
o-val-i-ty
o-var-i-an
o-var-i-ec-to-my
o-var-i-ole
o-var-i-ot-o-my
o-va-ri-tis
o-va-ry
ov-en
o-ver-head
o-ver-land-er
o-ver-se-er
o-ver-ture
o-vi-ci-dal
o-vic-u-lar
O-vid-i-an
o-vi-na-tion
o-vip-a-ra
o-vi-par-i-ty
o-vip-a-rous
o-vi-pos-i-tor
o-vu-lar
o-vu-la-to-ry
ow-ing
own-er
ox-a-late

ox-al-ic
ox-al-u-ric
ox-a-lyl
ox-am-ide
ox-am-i-dine
ox-an-i-late
ox-a-nil-ic
ox-a-zine
ox-a-zol-i-dine
ox-i-dant
ox-i-dase
ox-i-da-tion
ox-ide
ox-i-dim-e-try
ox-i-diz-a-ble
ox-i-diz-er
ox-id-u-lat-ed
ox-im-e-ter
ox-i-met-ric
ox-in-dole
ox-o-ni-um
ox-o-phen-ar-sine
ox-y-a-can-thine
ox-y-a-cet-y-lene
ox-y-gen
ox-y-gen-ate
ox-y-gen-ize
ox-y-lu-cif-er-in
ox-y-tet-ra-cy-cline
ox-y-to-cin
oys-ter
Oz-al-id
O-zark-i-an
o-zo-ke-rite
o-zon-ate
o-zon-ide
o-zon-iz-er
o-zon-ol-y-sis
o-zo-no-sphere

P

pab-u-lum
pac-er
pa-chi-si
pach-no-lite
pach-y-der-ma-tous
pa-chym-e-ter
pac-i-fi-a-ble
pa-cif-ic
pac-i-fi-ca-tion
pa-cif-i-ca-to-ry
pac-i-fist

pac-i-fy
pack-ag-er
pack-et
pad-dling
pa-dre
pa-dro-ne
Pad-u-an
pae-an
pa-gan-ism
pag-eant-ry

pag-er
pag-i-nal
pag-i-nate
pag-ing
pa-go-da
pains-tak-ing
paint-er
Pais-ley
Pak-i-stan-i
pal-ace
pa-la-ceous

pal-a-din
pal-an-quin
pal-at-a-bil-i-ty
pal-at-a-ble
pal-a-tal-ize
pal-ate (roof of mouth)
pa-la-tial
pa-lat-i-nate
pal-a-tine
pal-a-ti-tis
pal-a-to-gram
pa-lav-er
pa-le-a-ceous
pa-le-og-ra-pher
pa-le-ol-o-gy
pa-le-on-tol-o-gy
Pa-le-o-zo-ic
Pal-es-tin-i-an
pal-ette (artist's board)
pal-frey
pa-lil-o-gy
pal-imp-sest
pal-in-drome
pal-i-sade
pal-la-di-um
pal-let (a bed)
pal-let-ize
pal-lette (armor)
pal-li-a-tive
pal-mate
palm-er
pal-met-to
palm-is-try
pal-mit-ic
pal-mit-o-le-ic
pal-o-mi-no
pal-pa-ble
pal-pi-tate
pal-sy
pal-try
pal-u-drine
pa-lus-trine
pal-y-nol-o-gy
pam-a-quine
Pam-e-la
pam-pas
pam-pe-an
pam-per
pam-phlet
pam-phlet-eer
pam-phlet-ize
pan-a-ce-a

pa-nache (headdress)
pa-na-che (food)
Pan-a-ma-ni-an
pan-a-ry
pan-a-tel-a
pan-car-di-tis
pan-chro-mat-ic
pan-cre-as
pan-cre-a-tec-to-my
pan-cre-a-tin
pan-cre-a-ti-tis
pan-cre-o-zy-min
pan-dem-ic
pan-de-mo-ni-um
pan-der
pan-e-gyr-ic
pan-e-gy-rize
pan-el-ist
pan-go-lin
pan-icked
pan-i-cle
pa-nic-u-late
pan-mne-si-a
pan-nic-u-li-tis
pan-nier
pa-no-cha
pan-o-ply
pan-o-ram-a
pan-o-ram-ic
pan-soph-ic
pan-tag-a-my
Pan-ta-gru-el
pan-ta-loon
pan-tarch-y
pan-te-the-ine
pan-the-ism
pan-the-on
pan-ther
pant-i-soc-ra-cy
pan-to-chro-mism
pan-to-graph
pan-tog-ra-pher
pan-to-ic
pan-tol-o-gy
pan-tom-e-ter
pan-to-mime
pan-to-then-ic
pan-to-yl
pan-try
pa-pa-cy
pa-pa-in-ase
Pa-pa-ni-co-laou

pa-par-chy
pa-pav-er-ine
pa-paw
pa-pay-a
pa-per
pa-pier ma-che
pa-pil-la
pap-il-lar-y
pap-il-lo-ma-to-sis
pap-il-lom-a-tous
pa-pism
pa-poose
pa-pri-ka
Pap-u-an
pap-u-lar
pap-y-ra-ceous
pap-y-rin
pa-py-rus
par-a-ban-ic
par-a-ba-sic
pa-rab-a-sis
par-a-bi-o-sis
par-a-ble
pa-rab-o-la
par-a-bol-i-cal
pa-rab-o-loi-dal
par-a-chor
par-a-chord-al
pa-rach-ro-nism
par-a-chut-ist
par-a-clete
pa-rad-er
par-a-pdigm
par-a-dise
par-a-di-si-a-cal
par-a-dox
par-af-fin-ic
par-a-gly-co-gen
par-a-go-ge
par-a-gog-ic
par-a-gon
pa-rag-o-nite
par-a-graph-er
Par-a-guay-an
par-a-keet
par-al-de-hyde
par-al-lac-tic
par-al-leled
par-al-lel-e-pi-ped
par-al-lel-e-pip-e-don
par-al-lel-ing
par-al-lel-om-e-ter

pa-ral-o-gize
pa-ral-y-sis
par-a-lyt-ic
par-a-lyzed
pa-ram-e-ter
par-a-mide
par-a-mi-no-ben-zo-ic
par-a-mor-phism
par-a-mour
par-a-noi-a
par-a-noi-ac
par-a-noi-dal
par-ant-he-lion
par-a-pet-ed
par-a-pha-si-a
par-a-pher-na-lia
par-a-phrase
pa-raph-ra-sis
pa-raph-y-sis
par-a-ple-gi-a
par-a-ple-gic
pa-rap-sis
par-a-se-le-ne
par-a-sit-e-mi-a
par-a-sit-i-cal
par-a-sit-i-ci-dal
par-a-sit-ism
par-a-si-tize
par-a-si-to-sis
par-a-sol
pa-rat-ro-phy
par-celed
par-don-a-ble
par-e-gor-ic
pa-ren-chy-ma
par-en-chym-a-tous
par-ent-age
pa-ren-tal
par-en-ter-al
pa-ren-the-sis
par-en-thet-i-cal
par-er-gon
pa-re-sis
pa-ret-ic
par-he-lion
pa-ri-ah
pa-ri-e-tal
pa-ri-e-to-fron-tal
par-i-mu-tu-el
par-i-nar-ic
par-ing
Par-is

par-ish
pa-rish-ion-er
Pa-ri-sian
Pa-ri-si-enne
par-i-son
par-i-ty
Par-ker
park-er
par-lance
par-lia-men-tar-i-an
par-lia-men-ta-ry
par-lous
pa-ro-chi-al
par-o-dis-tic
par-o-dy
pa-rol
pa-role
pa-rol-ee
par-o-nych-i-a
par-o-nym
pa-ron-y-mous
pa-rot-id
pa-rot-i-dec-to-my
par-o-tit-ic
par-o-ti-tis
par-ox-ysm
par-ox-ys-mal
par-quet-ry
par-ri-ci-dal
par-si-mo-ni-ous
pars-ley
pars-nip
par-son-age
par-tage
par-tak-er
part-er
par-terre
Par-the-non
par-ti-al-i-ty
par-tial-ly
par-ti-bil-i-ty
par-tic-i-pant
par-tic-i-pa-tor
par-tic-i-ple
par-ti-ci-ple
par-ti-cle
par-tic-u-lar-i-ty
par-tic-u-late
par-ti-san
par-ti-tion-er
par-ti-tive

par-tu-ri-tion
pa-ru-lis
par-ve-nu
pas-chal
pa-sha
pas-i-graph-ic
pa-sig-ra-phy
pas-quin-ade
pass-a-ble
pas-sa-ca-glia
pas-sage
pas-sé
pas-sen-ger
pas-ser (bird)
pass-er
pas-si-ble
pas-sim-e-ter
pass-ing
pas-sion-ate
pas-si-va-tor
pas-siv-ist
pas-siv-i-ty
pas-som-e-ter
pass-o-ver
pas-tel
past-er
pas-tern
pas-teur-i-za-tion
pas-tiche
pas-tille
pas-time
pas-tor
pas-to-ral
pas-to-rale
pas-tor-ate
pas-tra-mi
pas-try
pas-tur-age
Pat-a-go-ni-an
Pa-taps-co
patch-er-y
patch-ou-li
pa-tel-la
pat-ent-ee
pat-en-tor
pa-ter-fa-mil-i-as
pa-ter-nal
pa-ter-ni-ty
pa-ter-nos-ter
pa-thet-ic
path-o-don-ti-a
path-o-gen-ic

path-o-ge-nic-i-ty
pa-thog-e-ny
pa-thog-no-my
path-o-log-i-cal
pa-thol-o-gist
pa-thol-o-gy
pa-thom-e-ter
pa-thos
pa-tho-sis
pa-tien-cy
pat-i-na
pat-i-o
pa-tois
pa-tri-ar-chal
pa-tri-arch-ate
pa-tri-arch-y
pa-tri-cian
pat-ri-cid-al
pat-ri-mo-ni-al
pat-ri-mo-ny
pa-tri-ot-ic
pa-tri-ot-ism
pa-tris-tic
pa-trolled
pa-trol-ling
pa-tron-age
pa-tron-ess
pat-ro-nite
pa-tron-ize
pat-ro-nym-ic
pa-tron-y-my
pa-troon
pat-terned
pau-ci-ty
Pau-li-na
Pau-line
Paul-ine (of Paul)
Paul-ist
pau-lo-post
pau-per-ize
paus-al
pav-er
pa-vil-ion
Pav-lov-i-an
pav-o-nite
pawn-ee (pledgee)
Paw-nee (Indian)
pay-ee
pay-o-la
peace-a-ble
peaked (topped)
peak-ed (pale)

pearl-es-cent
pearl-ite
peas-ant-ry
pe-can
pec-ca-ble
pec-ca-dil-lo
pec-cant
pec-ca-ry
pec-tin-ase
pec-ti-nate
pec-tin-ic
pec-to-lyt-ic
pec-to-ral
pec-to-ril-o-quy
pec-tous (chemistry)
pec-tus (zoology)
pe-cu-liar
pe-cu-li-ar-i-ty
pe-cu-ni-ar-y
ped-a-gog
ped-a-gog-i-cal
ped-a-gog-y
ped-aled
ped-al-ine
ped-ant
pe-dan-tic
ped-ant-ry
ped-dler
Pe-der-sen
ped-es-tal
pe-des-tri-an
pe-di-at-ric
pe-di-a-tri-cian
ped-i-cel
ped-i-cle
pe-dic-u-lar
Pe-dic-u-lar-is
pe-dic-u-lo-sis
pe-dic-u-lous (adj.)
Pe-dic-u-lus (n.)
ped-i-cure
ped-i-gree
ped-o-cal
pe-dol-o-gy
pe-dom-e-ter
ped-o-met-ri-cal
pe-dun-cu-lar
peel-er
peep-er
peer-age
pee-vish
Peg-a-sus

peg-ma-tite
peg-ma-tit-ic
peign-oir
pei-ram-e-ter
pej-o-ra-tive
Pe-king-ese
pe-koe
pe-lag-ic
pel-ar-go-nate
pel-ar-gon-ic
pel-ar-gon-i-din
pel-ar-go-nin
pel-er-ine
pel-i-can
pe-lisse
pel-la-gra
pel-let-er
pel-lu-cid-i-ty
pel-mat-o-gram
pe-lo-rus
pelt-er (n.)
pel-ter (v.)
pelt-ry
pel-vic
pel-vim-e-ter
pem-mi-can
pe-nal-ize
pen-al-ty
pen-ance
pe-na-tes
pench-ant
pen-ciled
pend-ant (n.)
pend-en-cy
pend-ent (adj.)
pen-du-los-i-ty
pen-du-lum
Pe-nel-o-pe
pen-e-tra-ble
pen-e-tram-e-ter
pen-e-tra-tive
pen-e-tra-tor
pen-e-trom-e-ter
pen-guin
pen-i-cil-lin
pen-i-cil-lin-ase
pen-i-cil-li-o-sis
pe-nin-su-lar
pen-i-tent
pen-i-ten-tia-ry
pen-ni-nite
Penn-syl-va-nian

83

Pe-nob-scot
pe-no-log-i-cal
pe-nol-o-gy
Pen-sa-co-la
pen-sive
pent-ac-id
pen-ta-cle
pen-tad
pen-ta-dec-ane
pen-ta-dec-yl
pen-ta-e-ryth-ri-tol
pen-ta-gon
pen-tag-o-nal
pen-ta-he-dral
pen-ta-hy-drite
pen-ta-mer
pen-tam-er-al
pen-tam-er-ous (adj.)
pen-tam-er-us (n.)
pen-tam-e-ter
pent-am-i-dine
pen-tane
pen-ta-no-ic
pen-ta-ploi-dic
pen-tarch-y
pen-ta-rone
Pen-ta-teuch
pen-tath-lon
pen-ta-tom-ic
pen-ta-va-lent
Pen-te-cos-tal
pen-te-nyl
pen-ti-tol
pen-to-bar-bi-tal
pen-tode
pen-tom-ic
pen-to-san
Pen-to-thal
pent-ox-ide
pen-tryl
pen-tu-lose
pen-tyl-ene
pen-tyl-i-dene
pe-nul-ti-mate
pe-num-bra
pe-nu-ri-ous
pen-u-ry
pe-on-age
pe-o-ny
peo-ple
Pe-o-ri-a
pe-pi-no

pep-lum
pep-si-gogue
pep-sin-if-er-ous
pep-sin-o-gen
pep-ti-dase
pep-to-nate
pep-to-nize
per-a-ce-tic
per-am-bu-la-tor
per-bo-rate
Per-bu-nan
per-ca-line
per-ceiv-a-ble
per-ceiv-er
per-cent-age
per-cent-ile
per-cep-ti-ble
per-cep-tive
per-cep-tu-al
perch-er
Per-che-ron
per-chlo-rate
per-chlo-ryl
per-cip-i-ent
per-co-la-tor
per-cu-ri-am
per-cus-sive
per-e-gri-nate
pe-rei-ra
pe-remp-tive
pe-remp-to-ry
pe-ren-ni-al
per-fect-er
per-fect-i-ble
per-fec-tor
per-fer-vid
per-fid-i-ous
per-fi-dy
per-fo-ra-tor
per-form-ance
per-form-er
per-fum-er-y
per-func-to-ry
per-i-anth
per-i-ar-thri-tis
per-i-as-tron
per-i-car-di-tis
per-i-car-di-um
per-i-cla-site
Per-i-cle-an
pe-ric-o-pe
per-i-cop-ic

pe-rid-i-um
pe-rid-o-tite
per-i-gee
pe-rig-y-nous
per-i-he-lion
per-iled
per-il-ous
pe-rim-e-ter
per-i-met-ri-cal
per-im-e-try
per-i-ne-al
per-i-ne-or-rha-ph
per-i-neph-ri-um
per-i-ne-um
pe-ri-od-ic (at int
pe-ri-od-ic (chem
pe-ri-od-i-cal
pe-ri-o-dic-i-ty
per-i-os-te-um
per-i-pa-tet-ic
per-i-pher-al-ly
pe-riph-er-y
per-i-phrase
pe-riph-ra-sis
pe-rip-ter-al
pe-rip-ter-y
pe-rique
pe-ris-cit
per-i-scop-ic
per-ish
per-i-som-al
pe-ris-sad
per-i-stal-tic
per-i-sta-sis
per-i-sty-lar
pe-rit-o-my
per-i-to-ne-os-co-
per-i-to-ne-um
per-i-to-nit-ic
per-i-to-ni-tis
per-i-win-kle
per-jur-er
per-ju-ri-ous
per-ju-ry
per-lite
per-ma-frost
Perm-al-loy
per-ma-nent
per-man-ga-nate
per-me-a-ble
per-me-am-e-ter
Per-mi-an

per-mis-si-ble
per-mit-tee
per-mut-a-ble
per-mu-ta-tor
per-ni-cious
per-ni-o-sis
per-o-ne-al
Pe-ro-nist
per-o-ra-tion
pe-ro-sis
per-ox-i-dase
per-ox-ide
per-ox-y-a-ce-tic
per-ox-y-di-sul-fate
per-pen-dic-u-lar
per-pe-tra-tor
per-pet-u-al
per-pe-tu-i-ty
per-qui-site
per-se-cu-tion
per-se-cu-to-ry
Per-se-id
per-se-i-tol
per-se-ver-ance
per-sev-er-a-tive
Per-shing
Per-sian
per-si-flage
per-sist-ence
per-sist-er
per-snick-e-ty
per-son-a-ble
per-son-al-i-ty
per-son-al-ty
per-son-nel
per-spec-tive
per-spec-tom-e-ter
per-spi-ca-cious
per-spi-cac-i-ty
per-spi-cu-i-ty
per-spic-u-ous
per-spir-a-ble
per-spi-ra-tion
per-spir-a-tive
per-spir-a-to-ry
per-suad-er
per-sua-si-ble
per-sua-sive
perth-ite
per-ti-na-cious
per-ti-nac-i-ty
per-ti-nent

per-turb-a-ble
per-tur-ba-tion
per-turb-er
pe-rus-al
Pe-ru-vi-an
per-va-sive
per-ver-sion
per-ver-si-ty
per-vert-i-ble
per-vi-ca-cious
per-vi-cac-i-ty
per-vi-ous
per-y-lene
pe-se-ta
Pe-sha-war
pes-sa-ry
pes-si-mis-tic
pes-tered
pes-ti-ci-dal
pes-tif-er-ous
pes-ti-lence
pes-tle
pes-tol-o-gy
pet-al-if-er-ous
pet-al-ite
pet-al-ous
pet-al-y
pe-tard
pe-te-chi-al
Pe-ter
pet-i-o-lar
pet-i-ole
pet-it
pe-tite
pe-ti-tion-er
Pe-trar-chan
Pe-trarch-ist
pe-trel
pe-tres-cence
pe-tri
pet-ri-fac-tion
pe-tro-chem-i-cal
pe-trog-e-ny
pet-ro-graph-i-cal
pe-trog-ra-phy
pet-rol
pet-ro-lage
pet-ro-la-tum
pet-ro-lene
pe-tro-le-um
pe-trol-ic

pet-ro-lif-er-ous
pet-ro-lize
pet-ro-log-ic
pe-trol-o-gy
pe-tro-sal
pet-rous
pe-trox-o-lin
pet-u-lant
pe-tu-nia
pe-yo-te
pha-com-e-ter
pha-e-ton
phag-o-cyte
phag-o-cyt-ic
phag-o-cy-to-sis
pha-lange
pha-lan-ge-al
pha-lanx
phal-loi-dine
phan-er-ite
phan-er-o-gam
phan-er-os-co-py
phan-er-o-sis
phan-o-tron
phan-tas-ma-go-ri-al
phan-tas-mal
phan-tom
phan-to-scope
Phar-aoh
phar-i-sa-i-cal
Phar-i-see
phar-ma-ceu-ti-cal
phar-ma-cist
phar-ma-cog-no-sy
phar-mac-o-lite
phar-ma-col-o-gy
phar-ma-co-pe1a
pha-ryn-ge-al
phar-yn-gi-tis
pha-ryn-go-log-i-cal
phar-yn-gol-o-gy
pha-ryn-go-scope
phar-ynx
phase-me-ter
pha-se-o-lin
phas-er (one who phases)
pha-sic
pha-si-tron
pha-sor (electrical)
pheas-ant
phel-lan-drene
phen-ac-e-tin

85

phen-a-cite
phen-a-cyl
phen-an-threne
phen-an-thri-dine
phe-nan-thri-din-i-um
phe-nan-thro-line
phe-nan-thryl
phen-ar-sa-zine
phen-a-zine
phe-net-i-dine
phen-e-tole
phe-nic
phen-mi-az-ine
phe-no-bar-bi-tal
phe-no-cop-ic
phe-no-crys-tic
phe-nol
phe-no-lase
phe-no-late
phe-no-lic
phe-no-log-i-cal
phe-nol-o-gy
phe-nol-phthal-ein
phe-nom-e-nal
phe-nom-e-no-log-i-cal
phe-nom-e-nol-o-gy
phe-no-plast
phe-no-type
phen-ox-ide
phe-nox-y-a-ce-tic
phen-tol-a-mine
phen-yl-ac-et-al-de-hyde
phen-yl-ate
phen-yl-ene
phen-yl-eph-rine
phen-yl-eth-yl-ene
phe-nyl-ic
phen-yl-ke-to-nu-ric
phe-nyt-o-in
phe-o-chro-mo-cy-to-ma
phe-o-phor-bide
phe-o-phy-tin
Phil-a-del-phi-an
phi-lan-der
phil-an-throp-ic
phi-lan-thro-pist
phi-lan-thro-py
phil-a-tel-ic
phi-lat-e-list
phi-lat-e-ly
phil-har-mon-ic
phil-i-a-ter

phi-lip-pic
Phil-ip-pine
Phil-is-tine
phil-o-den-dron
phil-o-graph
phi-log-y-ny
phil-o-log-i-cal
phi-lol-o-gy
phil-o-pe-na
phi-los-o-pher
phil-o-soph-i-cal
phi-los-o-phiz-er
phi-los-o-phy
phil-ter
phle-bit-ic
phle-bi-tis
phleb-o-graph-ic
phle-bog-ra-phy
phle-bot-o-my
phleg-mat-ic
phlo-em
phlo-gis-ton
phlog-o-pi-ti-za-tion
phlo-i-on-ic
phlor-e-tin
phlor-i-zin-ize
phlor-o-glu-cin-ol
phlo-rol
phlox-ine
pho-bi-a
pho-bo-tax-is
phoe-be
Phoe-ni-cian
Phoe-nix
phon-as-the-ni-a
phon-au-to-graph
pho-ne-mat-ic
pho-ne-mic
pho-ne-mic-i-ty
pho-nen-do-scope
pho-net-ic
pho-ne-ti-cian
Phone-vi-sion
pho-ni-at-ric
phon-ic
pho-no-gen-ic
pho-no-graph-i-cal
pho-nog-ra-phy
pho-no-lite
pho-nol-o-gy
pho-nom-e-ter

pho-nom-e-try
pho-no-phore
pho-noph-o-rous
pho-ny
phor-bin
pho-re-sis
pho-ret-ic
pho-rom-e-ter
pho-rom-e-try
pho-rone
pho-rop-tor
phos-gen-ite
phos-pham-ic
phos-pha-tase
phos-pha-te-mi-a
phos-phat-ic
phos-phi-nate
phos-phin-ic
phos-pho-a-mi-no-lip-ide
phos-pho-di-es-ter-ase
phos-pho-nate
phos-phon-ic
phos-pho-rate
phos-pho-re-al
phos-pho-res-cence
phos-phor-ic
phos-phor-o-gen
phos-pho-ro-gen-ic
phos-pho-rol-y-sis
phos-pho-rous (adj.)
phos-pho-rus (n.)
phos-pho-ryl-ase
phos-vi-tin
pho-tics
pho-to-chro-my
pho-to-gen-ic
pho-to-gram-me-try
pho-tog-ra-pher
pho-to-graph-ic
pho-tog-ra-phy
pho-to-gra-vure
pho-tol-y-sis
pho-to-lyt-ic
pho-tom-e-ter
pho-to-met-ric
pho-tom-e-try
pho-ton
pho-to-nas-tic
pho-top-a-thy
pho-to-pho-re-sis
phot-op-tom-e-ter

pho-to-stat-ed
pho-to-trop-ic
pho-tot-ro-pism
pho-tron-ic
phras-a-ble
phra-se-o-gram
phra-se-og-ra-phy
phra-se-ol-o-gy
phras-er
phras-ing
phren-ic
phren-i-cot-o-my
phre-ni-tis
phren-o-log-i-cal
phre-nol-o-gy
phren-o-sin
Phryg-i-an
phthal-am-ic
phthal-ate
phthal-ein
phthal-ic
phthal-im-ide
phthal-in
phthal-o-ni-trile
phthal-o-yl
phthi-o-col
phthi-ri-a-sis
phthis-ick-y
phthis-i-ol-o-gy
phthi-sis
phy-col-o-gy
phy-lac-tery
phyl-lo-por-phy-rin
phy-lo-ge-net-ic
phy-log-e-ny
phy-lum
phy-ma-to-sis
phys-i-at-rics
phys-ic
phys-i-cal
phy-si-cian
phys-i-cist
phys-i-og-no-my
phys-i-og-ra-phy
phys-i-ol-a-ter
phys-i-o-log-i-cal
phys-i-ol-o-gy
phys-i-om-e-try
phys-i-os-o-phy
phy-sique
phy-so-car-pous
phy-so-stig-mine

phy-tase
Phy-tin
phy-to-flu-ene
phy-tog-a-my
phy-to-gen-ic
phy-tol-o-gy
phy-tom-e-ter
phy-to-met-ric
phy-toph-a-gous
phy-to-sis
phy-tos-te-rol
phy-tyl
pi-a-nis-si-mo
pi-an-ist
pi-a-niste
pi-a-nis-tic
pi-an-o-for-te
pi-as-sa-va
pi-as-ter
pic-a-resque
pic-a-yune
Pic-ca-dil-ly
pic-ca-lil-li
pic-e-in
pi-cene
pick-et-er
pick-led
pick-ling
pic-nick-er
pic-o-line
pic-o-lin-ic
pic-ram-ic
pic-ram-ide
pic-rate
pic-ric
pic-ro-cro-cin
pic-ro-lon-ic
pic-rom-er-ite
pic-ryl
pic-to-graph-ic
pic-tog-ra-phy
pic-to-ri-al
pic-tur-a-ble
pic-tur-esque
pic-ul
pid-dler
pi-ece de re-sis-tance
piec-er
pierc-er
pi-e-ty
pi-e-zom-e-ter
pi-e-zom-e-try

pi-geon-eer
pig-men-tar-y
pi-gnon
pik-er
pi-las-ter
pil-chard
pil-er
pil-fer-age
pil-grim-age
pi-lif-er-ous
pil-lag-er
pil-lo-ry
pi-lo-car-pi-dine
pi-lose
pi-lo-sine
pi-los-i-ty
pi-lot-age
Pil-sner
pil-u-lar
pim-an-threne
pi-mar-ic
pim-e-late
pi-men-ta
pi-men-to
pi-mien-to
pim-ply
pin-a-coi-dal
pin-a-col
pi-nac-o-late
pi-nac-o-lone
pin-a-cy-a-nol
pi-nane
pin-cers
pinch-er
pin-e-al
pi-nene
pin-er-y
pi-nic
pin-ion
pi-nite
pi-ni-tol
pink-er
pin-na-cle
pi-no-cam-phe-ol
pi-noch-le
pi-no-lin
pi-ñon
pi-non-ic
pi-no-syl-vin
pin-tle
pi-nyl
pi-o-neered

87

pi-os-i-ty
pi-ous
pip-age
pi-pec-o-line
pip-er
pi-per-a-zine
pi-per-ic
pi-per-i-dine
pip-er-ine
pi-per-o-nyl-ic
pip-er-ox-an
pi-per-y-lene
pi-pet
pi-quan-cy
pi-quant
pl-qué (fabric)
pi-quet
pi-ra-cy
pi-ra-nha
pi-rat-i-cal
pi-rogue
pir-ou-ette
pis-ca-to-ri-al
Pis-ces
pis-cine
pi-si-form
pis-tach-i-o
pis-til-late
pitch-er
pit-e-ous
pith-e-can-thro-poid
pith-e-col-o-gy
pith-i-ness
pit-i-a-ble
pi-tom-e-ter
pi-ton
pi-tu-i-tar-y
Pi-tu-i-trin
pi-val-ic
piv-ot-al
piv-ot-er
pix-i-lat-ed
piz-ze-ri-a
plac-a-ble
plac-ard (n.)
pla-card (v.)
pla-cat-er
pla-ca-to-ry
place-a-ble
pla-ce-bo
pla-cen-ta
plac-en-tar-y

plac-en-ti-tis
plac-er
plac-id
pla-cid-i-ty
plack-et
pla-coi-dal
pla-gia-rism
pla-gia-rize
pla-gi-o-clase
pla-gi-o-nite
plagu-ed
pla-gui-ly
pla-guy
plain-tiff
plain-tive
plait-er
pla-nar-i-ty
pla-na-tion
plan-chet
plan-chette
pla-ner (tree)
plan-er
plan-et
plan-e-tar-i-um
plan-e-tar-y
plan-e-tes-i-mal
plan-et-oi-dal
plan-et-o-log-ic
plan-e-tol-o-gy
plan-gen-cy
pla-nig-ra-phy
pla-nim-e-ter
pla-ni-met-ric
plani-i-sphere
plank-tiv-o-rous
pla-no-con-cave
plan-o-graph
pla-nog-ra-phy
pla-nom-e-ter
plan-o-sol
plan-tain
plan-tar
plan-ta-tion
plant-er
pla-num
pla-quette
plas-ma-pher-e-sis
plas-min-o-gen
plas-mo-di-a-sis
plas-mo-di-um
plas-mol-y-sis
plas-mo-lyt-ic

plas-ter
plas-ti-ca-tor
plas-ti-cim-e-ter
plas-tic-i-ty
plas-ti-ciz-er
plas-ti-line
plas-ti-noid
plas-ti-sol
plas-to-mer
plas-tom-e-ter
plas-tron
pla-teau
plat-ed
plat-en
plat-er
pla-ti-na
pla-tin-ic
plat-i-no-type
plat-i-num
plat-i-tu-di-nar-i-a*
pla-ton-ic
Pla-to-nist
pla-toon
plat-y-nite
plat-y-pus
plau-dit
plau-si-ble
plead-er
pleas-ant-ry
pleas-ur-a-ble
pleat-er
ple-be-ian
pleb-i-scite
pledg-ee
pledge-or (law)
pledg-er
pledg-et
Ple-ia-des
plei-o-bar
plei-ot-ro-py
Pleis-to-cene
ple-na-ry
plen-i-po-ten-tia-ry
plen-i-tude
plen-te-ous
plen-ti-ful
ple-num
ple-o-nasm
ple-rot-ic
pleth-o-ra
ple-thor-ic
pleu-ral

pleu-ri-sy
pleu-rit-ic
pleu-ro-dont
plex-im-e-ter
plex-us
Pli-o-cene
plom-bage
plov-er
plu-ma-ceous
plum-age
plu-mate
plum-ba-gin
plum-ba-go
plum-bate
plumb-er
plum-bif-er-ous
plum-bite
plum-bous
plu-mose
plump-er
plun-der
plung-er
plu-ral-i-ty
plu-ri-va-lent
plu-tar-chy
plu-toc-ra-cy
plu-to-crat
plu-to-nism
plu-to-ni-um
plu-vi-og-ra-phy
plu-vi-om-e-ter
plu-vi-o-met-ric
plu-vi-ous
Plym-outh
pneu-drau-lic
pneu-mat-ic
pneu-ma-tic-i-ty
pneu-ma-tol-y-sis
pneu-ma-tom-e-ter
pneu-ma-to-sis
pneu-mec-to-my
pneu-mo-coc-cus
pneu-mol-y-sis
pneu-mo-nia
pneu-mon-ic
pneu-mo-ni-tis
poach-er
po-choir
pock-et
po-dal-ic
po-di-a-trist
po-di-a-try

po-di-um
po-do-lite
pod-zol-ize
po-et-as-ter
po-et-i-cal
po-et-ry
po-go-not-ro-phy
po-grom
poign-an-cy
poign-ant
poi-ki-lit-ic
poi-kil-o-cy-to-sis
poin-ci-an-a
poin-set-ti-a
point-er
Poi-ret
pois-er
poi-son-ous
pok-er
po-lar
po-lar-im-e-ter
po-lar-i-met-ric
Po-la-ris
po-lar-i-scope
po-lar-i-stro-bom-e-ter
po-lar-i-ty
po-lar-iz-er
po-lar-o-graph-ic
po-lar-og-ra-phy
Po-lar-oid
po-lar-on
po-lem-ic
pol-e-mize
pol-er
po-li-a-nite
po-lic-ing
pol-i-cy
po-li-o-my-e-li-tis
po-li-o-sis
Pol-ish
pol-ish-er
Po-lit-bu-ro
po-lit-i-cal
pol-i-ti-cian
pol-i-tics
po-litz-er
pol-len-iz-er
poll-er
pol-li-na-tion
pol-li-nif-er-ous
pol-lin-i-um
pol-li-no-sis

pol-lu-cite
pol-lut-ant
pol-lut-er
pol-lu-tion
po-lo-naise
po-lo-ni-um
pol-troon
pol-y-a-cryl-ic
pol-y-am-ide
pol-y-an-dry
pol-y-ar-gy-rite
pol-y-ba-site
pol-y-chro-mat-ic
pol-y-chro-my
pol-y-clin-ic
pol-y-crase
pol-y-cy-the-mi-a
po-lyd-y-mite
pol-y-ene
pol-y-es-ter
pol-y-eth-yl-ene
pol-y-gam-ic
po-lyg-a-my
po-lyg-e-ny
pol-y-glot
pol-y-gon
po-lyg-o-nal
pol-y-graph-ic
po-lyg-ra-phy
pol-y-he-dral
pol-y-hi-dro-sis
pol-y-i-so-bu-tyl-ene
pol-y-i-so-top-ic
pol-y-kar-y-on
pol-y-mer-ic
po-lym-er-i-za-tion
po-lym-er-iz-er
po-lym-er-ous
pol-y-me-ter
pol-ym-nite
pol-y-mor-phous
Pol-y-ne-sian
pol-y-no-mi-al
pol-y-nu-cle-o-sis
pol-yp-ec-to-my
po-lyph-a-gous
po-lyph-o-ny
pol-y-ploi-dic
pol-yp-ous
pol-yp-tych
pol-y-pus
pol-y-so-ma-ty

89

pol-y-sty-rene
pol-y-tech-ni-cal
pol-y-trop-ic
pol-y-u-ro-nide
pol-y-va-lent
pol-y-vi-nyl
pom-ace
po-made
po-ma-tum
pome-gran-ate
Pom-er-a-ni-an
pom-meled
po-mo-log-i-cal
po-mol-o-gy
pom-pa-dour
pom-pa-no
Pom-pe-ian
pom-pos-i-ty
pomp-ous
Pon-a-pe-an
pon-cho
pond-age
pon-der-o-sa
pon-der-os-i-ty
pon-der-ous
pon-iard
pon-tage
pon-tif-i-cal
pon-tif-i-ca-tor
poo-dle
pop-e-line
pop-lit-e-al
pop-ping
pop-u-lace
pop-u-lar-i-ty
pop-u-lar-ize
pop-u-lous
por-ce-lain
por-ce-la-ne-ous
por-cine
por-cu-pine
po-ri-ci-dal
po-rif-er-ous
po-ri-tes
por-nog-ra-pher
por-no-graph-ic
po-rom-e-ter
po-ro-scope
po-ros-co-py
po-rose
po-ro-sim-e-ter
po-ros-i-ty

po-rot-ic
po-rous
por-phin
por-phy-rin
por-phy-rit-ic
por-phyr-ox-ine
por-phy-ry
por-poise
port-a-ble
por-tage
por-tal
por-ten-tous
por-ter
port-fo-li-o
por-ti-co
por-tiere
port-man-teau
por-trai-ture
Por-tu-guese
por-tu-lac-a
pos-er
po-seur
po-si-tion-er
pos-i-ti-val
pos-i-tiv-ism
pos-i-tri-no
pos-i-tro-ni-um
po-sol-o-gy
pos-sessed
pos-sess-es
pos-ses-sive
pos-ses-sor
pos-si-bil-i-ty
post-age
post-al
post-er
pos-te-ri-or
pos-ter-i-ty
pos-ter-o-dor-sal
post-hu-mous
pos-tu-lant
pos-tur-al
po-ta-ble
po-tage
po-tam-ic
pot-a-mog-ra-phy
pot-a-mom-e-ter
pot-ash
pot-as-sam-ide
po-tas-sic
po-tas-si-um
po-ta-to-ry

Pot-a-wat-o-mi
po-ten-cy
po-ten-tate
po-ten-ti-al-i-ty
po-ten-ti-om-e-ter
po-tom-e-ter
pot-pour-ri
pot-sherd
poul-tice
poul-try
pounc-er
pound-age
pound-er
pour-par-ler
pousse ca-fe
pout-er
pov-er-ty
pow-dered
pow-ered
poz-zo-la-nic
prac-ti-ca-ble
prac-ti-cal-i-ty
prac-tic-er
prac-ti-tion-er
prae-ci-pe
prag-mat-ic
prag-ma-tism
prai-rie
prais-er
pra-line
pranc-er
pran-di-al
prank-ster
pra-se-o-dym-i-um
pras-oid
pra-tique
prat-tler
prax-e-ol-o-gy
pray-er
preach-er
pre-am-ble
pre-car-i-ous
prec-a-to-ry
pre-ced-a-ble
prec-e-dence
pre-ce-dent (adj.)
prec-e-dent (n., v.)
pre-ced-ing
pre-cep-tor
pre-ci-os-i-ty
pre-cious
prec-i-pice

pre-cip-i-tant
pre-cip-i-ta-tor
pre-cip-i-tin-o-gen
pre-cip-i-tous
Pre-cip-i-tron
pre-ci-sion
pre-ci-sive
pre-clu-sive
pre-co-cious
pre-coc-i-ty
pre-cor-di-um
pre-cur-sor
pre-da-ceous
pre-dac-i-ty
pred-a-to-ry
pred-e-ces-sor
pre-den-ta-ry
pred-i-ca-ble
pre-dic-a-ment
pred-i-cate
pred-i-ca-to-ry
pre-dict-able
pre-dic-tion
pre-dic-tor
pred-i-lec-tion
pred-nis-o-lone
pred-ni-sone
pre-dom-i-nance
pre-emp-to-ry
pre-fab-ri-ca-tor
pref-ace
pref-a-to-ry
pre-fec-ture
pre-fer
pref-er-a-ble
pref-er-ence
pref-er-en-tial
pre-fer-ment
pre-for-ma-tion
preg-nan-cy
preg-nen-in-o-lone
preg-nen-o-lone
pre-hen-si-ble
pre-hen-sile
prehn-ite
prehn-i-tene
prehn-it-ic
prej-u-di-cial
prel-ate
pre-lim-i-nar-y
prel-ude

pre-lu-di-al
pre-ma-ture
pre-med-i-ta-tive
pre-mier
pre-miere
prem-ise (n.)
pre-mise (v.)
pre-mi-um
pre-mo-ni-tion
pre-mon-i-to-ry
prep-a-ra-tion
pre-par-a-to-ry
pre-par-er
pre-pon-der-ant
pre-po-si-tion (before)
prep-o-si-tion
pre-pos-ter-ous
pre-puce
pre-req-ui-site
pre-rog-a-tive
pres-age (n.)
pre-sage (v.)
pres-by-o-phre-ni-a
pres-by-o-pi-a
Pres-by-te-ri-an
pres-by-ter-y
pre-science
pre-scient
pre-scis-sion
pre-scrib-er
pre-scrip-ti-ble
pre-scrip-tive
pres-ent (adj. and n.)
pre-sent (v.; also as n.,
   military term)
pre-sent-a-ble
pres-en-ta-tion
pre-sen-ta-tive
pre-sent-er
pre-sen-ti-ment
pre-sen-tive
pres-er-va-tion
pre-serv-a-tive
pre-serv-er
pres-i-den-cy
pres-i-den-tial
pre-sid-i-o
pre-sid-i-um
press-er
pres-sor
pres-sur-ize
pres-ti-dig-i-ta-tor

pres-tig-i-ous
Pres-tone
pre-sum-a-ble
pre-sump-tion
pre-sump-tive
pre-sump-tu-ous
pre-tend-er
pre-tense
pre-ten-tious
pret-er-it
pre-ter-i-tal
pre-ter-mit
pre-to-ri-al
pret-ti-ness
pret-zel
pre-vail
prev-a-lence
pre-var-i-ca-tor
pre-vent-a-tive
pre-vent-er
pre-ven-tive
pre-vi-ous
pric-er
prick-ling
pri-ma-cy
pri-ma fa-ci-e
pri-ma-quine
pri-mar-i-ly
pri-mar-y
pri-mate
Pri-ma-tes
pri-ma-tol-o-gy
pri-ma-ve-ral
prim-er
pri-me-val
prim-i-tiv-ism
pri-mo-gen-i-ture
pri-mor-di-al
prim-u-lav-er-in
prim-u-line
pri-mus
prin-cess
prin-ci-pal
prin-ci-ple
print-er-y
pri-or-i-ty
pri-o-ry
pris-mat-ic
pris-ma-toi-dal
pris-moi-dal
pri-som-e-ter
pris-on-er

pris-tine
pri-va-cy
pri-va-teer
pri-va-tion
priv-a-tive
pri-vat-ize
priv-et
priv-i-leged
priv-i-ty
priz-a-ble
prob-a-bil-i-ty
prob-a-ble
pro-ba-tion-er
pro-ba-tive
pro-bi-ty
prob-lem-at-i-cal
prob-o-la
pro-bos-cis
pro-caine
pro-ce-dur-al
pro-ce-dure,
proc-ess (n., v.)
proc-ess-ing
pro-ces-sion
proc-es-sor
pro-claim
proc-la-ma-tion
pro-clam-a-to-ry
pro-clit-ic
pro-cliv-i-ty
pro-cli-vous
proc-ne-mi-al
pro-cras-ti-na-tor
pro-cre-a-tor
pro-crus-te-an
proc-ti-tis
proc-to-log-i-cal
proc-tol-o-gy
proc-to-ri-al
proc-to-scop-ic
proc-tos-co-py
pro-cur-a-ble
proc-u-ra-cy
proc-u-ra-to-ry
pro-cur-er
pro-cur-ess
prod-i-gal-i-ty
pro-dig-i-o-sin
pro-di-gious
prod-i-gy
pro-drome
pro-duce (v.)

prod-uce (n.)
pro-duc-er
pro-duc-i-ble
prod-uct (n.)
pro-duct-i-ble
pro-duc-tion
pro-duc-tiv-i-ty
prof-a-na-tion
pro fan-i-ty
pro-fess-ant
pro-fessed
pro-fes-sion
pro-fes-sor
pro-fes-so-ri-al
prof-fered
pro-fi-cient
pro-fil-er
pro-fil-o-graph
pro-fi-lom-e-ter
prof-it-a-ble
prof-it-eer
prof-it-er
prof-li-ga-cy
prof-li-gate
prof-lu-ence
pro-fun-di-ty
pro-fu-sion
pro-gen-i-tor
prog-e-ny
pro-ges-ter-one
prog-na-thous
prog-no-sis
prog-nos-ti-ca-tor
pro-gramed
pro-gram-er
pro-gram-ing
pro-gram-ist
pro-gram-mat-ic
prog-ress (n.)
pro-gress (v.)
pro-gres-sion
pro-gres-sive
pro-hib-it-er
pro-hi-bi-tion
pro-hib-i-tive
pro-hib-i-to-ry
proj-ect (n.)
pro-ject (v.)
pro-jec-tile
pro-jec-tive
pro-jec-tor
pro-ji-cient

pro-lam-in
pro-la-tive
pro-le-gom-e-non
pro-lep-sis
pro-le-tar-i-an
pro-lif-er-a-tive
pro-lif-ic
pro-li-fic-i-ty
pro-line
pro-lix
pro-log
pro-lon-ga-tion
pro-lu-so-ry
prom-e-nad-er
Pro-me-the-us
pro-me-thi-um
prom-i-nence
prom-is-cu-i-ty
pro-mis-cu-ous
prom-is-ee
prom-i-sor
prom-is-so-ry
Prom-i-zole
prom-on-to-ry
pro-mot-er
prompt-er
promp-ti-tude
pro-mul-ga-tion
pro-mul-ga-tor
pro-na-tor
pro-nom-i-nal
pro-no-tum
pro-nounce-a-ble
pro-nun-ci-a-tion
proof-er
pro-pa-di-ene
prop-a-ga-ble
prop-a-gan-dist
prop-a-ga-tor
pro-pam-i-dine
pro-pa-no-ic
pro-pa-nol
pro-par-gyl
pro-par-ox-y-tone
pro-pel-lant (n.)
pro-pel-lent (adj.)
pro-pel-ler
pro-pel-ler
pro-pe-no-ic
pro-pen-si-ty
pro-pe-nyl
pro-per-din
prop-er-ly

prop-er-ty
proph-e-cy (n.)
proph-e-sy (v.)
proph-et
pro-phet-ic
pro-phy-lac-tic
pro-phy-lax-is
pro-pin-qui-ty
pro-pi-o-late
pro-pi-o-lic
pro-pi-o-nate
pro-pi-on-ic
pro-pi-o-ni-trile
pro-pi-o-nyl
pro-pi-on-y-late
pro-pi-ti-ate
pro-pi-tious
pro-po-de-um
pro-po-nent
pro-por-tion-ate
pro-pos-al
pro-pos-er
prop-o-si-tion
pro-pri-e-tar-y
pro-pri-e-tor
pro-pri-e-ty
pro-pox-y-ac-et-an-i-lide
pro-pul-sive
pro-pul-so-ry
pro-pyl-a-mine
pro-pyl-ene
pro-pyl-ic
prop-y-lite
pro ra-ta
pro-rat-a-ble
pro-rat-er
pro-ro-ga-tion
pro-rogue
pro-sa-i-cal-ly
pro-sce-ni-um
pro-scribe
pro-scrip-tive
pros-e-cu-to-ry
pros-e-cu-trix
pros-e-lyte
pros-e-lyt-iz-er
pro-sod-i-cal
pros-o-dy
pros-o-pite
pros-o-pla-si-a
pros-pect
pro-spec-tive

pros-pec-tor
pros-pec-tus
pros-per-i-ty
pros-per-ous
pro-spi-cience
pros-ta-tec-to-my
pros-tat-ic
pros-ta-ti-tis
pro-sthen-ic
pros-the-sis
pros-thet-ic
pros-the-tist
Pro-stig-min
pros-ti-tute
pros-tra-tor
prot-ac-tin-i-um
pro-ta-gon
pro-tag-o-nist
prot-a-mine
pro-ta-no-pi-a
pro-te-an
pro-te-ase
pro-tect-ant
pro-tec-tive
pro-tec-tor-ate
pro-te-ge
pro-te-ide
pro-tein
pro-tein-a-ceous
pro-tein-ase
pro tem-po-re
pro-te-ol-y-sin
Prot-er-o-zo-ic
pro-test
pro-tes-tant (law)
Prot-es-tant (religion)
prot-es-ta-tion
pro-test-er
pro-thon-o-tar-y
pro-throm-bin
pro-tide
pro-ti-um
pro-to-blast
pro-to-cat-e-chu-al-de-hyde
pro-to-clas-tic
pro-toc-neme
pro-to-col
pro-to-gen
pro-tog-y-ny
pro-ton-ate
pro-to-pine

pro-to-plas-mal
pro-to-trop-ic
pro-tot-ro-py
pro-to-type
pro-to-ver-a-trine
prot-ox-ide
pro-to-zo-a
pro-to-zo-i-a-sis
pro-tract-i-ble
pro-trac-tile
pro-trac-tor
pro-tru-si-ble
pro-tru-sive
pro-tu-ber-ance
proust-ite
prov-a-ble
prov-e-nance
prov-en-der
pro-ve-nience
prov-er
prov-erb
pro-ver-bi-al
pro-vide
prov-i-dence
prov-i-den-tial
pro-vid-er
prov-ince
pro-vin-cial
pro-vi-sion
pro-vi-so-ry
prov-o-ca-tion
pro-voc-a-tive
pro-voc-a-to-ry
pro-vost (military)
prov-ost-al
prow-ess
prowl-er
prox-i-mate
prox-im-i-ty
pru-dence
pru-den-tial
prud-er-y
prud-ish
pru-i-nes-cence
pru-na-sin
pru-nel-la
prun-er
pru-ne-tin
pru-ni-trin
pru-ri-ent
pru-rit-ic
pru-ri-tus

prus-si-ate
psalm-ist
psal-mod-ic
psal-ter-y
pseud-an-dry
pseud-ar-thro-sis
pseu-do-cu-mi-dine
pseu-do-i-o-none
pseu-do-ni-trole
pseu-do-nym
pseu-don-y-mous
pseu-dos-co-py
pseu-dos-to-ma
psil-an-thro-py
psi-lo-mel-ane
psi-lo-sis
psi-lot-ic
psit-ta-co-sis
psit-ta-cot-ic
pso-phom-e-ter
pso-ri-a-sis
pso-ro-sis
Psy-che
psy-che-om-e-try
psy-chi-at-ric
psy-chi-a-trist
psy-chi-a-try
psy-chi-cal
psy-cho-an-a-lyst
psy-cho-an-a-lyt-ic
psy-cho-an-a-lyze
psy-cho-gen-ic
psy-cho-ge-nic-i-ty
psy-cho-graph-ic
psy-chog-ra-phy
psy-cho-log-i-cal
psy-chol-o-gist
psy-chom-e-ter
psy-cho-met-ric
psy-chom-e-tri-cian
psy-chom-e-try
psy-cho-nom-ics
psy-cho-path-ic
psy-chop-a-thy
psy-cho-sis
psy-cho-so-mat-ic
psy-chot-ic
psy-cho-trine
psy-chrom-e-ter
psy-chrom-e-try
psyl-li-um
psyl-lyl

ptar-mi-gan
pter-i-dine
pter-o-dac-tyl
pte-ro-ic
pter-o-pod
Pte-rop-o-da
pter-o-yl
pte-ryg-i-um
pter-y-goid
Ptol-e-ma-ic
pto-maine
pto-sis
pu-ber-ty
pu-ber-u-lent
pu-ber-u-lon-ic
pu-bes-cent
pu-bic
pu-bi-ot-o-my
pub-li-ca-tion
pub-li-cist
pub-lic-i-ty
puck-ered
pu-den-dal
pueb-lo
pu-er-ile
pu-er-per-al
pu-er-pe-ri-um
puff-er
pu-gi-lism
pu-gi-list
pu-gi-lis-tic
pug-na-cious
pug-nac-i-ty
pu-is-sant
pul-chri-tu-di-nous
pu-le-gone
pu-li-cide
pul-ing
pull-er
pul-let
pul-lo-rum
pul-mom-e-ter
pul-mo-nar-y
pul-mon-ic
Pul-mo-tor
pulp-er
pul-pit-eer
pulp-ot-o-my
pulp-ous
pul-que
pul-sa-tance

pul-sa-to-ry
puls-er
pul-sim-e-ter
pul-som-e-ter
pul-ver-iz-er
pul-ver-u-lent
pul-vin-ic
pu-mi-cate
pum-ice
pu-mi-ceous
pump-age
pump-er
pum-per-nick-el
pun-cheon
punch-er
pun-chi-nel-lo
punc-tate
punc-ti-form
punc-til-i-o
punc-til-i-ous
punc-tu-al-i-ty
punc-tu-ate
punc-tur-a-ble
punc-tured
pun-dit
pun-gen-cy
Pu-nic
pu-nic-ic
pun-ish-er
pu-ni-tive
pun-ster
punt-er
Punx-su-taw-ney
pu-pa-tion
pu-pif-er-ous
pu-pil
pu-pil-late
pu-pil-lom-e-ter
pup-pet-eer
pup-pet-ry
pur-chas-er
pu-ree
pur-ga-tive
pur-ga-to-ry
purg-er
pu-ri-fi-ca-tion
pu-rine
pur-ist
pu-ris-tic
pu-ri-tan
pu-ri-ty

Pur-kin-je
pur-lieu
pur-lin
pur-loin
pu-ro-my-cin
pur-ples-cent
pur-plish
pur-pos-ive
pur-pu-ra
pur-pu-rin
pur-pu-rite
pur-pu-ro-gal-lin
pur-pu-rog-e-nous
purs-er
pur-su-ant
pur-suit-me-ter
pur-sui-vant
pur-te-nance
pu-ru-lence
pur-vey-or
pu-sil-la-nim-i-ty
pu-sil-lan-i-mous
pus-tu-lous
pu-ta-tive
pu-tre-fa-cient
pu-tre-fac-tion
pu-tres-cent
pu-tres-ci-ble
pu-tres-cine
pu-trid
put-ter (n., v.)
putt-er (golf club)
Puy-al-lup
puz-zler
pyc-nom-e-ter
pyc-no-sis
pyc-not-ic
py-e-lit-ic

py-e-li-tis
py-e-lo-graph-ic
Pyg-ma-li-on
pyg-my
pyk-rete
py-lor-ic
py-lo-ro-plas-ty
py-lo-rus
py-o-cy-a-nase
py-o-cy-a-nin
py-o-gen-ic
py-or-rhe-a
pyr-a-cene
Pyr-a-lin
pyr-a-mid
py-ram-i-dal
pyr-a-mid-er
pyr-a-mid-i-cal
py-ran
pyr-a-nom-e-ter
py-ran-o-side
pyr-ar-gy-rite
pyr-a-zin-a-mide
pyr-az-ine
pyr-az-ole
py-raz-o-lone
py-raz-o-lyl
py-rene
Pyr-e-ne-an
py-ren-em-a-tous
py-re-thrin
py-re-thrum
Py-rex
py-rex-in
pyr-ge-om-e-ter
pyr-he-li-om-e-ter
pyr-i-bole
py-rid-a-zine

py-rid-ic
pyr-i-dine
pyr-i-din-i-um
pyr-i-done
pyr-i-dyl
py-rim-i-dine
py-rite
py-ri-tes
py-rit-ic
py-rit-if-er-ous
py ri-to-he-dral
py-ro-cat-e-chu-ic
py-ro-gal-lol
py-ro-ge-na-tion
py-rog-ra-phy
py-ro-lu-site
py-rol-y-sis
py-ro-lyze
py-ro-ma-ni-a
py-rom-e-ter
py-rone
py-ro-sis
py-ro-sphere
py-ro-tech-nic
py-rox-ene
pyr-ox-i-dine
py-rox-y-lin
p**yr**-rhic
pyr-rol-i-dine
pyr-ro-line
pyr-ro-lo-pyr-i-dine
pyr-ro-lyl
pyr-uv-al-de-hyde
pyr-u-vic
py-ryl-i-um
Py-thag-o-re-an
Pyth-i-an
py-thon-ic

Q

quack-er-y
quad-ded
quad-ra-ges-i-mal
quad-ran-gle
quad-ran-gu-lar
quad-rant
quad-rat-ic
quad-ra-ture
quad-ra-tus
quad-ren-ni-al
quad-ric
quad-rille

quad-ril-lion
quad-ri-ple-gic
quad-ri-va-lent
quad-roon
quad-ru-ped
quad-ru-ple
quad-ru-plet
quad-ru-plex
quad-ru-pli-cate
quak-er
qual-i-fi-ca-tion
qua-lim-e-ter

qual-i-ta-tive
qualm-ish
quan-da-ry
quan-tile
quan-tim-e-ter
quan-ti-ta-tive
quan-ti-ty
quan-ti-za-tion
quan-tize
quan-tum
quar-an-tin-er
quar-reled

quar-tan
quar-tered
quar-tern
quar-tet
quar-tile
quartz-ite
quartz-it-ic
quartz-ose
qua-si
quas-si-a
qua-ter-nar-y
qua-ter-ni-on
qua-ter-ni-ty
qua-ter-ni-za-tion
qua-ter-phen-yl
qua-torze
quat-rain
qua-vered
que-brach-i-tol
que-bra-cho
quell-er
quench-er
quen-stedt-ite
quer-ce-tin
quer-ci-mer-i-trin
que-rist

quer-u-lous
que-ry
ques-tion-naire
quet-zal
queu-er
queu-ing
quib-bler
quick-en-ing
qui-es-cent
qui-e-tude
qui-e-tus
quin-a-chrine
quin-al-din-i-um
quin-a-mine
qui-naph-thol
qui-na-ry
quin-az-o-line
quin-i-dine
qui-nine
qui-nin-ic
qui-niz-a-rin
qui-noi-dine
quin-o-line
quin-o-lin-yl
qui-nol-o-gy
quin-o-lyl

qui-none
qui-non-ize
qui-no-nyl
qui-no-va-tan-nic
qui-no-vose
quin-sy
quin-tal
quin-tant
quin-ter-ni-on
quint-es-sence
quin-tet
quin-tile
quin-tu-ple
quin-tu-plet
qui-nu-cli-dine
quip-ster
quiv-o-ered
quix-ot-ic
quix-o-tism
quiz-zi-cal
quon-dam
quo-rum
quot-a-ble
quo-ta-tion
quot-er
quo-tient

R

rab-bet-ed
rab-bin-ate
rab-id
ra-bid-i-ty
ra-bies
rac-coon
rac-e-mate
ra-ceme
ra-ce-mic
rac-e-mi-za-tion
rac-e-mose
ra-chi-om-e-ter
ra-chis
ra-chit-ic
ra-chi-tis
ra-cial-ism
rac-ing
rac-ist
rack-et-eer
rack-et-y
ra-con
rac-on-teur
ra-dar

ra-di-ac
ra-di-al
ra-di-ant
ra-di-a-tor
rad-i-cal
rad-i-cand
rad-i-cle
ra-di-o
ra-di-o-graph-ic
ra-di-og-ra-phy
ra-di-o-i-so-tope
ra-di-o-log-i-cal
ra-di-ol-o-gy
ra-di-ol-y-sis
ra-di-om-e-ter
ra-di-o-met-ric
ra-di-on-ic
ra-di-o-nu-clide
ra-di-os-co-py
ra-di-o-sonde
rad-ish
ra-di-um
ra-di-us
ra-dome

ra-don
raf-fi-a
raf-fi-nase
raf-fi-nate
raf-fi-nose
raf-fled
raf-ter (roof)
raft-er (worker on raft)
ra-gout
raid-er
rail-ler-y
rai-ment
rais-er
rai-sin
rais-ing
ra-jah
rak-er
rak-ish
Ra-leigh
ral-ston-ite
ram-bler
ram-bunc-tious
ram-e-kin

ram-ie
ram-i-fi-ca-tion
ra-mose
ram-pa-geous
ram-pag-er
ramp-ant
ram-part
ra-na-les
ranch-er
ran-che-ro
ran-cho
ran-cid-i-ty
ran-cor-ous
ran-dom-ize
rang-er
rang-ette
ra-nine
rank-er
ran-kled
ran-som-er
rant-er
ra-pa-cious
ra-pac-i-ty
ra-pa-ki-vi
rap-er
Raph-a-el
rap-id
ra-pid-i-ty
ra-pi-er
rap-ine
rap-proche-ment
rap-tur-ous
rar-e-fy
rar-i-ty
ras-cal-i-ty
rash-er
rasp-er
ras-ter
rat-a-ble
rat-a-fi-a
ratch-et
rat-er
rath-er
rat-i-fy
ra-tio
ra-ti-oc-i-na-tion
ra-ti-om-e-ter
ra-tion-ale
ra-tion-al-ize
rat-tler
rau-cous
rau-vite
Rau-wol-fi-a
rav-ag-er

rav-eled
rave-lin
rav-el-ing
ra-ven (bird)
rav-en (other meanings)
rav-en-ing
rav-en-ous
ra-vine
rav-ing
rav-ish-er
ra-win-sonde
ra-zon
ra-zor
re-act-ance
re-ac-tion-ar-y
re-ac-tive
re-ac-tor
read-er
read-i-ness
re-a-gent
re-a-gin
re-al-gar
re-al-ism
re-al-is-tic
re-al-ize
re-al-tor
ream-er
reap-er
rea-son-a-ble
Re-au-mur
re-bat-er
re-bel (v.)
reb-el (adj., n.)
re-bel-lious
re-but-ta-ble
re-cal-ci-trant
re-ca-les-cence
re-can-ta-tion
re-ca-pit-u-late
re-ced-ence
re-ced-er
re-ceipt-or
re-ceiv-a-ble
re-ceiv-er
re-cen-sion
re-cep-ta-cle
re-cep-ti-ble
re-cep-tiv-i-ty
re-cep-tor
re-cess-er
re-ces-sion-al
re-ces-sive
re-cher-che
re-cid-i-vist

Re-ci-fe
rec-i-pe
re-cip-i-ent
re-cip-ro-ca-ble
re-cip-ro-cal
rec-i-proc-i-ty
re-ci-sion
re-cit-al
rec-i-ta-tive
reck-on-ing
re-claim
rec-la-ma
rec-la-ma-tion
re-clin-a-ble
rec-li-na-tion
re-clin-er
rec-luse
re-clu-sive
rec-og-ni-tion
re-cog-ni-zance
rec-og-nize
re-cog-ni-zee
rec-og-niz-er
re-cog-ni-zor
re-col-lect (collect
    again)
rec-ol-lect (remember)
rec-om-men-da-tion
rec-om-mend-a-to-ry
rec-om-pens-er
re-con-cen-tra-do
rec-on-cil-a-ble
rec-on-cil-er
rec-on-cil-i-a-tion
rec-on-dite
re-con-nais-sance
rec-on-noi-ter
rec-ord (adj., n.)
re-cord (v.)
re-cord-a-ble
rec-or-da-tion
re-cord-er
re-coup
re-cov-er-y
rec-re-ant
rec-re-ate (refresh)
re-cre-ate (create again)
rec-re-a-tion
rec-re-a-tion
re-crim-i-na-to-ry
re-cru-des-cence
re-cruit-er
rec-tan-gle
rec-tan-gu-lar

97

rec-tan-gu-lom-e-ter
rec-ti-fi-er
rec-ti-lin-e-ar
rec-ti-tude
rec-tor-ate
rec-to-ry
rec-tum
re-cum-bent
re-cu-per-a-tive
re-cur-rence
re-cur-sive
rec-u-sant
re-dac-tor
re-demp-ti-ble
re-demp-tive
re-demp-tor
red-in-gote
red-o-lent
re-doubt-a-ble
re-dox
re-dress-a-ble
re-dress-er
re-duc-er
re-duc-i-ble
re-duc-tase
re-duc-tone
re-duc-tor
re-dun-dan-cy
reef-er
reel-er
re-fec-to-ry
ref-er-a-ble
ref-er-ee
ref-er-ence
ref-er-en-dum
ref-er-en-tial
re-fer-ring
re-fin-er-y
re-flec-tance
re-flect-i-ble
re-flec-tive
re-flec-tom-e-ter
re-flec-tom-e-try
re-flec-tor-ize
re-flex-iv-i-ty
ref-lu-ent
re-for-est-a-tion
re-form-a-ble
ref-or-ma-tion
re-form-a-to-ry
re-form-er
re-frac-tive
re-frac-tom-e-ter
re-frac-to-met-ric

re-frac-tom-e-try
re-frac-to-ry
re-fran-gi-ble
ref-re-na-tion
re-frig-er-ant
re-frig-er-at-ing
re-frig-er-a-tion
re-frig-er-a-tor
ref-uge
ref-u-gee
re-ful-gent
re-fus-al
ref-use (adj., n.)
re-fuse (v.)
re-fut-a-ble
ref-u-ta-tion
re-fut-er
re-ga-lia
re-gal-i-ty
re-ge-late
re-gen-cy
re-gen-er-a-tive
re-gen-er-a-tor
reg-i-cide
re-gime
reg-i-men
reg-i-men-tal
reg-i-men-ta-ry
Re-gi-na
re-gion-al
reg-is-tered
reg-is-tra-ble
reg-is-trar
reg-is-trate
reg-let
Re-gnault
reg-o-sol
re-gres-sive
re-gret-ta-ble
reg-u-lar-i-ty
reg-u-la-tive
reg-u-la-to-ry
reg-u-lus
re-gur-gi-tate
re-ha-bil-i-ta-tive
re-hears-al
re-hears-er
Re-ho-both
Reichs-tag
re-im-burs-a-ble
Rei-nec-ke
re-in-forced
re-it-er-ate
re-ject-a-ble

re-ject-er (one that rejects)
re-jec-tor (circuit)
re-joic-ing
re-join-der
re-ju-ve-na-tor
re-ju-ve-nes-cence
re-laps-er
re-lat-er
rel-a-tiv-ism
rel-a-tiv-i-ty
re-la-tor (law)
re-lax-om-e-ter
re-leas-er
rel-e-ga-ble
rel-e-vant
rel-ict (n.)
re-lict (adj.)
re-lief-er
re-liev-er
re-li-gion
re-li-gi-os-i-ty
re-li-gious
re-lin-quish
rel-i-quar-y
rel-ish
re-lu-cence
re-luc-tance
rel-uc-tiv-i-ty
re-lu-mine
re-main-der
rem-a-nence
re-mark-a-ble
re-me-di-a-ble
re-me-di-al
rem-e-di-less
rem-e-dy
re-mem-brance
re-mind-er
rem-i-nis-cence
rem-i-nis-cer
re-miss-i-ble
re-mis-sive
re-mit-tee
re-mod-eled
re-mon-strance
re-mon-stra-tive
re-mon-stra-tor
re-mov-al
re-mu-ner-a-ble
re-mu-ner-a-tive
ren-ais-sance
Re-nais-sant
re-nal

98

re-nas-cence
ren-der (v.)
rend-er (n.)
ren-dez-vous
rend-i-ble
ren-di-tion
ren-dzi-na
ren-e-gade
re-nege
ren-gue
re-nin
ren-o-va-tor
re-nowned
rent-al
rent-er (n.)
ren-ter (v.)
re-nun-ci-a-to-ry
re-pair-a-ble
rep-a-ra-ble
rep-a-ra-tion
rep-ar-tee
re-pa-tri-ate
re-peal-er
re-peat-er
re-pel-lant (n.)
re-pel-lent (adj.)
re-pent-ance
re-per-cus-sion
rep-er-to-ry
rep-e-tend
rep-e-ti-tion
re-pet-i-tive
re-place-a-ble
re-plen-ish-er
re-ple-tive
re-plev-in
re-plev-i-sor
rep-li-ca
rep-li-cate
re-port-er
rep-or-to-ri-al
rep-o-si-tion (n.)
re-po-si-tion (v.)
re-pos-i-to-ry
rep-re-hen-si-ble
rep-re-hen-so-ry
rep-re-sen-ta-tion
rep-re-sent-a-tive
rep-re-sent-er
re-press-er
re-press-i-ble
re-pres-sive
re-priev-al
rep-ri-mand

re-pris-al
rep-ro-ba-cy
rep-ro-bate
re-pro-duc-er
re-pro-duc-i-ble
rep-til-i-an
re-pub-li-can
re-pu-di-a-tor
re-pug-nant
re-pul-sive
rep-u-ta-ble
rep-u-ta-tion
re-pute
re-quest-er
req-ui-em
re-qui-es-cat
re-quir-er
req-ui-site
req-ui-si-tion
re-quit-al
res-az-ur-in
re-scind
re-scis-sion
re-scrip-tive
res-cu-a-ble
re-sect-a-ble
re-sem-blance
re-sem-bler
res-ene
re-ser-pic
Re-ser-pine
res-er-va-tion
re-served
re-serv-ist
res-er-voir
re-side
res-i-dence
res-i-den-tial
re-sid-u-al
re-sid-u-ar-y
res-i-due
re-sid-u-um
re-sign
res-ig-na-tion
re-sil-ience
re-sil-ien-cy
re-sil-i-om-e-ter
rés-in-a-ceous
res-in-ate
res-in-ic
res-in-if-er-ous
re-sin-i-fi-ca-tion
res-in-og-ra-phy
res-in-oid

res-in-ol
res-in-ous
res-i-pis-cence
re-sist-ance
re-sist-er (one that re-
   sists)
re-sist-i-ble
re-sis-tiv-i-ty
re-sis-tor (device)
res-ite (resin)
res-i-tol
res ju-di-ca-ta
res-ol
re-sol-u-ble
res-o-lute
re-sol-u-tive
re-solv-ent
re-solv-er
res-o-nance
res-o-na-tor
res-or-cin-ol
res-or-cyl-ic
re-sorp-tive
res-o-ru-fin
re-spect-a-ble
re-spect-er
re-spec-tive
res-pi-ra-ble
res-pi-ra-tion
res-pi-ra-tor
res-pi-ra-to-ry
res-pi-rom-e-ter
res-pite
re-splend-ent
re-spond-ent
re-spond-èr
re-spons-er
re-spon-si-ble
re-spon-sive
re-spon-sor
re-spon-so-ry
res-tau-rant
res-tau-ra-teur
res-ti-tu-tion
res-tive
res-to-ra-tion
re-stor-a-tive
re-stric-tive
re-sult-ant
rè-sume (v.)
ré-su-mé (n.)
re-sump-tive
re-sur-gent
res-ur-rec-tor

99

re-sus-ci-ta-ble
re-sus-ci-ta-**tor**
re-tal-i-a-to-ry
re-tard-ant
re-tar-da-tion
re-tard-ed
re-tene
re-**ten-tive**
re-ten-tor
ret-ger-site
re-ti-ar-y
ret-i-cence
ret-i-cle
re-tic-u-late
ret-i-**cule**
re-tic-u-lin
re-tic-u-li-tis
re-tic-u-lo-cy-to-sis
re-tic-u-lose
ret-i-form
ret-i-na
re-tin-a-lite
ret-i-nene
ret-i-ni-tis
ret-i-no-cho-roid-i-tis
ret-i-nop-a-thy
ret-i-nos-co-py
ret-i-nue
re-tir-al
re-tir-ee
ret-o-na-tion
re-tort-er
re-tract-a-ble
re-trac-tile
re-trac-tion
re-trac-tive
re-trac-tor
ret-ri-bu-tion
re-trib-u-tive
re-trib-u-to-ry
re-triev-a-ble
re-triev-al
re-triev-er
ret-ro-ac-tive
ret-ro-cede (v.i.)
re-tro-cede (v.t.)
ret-ro-ced-ence
ret-ro-ces-sion
ret-ro-gra-da-to-**ry**
ret-ro-gres-sive
ret-ro-ne-cine
re-tror-sine
ret-ro-spec-tive
ret-ro-stal-sis

ret-rous-**sé**
ret-ro-vert-ed
re-turn-ee
re-un-ion
re-vanche
rev-eil-le
rev-e-la-tion
re-vel-a-to-ry
rev-eled
rev-el-ry
re-veng-er
rev-e-nue
re-ver-a-ble
re-ver-ber-a-to-ry
re-vere
rev-er-ence
rev-er-ie
re-ver-sal
re-vers-er
re-vers-i-ble
re-ver-sion
re-vert-er
re-vert-i-ble
re-vet-ment
re-vil-er
rev-i-res-cent
re-vised
re-vis-er
re-vi-sion
re-vi-so-ry
re-viv-al
re-viv-i-fy
rev-i-vis-cent
re-vi-vor
rev-o-ca-ble
rev-o-ca-tion
rev-o-ca-to-ry
re-vok-a-ble
re-vok-er
re-volt-er
rev-o-lu-ble
rev-o-lu-tion
re-volv-er
re-vul-sive
Rey-kja-vik
rey-nard
Reyn-olds
rhab-do-man-cer
rham-na-zin
rham-ni-nose
rham-no-side
rha-pon-ti-gen-in
rhap-sod-i-cal
rhap-so-dy

rhe-a-dine
rhe-ni-um
rhe-ol-o-gy
rhe-om-e-ter
rhe-o-stat
rhe-sus
rhet-o-ric
rhe-tor-i-cal
rhet-o-ri-cian
rheu-mat-ic
rheu-ma-tism
rheum-ic
rhig-o-lene
rhi-ni-tis
rhi-noc-er-os
rhi-nol-o-gy
rhi-nos-co-py
rhi-zoi-dal
rhi-zom-a-tous
rhi-zome
rhi-zop-ter-in
rhi-zot-o-my
rho-da-mine
rho-da-nate
Rho-de-sian
rho-di-nol
rho-dite
rho-di-um
rho-di-zon-ic
rho-do-chro-site
rho-do-den-dron
rhom-bo-clase
rhom-bo-he-dral
rhom-boi-dal
rhum-ba-tron
rhyme-ster
rhy-o-lite
rhyth-mi-cal
rib-al-dry
ri-bi-tyl
ri-bo-fla-vin
ri-bo-nu-cle-ase
ri-bo-side
ri-bu-lose
ric-er
ri-chell-ite
ric-in-o-le-ic
rick-ett-si-al
ric-o-cheted
rid-dled
rid-er
rid-i-cule
ri-dic-u-lous
rid-ing

ri-ding (political division)
rif-fling
ri-fling
right-cous
right-er
ri-gid-i-ty
rig-id-ly
rig-ma-role
rig-or-ous
ri-mose
rin-der-pest
ring-er
rins-a-ble
rins-er
ri-ot-ous
ri-par-i-an
rip-en
ri-pid-o-lite
rip-pled
ris-er
ris-i-bil-i-ty
ris-ing
ris-que
rit-u-al
ri-valed
ri-val-ry
riv-et-er
Riv-i-er-a
riv-u-let
Ri-yadh
road-ster
Ro-a-noke
roam-er
roast-er
Rob-ert
rob-in (bird)
ro-bin (chemistry)
ro-bi-nose
ro-bust
Ro-chelle
Roch-es-ter
rock-et-eer
rock-et-er
rock-et-ry
rock-oon
ro-co-co
ro-den-ti-ci-dal
Rod-er-ick
roe-bling-ite
roent-gen-o-graph
roent-gen-og-ra-phy
roent-gen-ol-o-gy
roent-gen-om-e-ter

roent-gen-om-e-try
roent-gen-o-scope
roent-gen-os-co-py
rog-a-to-ry
Rog-er
ro-gnon
rogu-er-y
rogu-ish
roist-er-er
Ro-land
roll-er
rol-lick-ing
ro-maine
ro-manc-er
Ro-man-esque
Ro-man-ism
ro-ma-ni-um
ro-man-ti-cism
ro-man-ti-cist
Rom-a-ny
ro-me-ite
Ro-me-o
Rom-ish
romp-er
ron-deau
ro-ne-o-graph
ron-geur
roof-er
rook-er-y
Roo-se-velt
roost-er
rop-er
Roque-fort
ro-rif-er-ous
Ror-schach
ro-sa-ceous
Ros-a-lind
Ros-a-mond
ro-sa-ry
rosch-er-ite
ro-se-ate
ro-se-o-la
ro-sette
Rosh Ha-sha-na
Ros-i-cru-cian
ros-in-ate
ros-i-ness
ro-sol-ic
ros-ter
ros-trum
ros-y
ro-tal
ro-tam-e-ter
Ro-tar-i-an

ro-ta-ry
ro-tat-a-ble
ro-ta-tive
ro-ta-tor
ro-ta-to-ry
ro-te-nold
ro-te-none
Ro-tif-er-a
ro-tis-ser-ie
ro-to-graph
ro-to-gra-vure
ro-tor
ro-tun-da
ro-tun-di-ty
rough-en
rough-er
rough-om-e-ter
rou-lade
rou-leau
rou-lette
round-el
round-er
rout-er
rou-tine
ro-ver (robber)
rov-er
row-dy-ism
row-eled
roy-al-ist
ru-ba-to
ru-be-an-ic
ru-be-fa-cient
ru-be-o-la
rub-e-ryth-ric
ru-bes-cent
ru-bi-cun-di-ty
ru-bid-i-um
ru-big-i-nous
ru-ble
ru-brene
ru-bric
ru-bri-ca-tor
ru-di-men-ta-ry
ru-fes-cence
ruf-fi-an
ruf-fler
ruf-fling
ru-fos-i-ty
ru-fous
ru-gos-i-ty
ru-gu-lose
ru-ined
ru-in-ing
ru-in-ous

101

rul-a-ble
rul-er
Ru-ma-ni-an
rum-bler
ru-mi-nant
rum-mag-er
ru-mor
rump-er
rum-pled
rum-pus
run-ci-ble
ru-nic

ru-pee
ru-pic-o-lous
rup-tured
ru-ral
ru-rig-e-nous
Rus-sian
rus-ti-ca-tor
rus-tic-i-ty
rust-i-ness
rus-tler
rus-tling
ru-ta-ba-ga

ru-ta-ceous
ru-te-car-pine
Ru-the-ni-an
ru-then-ic
ru-the-ni-um
ruth-er-ford-ine
ru-tile
ru-tin-ose
ru-ty-lene
Rwan-dan
ry-an-o-dine
Ry-u-kyu-an

S

sab-a-dine
Sab-ba-tar-i-an
sab-bat-i-cal
sa-ber
Sa-bine
sab-ine (pine)
sab-i-nene
sa-bi-no
sab-o-tage
sa-bra
sab-u-lous
sa-bu-tan
sac-cha-rate
sac-char-ic
sac-cha-ride
sac-cha-rif-er-ous
sac-cha-rim-e-ter
sac-cha-rin-ate
sac-cha-rin-ic
sac-cha-rom-e-ter
sac-cha-rose
sac-er-do-tal
sa-chem
sa-chet
sac-ral
sac-ra-men-tal
sac-ra-men-ta-ry
sa-cred
sac-ri-fi-cial
sac-ri-fic-ing
sac-ri-le-gious
sac-ris-tan
sac-ris-ty
sac-ro-il-i-ac
sac-ro-sanct
sac-rum
sad-dler-y
sa-dism
sa-dis-tic
Saeng-er-fest

sa-fa-ri
safe-ty
saf-flor-ite
saf-fron
saf-ra-nine
sa-ga-cious
sa-gac-i-ty
sag-a-more
sag-a-pe-num
sag-e-nite
Sag-it-tar-i-us
Sa-ha-ra
sail-or
sa-laam
sal-a-ble
sa-la-cious
sal-ad
sal-a-man-der
sa-la-mi
sal-a-ried
sal-e-ra-tus
sal-i-cin
sal-i-cyl-am-ide
sa-lic-y-late
sal-i-cyl-ic
sa-lic-y-lide
sal-i-cyl-ize
sal-i-cyl-o-yl
sal-i-cyl-u-ric
sa-lient
sal-i-gen-in
sa-lim-e-ter
sal-i-na-tion
sa-line
sa-lin-i-ty
sal-in-o-gen-ic
sal-i-nom-e-ter
Salis-bur-y
sa-li-va
sal-i-var-y

sal-i-va-tion
sa-li-vous
salm-on
Sal-mo-nel-la
sal-mo-nel-lo-sis
salm-ons-ite
Sal-ol
Sa-lo-me
sa-lon
sal-pin-gec-to-my
sal-pin-gi-tis
sal-si-fy
sal-ta-to-ri-al
salt-er-y
salt-pe-ter
sa-lu-bri-ous
sa-lu-bri-ty
sal-u-tar-y
sal-u-ta-tion
sa-lu-ta-to-ry
sa-lute
sal-va-ble
Sal-va-dor-an
sal-vage-a-ble
sal-vag-er
Sal-var-san
sal-ver
sal-vi-a-nin
sal vo-la-ti-le
sal-vor
sam-a-ra
Sa-mar-i-tan
sa-mar-i-um
sam-bu-ni-grin
Sa-mo-an
sam-o-var
Sam-o-yed
sam-pler
sa-mu-rai
san-a-to-ri-um

sanc-ti-fi-ca-tion
sanc-ti-mo-ni-ous
sanc-tion-er
sanc-ti-ty
sanc-tu-ar-y
sanc-tum
san-daled
sand-er
sand-i-ness
san-dust
San-for-ize
san-guin-a-rine
san-gui-nar-y
san-guin-e-ous
san-guin-o-lent
San-he-drin
san-i-dine
san-i-tar-i-um
san-i-tar-y
san-i-tiz-er
san-i-ty
San-skrit
san-ta-lene
san-ta-lol
san-te-none
san-to-nin
sa-phe-nous
sap-id
sa-pid-i-ty
sa-pi-ence
sap-o-gen-in
sap-o-na-ceous
sa-pon-i-fi-ca-tion
sap-o-nin
sap-o-rif-ic
sap-phir-ine
sap-ro-gen-ic
sap-ro-ge-nic-i-ty
sa-prog-e-nous
sap-ro-pel-ic
Sar-ah
Sa-ran
sar-casm
sar-cas-tic
sar-coid-o-sis
sar-col-y-sis
sar-co-ma
sar-co-ma-to-sis
sar-com-a-tous
sar-coph-a-gus
sar-cop-side
sar-co-sine
sar-dine
sar-don-ic

sar-don-yx
sar-ki-nite
sar-men-to-gen-in
sa-rong
sar-sa-pa-ril-la
sar-to-ri-al
sar-to-ri-us
Sar-tri-an
sas-sa-fras
sas-so-lite
sa-tan-i-cal
satch-el
sa-teen
sat-el-lit-ed
sat-el-lit-oid
sat-el-lit-o-sis
sat-el-loid
sa-tia-ble
sa-ti-ate
sa-ti-e-ty
sat-in-et
sat-in-ize
sat-ire
sa-tir-i-cal
sat-i-rize
sat-is-fac-to-ri-ly
sat-is-fy
sa-trap
sat-u-ra-ble
sat-u-ra-tor
Sat-ur-day
Sat-urn
sat-ur-na-lian
Sa-tur-ni-an
sat-ur-nine
sat-yr
sa-tyr-ic
sau-cer
sau-ci-ness
Sau-di A-ra-bi-a
sau-er-bra-ten
sau-er-kraut
saun-ter
sau-rel
sau-ri-an
sau-sage
saus-su-rite
sau-ted
sau-terne
sav-a-ble
sav-age-ry
sa-van-na
sa-vant
sav-ing

sav-ior
Sav-iour
sa-voir faire
sa-vor-y
Sa-voy-ard
sax-i-frage
sax-o-phone
scab-bler
sca-bies
sca-bres-cent
scab-rous
sca-lar
scald-er
sca-le-no-he-dral
scal-er
scal-loped
scal-pel
scalp-er
scam-per
scan-dal-ize
scan-dal-ous
Scan-di-na-vi-an
scan-di-um
scan-ner
scant-ling
scap-o-lite
scap-u-la
scar-ab
scar-ci-ty
scarf-er
scar-i-fy
scar-i-ous
scar-la-ti-na
scar-let
scat-o-log-i-cal
sca-tol-o-gy
scat-tered
scav-eng-er
sce-nar-i-o
sce-nar-ist
sce-ner-y
sce-ni-cal
sce-no-graph
sce-nog-ra-phy
scent-er
scep-ter
sched-ule
schee-lite
sche-ma
sche-mat-ic
sche-ma-tist
sche-mat-o-graph
Sche-ring
schiff-li

schis-mat-ic
schist-oid
schist-ose
schis-to-some
schis-to-so-mi-a-sis
schiz-oid-ism
schiz-o-phre-ni-a
schiz-o-phren-ic
schle-miel
schlie-ren
Schnei-der
scho-la can-to-rum
schol-ar
scho-las-tic
schoo-ner
schor-la-ceous
schot-tische
schra-dan
schrei-ner-ize
Schro-ding-er
schroec-king-er-ite
Schweit-zer
schwei-zer
sci-at-i-ca
sci-en-tif-ic
sci-en-tist
scil-i-cet
scil-li-ro-side
scim-i-tar
scin-tig-ra-phy
scin-til-la-tor
scin-til-lom-e-ter
sci-oph-i-lous
sci-re fa-ci-as
scis-sors
sclar-e-ol
scle-rec-to-my
scle-ren-chy-ma
scle-ri-tis
scle-ro-ma
scle-rom-e-ter
scle-ro-sis
scle-ro-tal
scle-rot-ic
scle-rot-o-my
scob-i-nate
scoff-er
scold-er
scol-e-cite
sco-li-o-sis
sconc-i-ble
scoop-er
scoot-er
sco-pa-rin

scoph-o-ny
sco-pine
sco-pol-a-mine
sco-po-le-tin
scop-u-lite
scor-bu-tic
sco-ri-a-ceous
sco-ri-fi-ca-tion
scorn-er
scor-o-dite
scor-per
Scor-pi-o
scor-pi-on
scor-za-lite
sco-to-ma
sco-tom-a-tous
scoun-drel
scourg-er
scrab-bler
scram-bling
scrap-er
scratch-er
scrawl-er
scream-er
screen-er
scrib-bler
scrib-er
scrip-tur-al
scriv-en-er
scrof-u-la
scrof-u-lo-sis
scro-tum
scru-ple
scru-pu-lous
scru-ti-nize
scru-ti-ny
scuf-fling
scul-ler-y
sculp-tor
sculp-tur-al
scum-bled
scur-ril-i-ty
scur-ri-lous
scur-vi-ly
scut-tle-butt
scu-tum
seal-ant
seal-er
seal-ine
seam-stress
se-ance
sea-son-a-ble
seat-er
seb-a-cate

se-ba-ceous
se-bac-ic
seb-or-rhe-a
sec-a-lose
se-cant
se-ced-er
se-clu-sive
Sec-o-nal
sec-ond-ar-i-ly
sec-ond-ar-y
sec-ond-er
se-cre-cy
se-cret
se-cre-ta-gogue
sec-re-tar-i-al
se-cre-tin
se-cre-tive
se-cre-to-ry
sec-tar-i-an
sec-til-i-ty
sec-tion-al-ize
sec-tor-al
sec-to-ri-al
sec-u-lar-ize
se-cund
se-cun-date
se-cu-ri-ty
se-dan
se-date
sed-a-tive
sed-en-tar-y
sed-i-men-ta-ry
se-di-tious
se-duc-er
se-duc-i-ble
se-duc-tive
se-du-li-ty
sed-u-lous
seed-ling
seek-er
seep-age
seg-men-tal
seg-re-ga-ble
Seid-litz
sei-gnior-age
sei-sin
seis-mic-i-ty
seis-mo-graph
seis-mog-ra-phy
seis-mo-log-i-cal
seis-mol-o-gy
seis-mom-e-ter
seis-mo-met-ric
seiz-er

sei-zin
seiz-ing
sei-zor (law)
sei-zure
sel-dom
se-lect-ance
se-lect-ee
se-lec-tiv-i-ty
se-lec-tor
sel-e-nate
se-len-ic
sel-e-nide
se-le-ni-ous
sel-e-nite
se-le-ni-um
se-le-no-bis-muth-ite
se-le-no-graph-ic
sel-e-nog-ra-phy
se-le-no-lite
se-le-no-log-i-cal
sel-e-nol-o-gy
sel-e-no-ni-um
sel-e-no-sis
self-ish
sell-er
sel-syn
Selt-zer
sel-vage
se-man-ti-cist
sem-a-phor-ist
se-ma-si-ol-o-gy
sem-blance
se-mei-ol-o-gy
se-mes-ter
sem-i-dine
sem-i-nal
sem-i-nar-y
sem-i-nif-er-ous
Sem-i-nole
Sem-ite
Se-mit-ic
Sem-i-tism
sem-o-li-na
sen-a-ry
sen-a-to-ri-al
send-er
se-ne-cic
se-ne-ci-o-nine
se-ne-ci-o-sis
Sen-e-gal-ese
se-nes-cence
sen-e-schal
se-nhor (Portuguese)
se-nile

se-nil-i-ty
sen-ior
se-nior-i-ty
se-nor
se-no-ri-ta
sen-sa-tion
sen-si-bil-i-ty
sen-sile
sen-si-tiv-i-ty
sen-si-tiz-er
sen-si-tom-e-ter
sen-so-ri-um
sen-so-ry
sen-su-al-i-ty
sen-su-ous
sen-tence
sen-ten-tious
sen-tience
sen-ti-men-tal
sen-ti-neled
sen-try
se-paled
sep-al-oid
sep-a-ra-ble
sep-a-ra-tee
sep-a-rat-ist
sep-a-ra-tor
se-phar-dic
se-pi-a
Sep-tem-ber
sep-ten-a-ry
sep-ti-ce-mi-a
sep-ti-mal
sep-tu-a-ge-nar-i-an
sep-tu-a-ges-i-ma
sep-tu-ple
sep-tu-plet
sep-tu-pli-cate
sep-ul-cher
se-pul-chral
sep-ul-ture
se-quac-i-ty
se-que-la
se-quen-tial
se-ques-tered
se-ques-tra-tor
se-ra-glio
ser-al
ser-aph
se-raph-ic
ser-a-phim
Ser-bi-an
ser-e-nad-er
ser-en-dip-i-ty

se-rene
se-ren-i-ty
ser-geant
se-ri-al
se-ri-a-tim
se-ri-ceous
ser-i-cin
ser-i-cite
se-ries
ser-i-graph
se-rig-ra-pher
se-rig-ra-phy
ser-ine
se-rin-ga
se-rin-gal
se-ri-ous
ser-mon-ize
se-ro-log-ic
se-rol-o-gy
se-ro-si-tis
se-ro-ton-in
se-rous
ser-pen-tin-ite
ser-pig-i-nous
se-rum
serv-ant
serv-er
serv-ice-a-ble
ser-vi-ent
ser-vile
ser-vil-i-ty
ser-vi-tor
ser-vi-tude
ser-vo-mo-tor
ses-a-me
ses-a-min
ses-a-moid-i-tis
ses-a-mo-lin
ses-qui-pe-da-lian
ses-sile
ses-sion
se-ta-ceous
se-ti-ger
se-tig-er-ous
set-tler
sev-en-ti-eth
sev-er-al
sev-ered
sev-er-i-ty
sew-age
sew-er-age
sex-a-ge-nar-i-an
sex-ag-e-nar-y
sex-tant

sex-tu-ple
sex-tu-plet
sex-tu-pli-cate
sfer-ics
sfor-zan-do
shack-led
shad-er
shad-ow
Sha-drach
sha-green
shak-er
Shake-spear·e-an
sham-bles
shank-er
shap-er
shap-om-e-ter
shar-a-ble
sharp-en-ing
sharp-er
shat-tered
shav-er
sheath-er
sheep-ish
sheet-age
shek-el
shel-lack-ing
shel-tered
shelv-ing
she-nan-i-gan
shep-herd
Sher-a-ton
sher-bet
sher-iff
shib-bo-leth
shield-er
shift-er
shi-kim-ic
shil-le-lagh
shil-ling
shin-er
shin-gled
shirk-er
shirr-ing
shiv-ered
shock-er
sho-far
shoot-er
sho-ran
short-en
short-om-e-ter
Sho-sho-ne
shoul-dered
shov-eled
shov-er

show-er-y
shriev-al-ty
Shrin-er
shrink-age
shrink-er
shriv-eled
shriv-ing
Shrop-shire
shuf-fled
shy-ster
si-a-log-ra-phy
si-al-o-li-thi-a-sis
Si-a-mese
Si-be-ri-an
sib-i-lant
sib-i-la-to-ry
sib-ling
sib-yl-line
Si-cil-ian
sick-en-ing
sick-led
si-de-re-al
sid-er-ite
sid-er-og-ra-pher
sid-er-o-graph-ic
sid-er-o-na-trite
sid-er-o-sis
sid-ing
si-dled
si-er-o-zem
Si-er-ra Le-one
siev-er
sift-er
sight-er
sig-ma-tism
sig-moid-ec-to-my
sig-moid-os-to-my
sig-naled
sig-nal-ize
sig-na-to-ry
sig-nif-i-cant
sig-ni-fi-ca-tion
si-gnor
si-gno-ra
si-lage
sil-ane
si-lenc-er
si-le-si-a
si-lex
sil-hou-ette
sil-i-cate
sil-i-ca-ti-za-tion
sil-i-ca-tor
sil-li-ceous

si-lic-ic
sil-i-cide
si-lic-i-dize
sil-i-cif-er-ous
si-lic-i-fy
sil-i-co-mag-ne-sio-flu-o-
    rite
sil-i-con
sil-i-cone
sil-i-co-sis
sil-i-cot-ic
silk-en
sil-li-man-ite
si-lox-ane
sil-ta-tion
Si-lu-ri-an
sil-ver
sil-vi-cul-tur-al
sim-i-lar-i-ty
sim-i-le (like)
si-mi-le (music)
si-mil-i-tude
si-mon-ize
si-mo-ny
si-moom
sim-pat-i-co
sim-per
sim-pler
sim-plex
sim-plic-i-ty
sim-pli-fy
sim-u-la-crum
sim-u-la-tor
si-mul-cast
si-mul-ta-ne-ous
Si-na-it-ic
si-nap-ic
sin-a-pine
sin-ar-quism
sin-cer-i-ty
si-ne-cure
sin-ew
sing-er
sin-gly
sin-gu-lar-i-ty
Sin-ha-lese
sin-is-tral
sink-age
sink-er
si-nom-e-nine
sin-ter
sin-u-ous
si-nus-i-tis
si-nus-oi-dal

si-phon-age
si-pid-i-ty
si-ren
si-ri-a-sis
Sir-i-us
si-roc-cos
sir-up
si-sal
sis-y-phe-an
si-tol-o-gy
si-to-ste-rol
sit-u-at-ed
si-tus
siz-a-ble
siz-zled
skat-ole
skeet-er
skel-e-ton-ize
skep-ti-cal
skep-ti-cism
skew-er
ski-am-e-try
ski-as-co-py
skill-ful-ness
skimp-i-ly
skir-mish
skirt-er
skit-tish
skiv-er
skul-dug-ger-y
skulk-er
slack-ened
slak-er
slan-der-ous
slat-tern
slaugh-ter
slav-er-y
slav-ish
Sla-von-ic
sleep-er
slen-der
slic-er
slick-en-side
slick-er
slid-a-ble
slid-om-e-ter
sling-er
slith-er-y
sliv-er
slo-gan
slop-ing
Slo-vak-i-an
slov-en
Slo-ve-ni-an

sludg-er
slum-ber-ous
smart-en
smell-er
smelt-er
smi-la-gen-in
smi-lax
smith-er-eens
Smith-so-ni-an
smok-er
smol-dered
smor-gas-bord
smoth-ered
smudg-er
smug-gler
snarl-ish
snatch-er
sneak-i-ness
sneez-er
snick-er-ing
sniff-er
snif-ter
snip-er
sniv-el-er
snob-ber-y
Sno-ho-mish
snoop-er-y
snor-kel
snort-er
snuf-fled
snug-gled
soak-age
soap-er
so-ber
so-bri-e-ty
so-bri-quet
so-cia-ble
so-cial-is-tic
so-ci-a-try
so-ci-e-ty
so-ci-oc-ra-cy
so-ci-o-log-ic
so-ci-ol-o-gist
so-ci-om-e-try
so-ci-op-a-thy
sock-dol-a-ger
sock-et
Soc-ra-tes
So-crat-ic
so-da-lite
so-dal-i-ty
so-dam-ide
so-dar
so-di-um

sod-om-y
so-far
soft-en-er
soi-gne
soi-ree
so-journ-er
sol-ace
so-lan-der
so-lan-i-dine
so-la-nine
so-la-no
so-lar
so-lar-ism
so-lar-i-um
so-lar-i-za-tion
so-las-o-nine
sol-dered
sol-dier
sol-e-cism
sol-emn
so-lem-ni-ty
sol-em-nize
so-le-noi-dal
sol-fe-ri-no
so-lic-i-ta-tion
so-lic-i-tor
so-lic-it-ous
so-lic-i-tude
sol-id
sol-i-dar-ic
sol-i-da-ris-tic
sol-i-dar-i-ty
so-lid-i-fy
so-lid-i-ty
sol-i-dus
so-lig-e-nous
so-lil-o-quy
so-li-lu-nar
sol-ip-sism
sol-i-taire
sol-i-tar-y
sol-i-tude
so-lod-ize
so-lo-ist
Sol-o-mon
sol-o-netz
so-lo-ni-an
sol-stice
sol-sti-tial
sol-u-bil-i-ty
sol-u-bi-liz-er
so-lum
sol-ute
so-lu-tion

sol-u-tiz-er
solv-a-ble
sol-ven-cy
sol-vent
sol-vol-y-sis
So-ma-li
so-mat-ic
so-ma-ti-za-tion
so-ma-to-gen-ic
som-bre-ro
som-er-sault
som-nam-bu-list
som-nil-o-quy
som-niv-o-len-cy
som-no-lent
so-na-ble
so-nar
so-na-ta
song-ster
son-ic
so-nif-er-ous
son-net-eer
son-o-buoy
so-nom-e-ter
So-no-ra
so-no-rant
son-o-res-cent
son-o-rif-er-ous
so-nor-i-ty
so-no-rous
soon-est
Soph-ist
so-phis-ti-cat-ed
soph-ist-ry
soph-o-mor-ic
sop-o-rif-er-ous
sop-o-rif-ic
so-pra-no
sor-be-fa-cient
sor-bent
sorb-ic
sor-bi-tan
sor-bite
sor-bi-tol
sor-bose
sor-bo-side
sor-cer-er
sor-cer-y
sor-did
sor-ghum
so-ri-tes
so-rit-i-cal
So-rop-ti-mist
so-ror-i-cide

so-ror-i-ty
so-ro-sis
sort-er
sor-tie
sor-ti-lege
so-ste-nu-to
sou-brette
souf-fle
soun-der (herd of swine)
sound-er
sou-tache
south-er-ly
south-ern-er
sou-ve-nir
sov-er-eign
so-vi-et-ism
sov-khoz
Soxh-let
so-zol-ic
spa-cious
spa-cis-tor
spa-ghet-ti
spall-er
span-drel
span-gled
Span-iard
span-iel
spank-er
sparg-er
spark-let
spar-kling
spar-si-ty
Spar-tan
spar-te-ine
spas-mod-ic
spas-mol-y-sis
spas-mo-lyt-ic
spas-tic-i-ty
spa-tial
spa-ti-og-ra-phy
spat-u-la
spav-in
spawn-er
speak-er
spe-cial-ist
spe-ci-al-i-ty
spe-cial-i-za-tion
spe-cial-ty
spe-ci-e (in sort)
spe-cie (coin)
spe-cif-i-cal-ly
spec-i-fi-ca-tion
spec-i-fic-i-ty
spec-i-fi-er

spec-i-men
spe-ci-os-i-ty
spe-cious
speck-led
spec-ta-cle
spec-tac-u-lar
spec-ta-tor
spec-ter
spec-trog-ra-phy
spec-trom-e-ter
spec-trom-e-try
spec-tro-scope
spec-tros-co-py
spec-trum
spec-u-la-tive
spec-u-la-tor
spec-u-lum
speed-er
speed-om-e-ter
speed-ster
spe-le-ol-o-gy
spel-ter
spe-lunk-er
Spen-ce-ri-an
spend-er
Spen-gle-ri-an
sper-ma-ce-ti
sper-mat-ic
sper-ma-tif-er-ous
sper-ma-tin
sper-ma-ti-za-tion
sper-ma-to-cele
sper-ma-to-ci-dal
sper-ma-to-cyte
sper-ma-tor-rhe-a
sper-ma-to-zo-id
sperm-ine
sperm-ism
sphal-er-ite
sphe-nog-ra-phy
sphe-noi-dal
spher-al
spher-i-cal
spho-ric-i-ty
sphe-roi-dal
sphe-roid-ic-i-ty
sphe-rom-e-ter
spher-u-lite
sphinc-ter-ot-o-my
sphin-gom-e-ter
sphin-go-sine
sphyg-mo-ma-nom-e-ter
sphyg-mom-e-ter
spic-i-ness

spic-u-lar
spi-der
spie-gel-ei-sen
spiel-er
spig-ot
spike-nard
spik-i-ness
spi-lite
spill-er
spil-ler (fish)
spi-lo-ma
spi-lo-site
spi-na-ceous
spin-ach
spi-nal
spi-na-ste-rol
spi-nate
spin-dler
spi-nel
spi-nes-cence
spin-et
spin-or
spi-nose
spi-nos-i-ty
spi-nous
spin-ster
spin-thar-i-scope
spi-nu-les-cent
spir-a-cle
spi-rac-u-lar
spi-raled
spi-re-a
spi-reme
Spi-ri-fer
spi-rif-er-ous
spir-it-ed
spir-it-u-al
spir-i-tu-el
spir-it-u-ous
spi-ro-chete
spi-ro-chet-o-sis
spi-ro-graph
spi-rom-e-ter
spi-ro-met-ric
spi-ro-pen-tane
splanch-ni-cec-to-my
splen-dent
splen-did
splen-dif-er-ous
splen-dor-ous
sple-net-ic
sple-nic
sple-ni-tis
sple-ni-um

splic-er
splin-tered
spo-di-um
spod-u-mene
spoil-age
spoil-er
spo-ken
spo-li-a-tion
spon-dy-li-tis
spong-er
spon-gi-ness
spon-gi-ol-o-gy
spon-si-ble
spon-sor
spon-ta-ne-i-ty
spon-ta-ne-ous
spoon-er-ism
spo-rad-ic
spo-ri-ci-dal
spo-rif-er-ous
spo-ro-gen-ic
spo-ro-phyll
spo-ro-zo-an
spor-tive
spor-u-la-tion
spor-ule
spout-er
spring-er
sprin-kler
sprin-kling
sprint-er
sprock-et
spu-mes-cence
spu-mous
spu-ri-ous
spur-tive
spu-tum
squad-ron
squa-lene
squal-ld-i-ty
squal-or
squa-mous
squan-dcred
squawk-er
squeal-er
squeam-ish
squce-gee
squeez-er
squint-er
squirt-er
sta-bi-la-tor
sta-bile
stab-i-lim-e-ter
sta-bil-i-ty

sta-bi-li-za-tion
sta-bi-liz-er
sta-bled
stac-ca-to
stach-y-drine
sta-dim-e-ter
sta-di-um
staff-er
stag-mom-e-ter
stain-er
Sta-kha-nov-ite
sta-lac-tite
stal-ac-tit-ic
sta-lag-mite
stal-ag-mit-ic
stal-ag-mom-e-ter
Sta-lin-grad
sta-men
stam-i-na
stam-pede
stamp-er
stan-chion
stand-ard-i-za-tion
stand-ing
sta-nine
stan-nite
sta-pes
Staph-y-lo-coc-cus
staph-y-lot-o-my
sta-pler
starch-er
sta-re de-ci-sis
star-ling
star-lite
start-er
star-tling
star-va-tion
sta-sis
stat-ed
stat-i-cal-ly
sta-tion-ar-y
sta-tion-er-y
sta-tis-ti-cal
stat-is-ti-cian
stat-i-tron
sta-tom-e-ter
sta-tor
stat-o-scope
stat-u-ar-y
stat-u-esque
stat-ure
sta-tus
stat-ute
stat-u-to-ry

stau-ro-lite
stau-ro-scop-ic
stead-i-ness
stealth-i-ness
steam-er
ste-a-rate
ste-ar-ic
ste-a-rin
ste-a-rit-ic
ste-ar-o-yl
ste-a-ryl
ste-a-tite
ste-a-tol-y-sis
ste-a-to-sis
steep-er
stee-ple
steer-age
Ste-fan
Stel-lite
sten-ciled
ste-nog-ra-pher
sten-o-graph-ic
ste-nog-ra-phy
sten-o-ha-line
ste-nom-e-ter
ste-no-sis
sten-o-typ-ist
sten-to-ri-an
Ste-phen
ste-ra-di-an
ster-co-bi-lin-o-gen
ster-co-rite
ster-cu-lic
ster-e-og-no-sis
ster-e-og-ra-pher
ster-e-o-graph-ic
ster-e-om-e-ter
ster-e-om-e-try
ster-e-o-phon-ic
ster-e-oph-o-ny
ster-e-op-ti-con
ster-e-o-scope
ster-e-os-co-py
ster-e-ot-o-my
ster-e-o-typ-er
ster-ic
ster-ile
ste-ril-i-ty
ster-i-li-za-tion
ster-i-liz-er
ster-let
ster-ling
ster-num
ster-nu-ta-to-ry

ste-roi-dal
ste-rol
ster-to-rous
ste-thom-e-ter
steth-o-scope
ste-thos-co-py
Steu-ben
ste-ve-dore
Ste-ven-son
ste-vi-o-side
stew-ard
sthen-ic
stib-a-mine
stib-ine
sti-bin-ic
stib-i-o-pal-la-di-nite
sti-bon-ic
sti-bo-ni-um
stib-o-phen
sti-chom-e-try
stick-ler
stiff-en-er
sti-fling
stig-mas-ter-ol
stig-mat-ic
stig-ma-tism
stig-ma-tize
stil-bene
stil-bes-trol
sti-let-to
stilp-no-mel-ane
stim-u-lant
stim-u-la-tive
stim-u-la-tor
stim-u-lus
sting-er
sting-y (stinging)
stin-gy (close)
stink-er
sti-pend
sti-pen-di-ar-y
sti-pes
stip-i-tat-ic
stip-pled
stip-u-la-tion
stip-ule
stitch-er
stock-ade
sto-gy
sto-i-cal
stoi-chi-o-met-ric
stoi-chi-om-e-try
stok-er
stol-id

sto-lid-i-ty
stom-ach
sto-mach-ic
sto-ma-ti-tis
sto-ma-tol-o-gy
ston-i-ness
stop-pled
stor-age
sto-ried
sto-ri-ette
storm-i-ness
sto-ver
stow-age
stra-bis-mom-e-ter
stra-bis-mus
strad-dler
strag-gler
straight-en-er
strain-er
strait-ened
stra-mo-ni-um
strand-er
stran-ger (n.)
strang-er (adj.)
stran-gler
stran-gu-late
strat-a-gem
stra-te-gi-cal
strat-e-gist
strat-e-gy
strat-i-fi-ca-tion
strat-i-graph-ic
stra-tig-ra-phy
stra-to-cu-mu-lus
strat-o-sphere
strat-o-spher-ic
stra-tum
stra-tus
streak-i-ness
stream-er
strength-en-ing
stren-u-ous
strep-o-gen-in
strep-ta-mine
strep-to-coc-cic
strep-to-coc-co-sis
strep-to-my-cin
strep-to-thri-cin
stretch-er
stri-at-ed
stric-ture
stri-dent
strid-u-lous
stri-gose

110

strik-er
strin-gent
string-er
strip-er
strob-i-la-ceous
strob-o-scop-ic
strob-o-tron
stro-ga-noff
strok-er
stro-mat-ic
stro-ma-tin
stron-gy-lo-sis
stron-ti-an-if-er-ous
stron-ti-an-ite
stron-ti-um
stro-phan-thi-din
stro-phe
stroph-ic
struc-tur-al
strug-gled
strum-pet
strych-nine
stub-born-ness
stu-dent
stud-ied
stu-di-ous
stul-ti-fy
stum-bling
stump-age
stu-pe-fa-cient
stu-pe-fy
stu-pen-dous
stu-pid-i-ty
stu-por
stur-di-ly
stur-geon
stut-tered
Styg-i-an
sty-let
styl-ish
sty-lis-tic
styl-ize
sty-lo-graph-ic
sty-lom-e-try
sty-lus
sty-mie
styp-tic
sty-rac-i-tol
styr-e-nate
sty-rene
sty-ryl
sua-si-ble
suav-i-ty
su-ber-ate

su-ber-ic
su-ber-in
su-ber-ose
su-ber-yl-ar-gi-nine
sub-jec-tiv-ism
sub-ju-gate
sub-junc-tive
sub-lim-a-ble
sub-li-mate
sub-lime
sub-lim-i-nal
sub-lim-i-ty
sub-li-mize
sub-merged
sub-mer-gence
sub-mer-gi-ble
sub-mer-sal
sub-mersed
sub-mers-i-ble
sub-or-di-nate
sub-or-na-tion
sub-pe-naed
sub-ro-gate
sub-scrib-er
sub-ser-vi-ent
sub-sid-ence
sub-sid-i-ar-y
sub-si-dize
sub-sist-ence
sub-son-ic
sub-stan-tial
sub-stan-tive
sub-stit-u-ent
sub-sti-tut-a-ble
sub-sti-tu-tive
sub-sump-tive
sub-ter-fuge
sub-ti-lin
sub-tle-ty
sub-tract-er
sub-trac-tive
sub-ur-ban
sub-ver-sive
sub-vert-er
sub-vert-i-ble
suc-ce-da-ne-ous
suc-ce-dent
suc-ces-sive
suc-ces-sor
suc-cin-a-mate
suc-ci-nam-ic
suc-cin-a-mide
suc-ci-nate
suc-cin-ic

suc-ci-nyl
suc-cu-lence
suck-ler
su-cre
su-crose
suc-to-ri-al
su-da-men
Su-da-nese
su-da-to-ry
su-do-rif-er-ous
suf-fic-er
suf-fi-cien-cy
suf-fo-ca-tive
suf-fra-gist
suf-fus-a-ble
suf-fu-sive
sug-ar
sug-gest-i-ble
sug-ges-tive
su-i-ci-dal
sui ge-ner-is
suit-a-ble
suit-or
su-ki-ya-ki
sul-fa-cet-a-mide
sul-fa-di-az-ine
sul-fa-gua-ni-dine
sul-fa-mer-a-zine
sul-fa-meth-yl-thi-az-ole
sul-fam-ic
sulf-am-ide
sul-fam-o-yl
sul-fa-nil-a-mide
sul-fa-nil-ic
sul-fan-i-lyl
sul-fa-pyr-i-dine
sulf-ars-phen-a-mine
sul-fat-ase
sul-fa-thi-az-ole
sul-fen-ic
sulf-hy-dryl
sul-fide
sul-fi-nyl
Sul-fo-nal
sul-fon-a-mide
sul-fo-nat-ed
sul-fo-na-tor
sul-fon-eth-yl-meth-ane
sul-fon-ic
sul-fo-ni-um
sulf-ox-ide
sul-fu-re-ous
sul-fu-ret-ed
sul-fu-ric

111

sul-fu-rize
sul-fu-rous
sul-fur-yl
sulk-i-ness
sul-tan-ate
sul-try
su-mac
Su-ma-tran
sum-mar-i-ly
sum-ma-rize
sum-ma-ry
sum-mit-ry
sump-tu-ar-y
sun-der
sun-dry
sunk-en
su-per-a-ble
su-perb
su-per-cil-i-ous
su-per-er-o-gate
su-per-e-rog-a-to-ry
su-per-fi-cial
su-per-flu-ous
su-per-in-tend-ent
su-pe-ri-or-i-ty
su-per-la-tive
su-per-nal
su-per-na-tant
su-per-nat-u-ral
su-per-nu-mer-ar-y
su-per-se-de-as
su-per-se-dure
su-per-sen-si-ble
su-per-son-ic
su-per-sti-tious
su-per-ve-nience
su-per-vis-ee
su-per-vi-so-ry
su-pi-na-tor
sup-ple-men-tal
sup-ple-men-ta-ry
sup-ple-tive
sup-pli-ca-to-ry
sup-port-ive
sup-pos-al
sup-po-si-tion
sup-pos-i-ti-tious
sup-pos-i-to-ry
sup-press-i-ble
sup-pres-sor
sup-pu-ra-tive
su-pra
su-prem-a-cy
sur-a-min

sur-cin-gle
sur-e-ty
sur-fac-er
sur-fac-ing
sur-fac-tant
sur-feit
sur-geon
sur-ger-y
sur-gi-cal
Su-ri-nam-ese
sur-li-ness
sur-mis-a-ble
sur-plice
sur-plus-age
sur-pris-a-ble
sur-re-al-ist
sur-ren-der
sur-rep-ti-tious
sur-ro-gate
sur-veil-lance
sur-viv-al
sur-vi-vor
sus-cep-ti-bil-i-ty
sus-pend-er
sus-pend-i-ble
sus-pen-si-ble
sus-pen-so-ry
sus-pi-cious
sus-pi-ra-tion
sus-te-nance
su-sur-rus
su-tur-al
su-ze-rain
swad-dled
swamp-er
swank-i-ness
swarth-i-ness
swas-ti-ka
sweat-er
Swe-den
Swed-ish
sweep-er
sweet-ened
swel-ter
swift-er
swin-dler
swin-dling
swin-ish
switch-er
Swit-zer-land
swiv-eled
Syb-a-rite
Syb-a-rit-ic
syc-a-more

sych-no-car-pous
syc-o-phan-cy
sy-co-sis
sy-e-nite
syl-la-bar-y
syl-lab-ic
syl-lab-i-fi-ca-tion
syl-la-bize
syl-la-ble
syl-lo-gism
syl-lo-gis-ti-cal
Syl-phon
syl-van-ite
Syl-ves-ter
syl-ves-trene
syl-vite
sym-bi-o-sis
sym-bi-ot-ic
sym-bol-i-cal
sym-bol-ism
sym-bol-ize
sym-bol-o-gy
sym-met-ri-cal
sym-me-trize
sym-me-try
sym-pa-thec-to-my
sym-pa-thet-ic
sym-path-i-co-trop-ic
sym-pa-thin
sym-pa-thiz-er
sym-pa-tho-lyt-ic
sym-pa-thy
sym-phon-ic
sym-pho-ni-ous
sym-pho-nize
sym-pho-ny
sym-phy-sis
sym-phyt-ic
sym-po-si-um
symp-to-mat-ic
symp-tom-a-tize
symp-tom-a-tol-o-gy
syn-a-gogue
syn-apse
syn-ar-thro-sis
syn-chon-drot-o-my
syn-chro-nism
syn-chro-ni-za-tion
syn-chro-niz-er
syn-chron-o-graph
syn-chro-nous
syn-chro-ny
syn-chrop-ter
syn-chro-scope

syn-chro-tron
syn-cli-nal
syn-co-pa-tion
syn-co-pe
syn-des-mo-sis
syn-di-cal-ism
syn-di-cate
syn-drome
syn-ec-do-che
syn-e-col-o-gy
syn-er-e-sis
syn-er-gis-ti-cal
syn-es-the-si-a
syn-ge-nite
syn-od-al
syn-od-i-cal

syn-o-nym
syn-on-y-mous
syn-on-y-my
syn-op-sis
syn-op-tic
syn-o-vi-tis
syn-tec-tic
syn-the-sis
syn-the-siz-er
syn-the-tase
syn-thet-i-cal
syn-thol
syn-to-ni-za-tion
syph-i-lit-ic
syph-i-lol-o-gy
Syr-a-cuse

Syr-i-an
sy-rin-ga
sy-ringe
sy-rin-ge-al
sy-rin-gic
sy-rin-gin
syr-in-gi-tis
syr-in-got-omy
syr-inx
sys-tem-at-i-cal
sys-tem-a-tize
sys-tem-ic
sys-to-le
sys-tol-ic
sy-zyg-i-al
syz-y-gy

T

tac-tom-e-ter
tac-to-sol
taf-fe-ta
Ta-ga-log
tag-a-tose
tag-e-tone
Ta-hi-tian
tail-er
tai-lored
Tai-wan-ese
tak-ing
talc-ose
tal-ent
ta-les (law)
tal-i-pes
tal-is-man
tal-i-tol
talk-a-tive
talk-er
tal-lage
tall-ate
tall-lith
Tal-mud-ic
tal-on
ta-lon-ic
tal-ose
ta-lus
ta-ma-le
tam-a-rack
tam-a-rind
tam-bour
tam-bou-rine
tamp-er (n.)
tam-per (v.)
Tam-pi-co
tam-pon-ade

tab-ard
Ta-bas-co
tab-er-na-cle
tab-er-nan-thine
ta-bes dor-sa-lis
ta-bet-ic
tab-i-net
tab-leaux
ta-ble d'hote
tab-let
ta-bling
tab-loid
ta-boo
tab-o-ret
tab-u-lar
tab-u-la-tor
ta-chis-to-scope
tach-o-graph
ta-chom-e-ter
tach-o-met-ric
ta-chom-e-try
tach-y-car-di-a
tach-y-gen-ic
tach-y-graph-om-e-ter
ta-chyg-ra-phy
ta-chym-e-ter
tach-y-met-ric
ta-chys-ter-ol
tac-it
tac-i-tur-ni-ty
tack-ling
tac-o-nite
tac-ti-cal
tac-ti-cian
tac-tic-i-ty
tac-til-i-ty

tan-a-ce-tin
tan-a-ger
Ta-nan-a-rive
tan-dem
Tan-gan-yi-kan
tan-ge-los
tan-gen-tial
tan-ger-e-tin
tan-ger-ine
tan-gi-ble
tan-gled
tank-age
tan-kard
tank-er
tan-nom-e-ter
tan-ta-lite
tan-ta-liz-er
tan-ta-lum
tan-ta-mount
tan-trum
Tan-za-ni-a
ta-per
tap-er (device; one who tapes)
tap-es-try
ta-pe-tum
tap-i-o-ca
ta-pir
tap-ster
tar-an-tel-la
ta-ran-tu-la
ta-rax-e-in
tar-di-ness
tar-get-eer
tar-iff
tar-nish

113

tar-pau-lin
tar-pon
tar-sal
tars-ec-to-my
tar-sor-rha-phy
tar-sus
tar-tan
tar-tar-e-ous
tar-tar-ic
tar-tar-ous
tar-tram-ic
tar-tra-mide
tar-trat-ed
ta-sim-e-ter
Tas-ma-ni-an
tas-ma-nite
tas-seled
tast-er
tat-ter-de-ma-lion
tat-too-er
tau-rine
tau-ro-cho-late
tau-rom-a-chy
Tau-rus
tau-ryl
tau-to-log-i-cal
tau-tol-o-gy
tau-to-mer-ic
tau-tom-er-ism
tau-to-met-ric
tau-toph-o-ny
tav-ern
taw-dry
tax-i-der-mist
tax-ied
tax-i-fo-lin
tax-i-ing
tax-i-me-ter
tax-o-nom-ic
tax-on-o-my
Tche-by-cheff
team-ster
tea-seled
teas-er
tech-ne-ti-um
tech-ni-cal
tech-ni-cian
tech-nique
tech-noc-ra-cy
tech-no-log-i-cal
tech-nol-o-gy
tec-ton-ics
tec-ton-ite
te-di-ous

te-di-um
tee-ter
tee-to-tal-er
Tef-lon
teg-men-tal
Te-he-ran
Te-huan-te-pec-er
Tel-Au-to-graph
te-leg-ra-pher
tel-e-graph-ic
tel-e-ki-ne-sis
tel-em-e-ter
tel-e-met-ric
te-lem-e-try
te-lem-o-tor
tel-e-o-log-i-cal
tel-e-ol-o-gy
tel-e-path-ic
tel-e-phon-ic
te-leph-o-ny
tel-e-ran
tel-e-scope
tel-e-scop-ic
te-les-co-py
tel-es-the-si-a
tel-e-vi-sion
tel-e-vi-sor
tell-er
tel-lu-ri-an
tel-lu-ride
tel-lu-ri-um
tel-lu-rom-e-ter
tel-lu-ro-ni-um
te-lome
tel-o-mer-i-za-tion
tel-pher-age
tem-blor
te-mer-i-ty
tem-per-a-men-tal
tem-per-ate
tem-per-a-ture
tem-pered
tem-pes-tu-ous
tem-plar
tem-plet
tem-po-ral
tem-po-rar-i-ly
tem-po-rar-y
tem-po-riz-er
tempt-a-ble
tempt-er
tempt-ress
ten-a-ble

te-na-cious
te-nac-i-ty
ten-an-cy
ten-ant-ry
tend-en-cy
tend-er (one wh‹
    tends; ship)
ten-der (soft; offer‹
ten-der-iz-er
ten-der-om-e-ter
ten-di-ni-tis
ten-don
ten-dril
ten-e-bres-cence
ten-e-brous
ten-e-ment
Ten-er-iffe
ten-et
te-nien-te
Ten-ite
Ten-nes-se-an
ten-o-de-sis
ten-on
ten-or
te-not-o-my
ten-si-ble
ten-sil-i-ty
ten-sim-e-ter
ten-si-om-e-ter
ten-so-ri-al
ten-ta-cle
ten-ta-tive
tent-age
ten-ter (drying fra‹
tent-er
ten-ter-hook
te-nu-i-ty
ten-u-lin
ten-u-ous
ten-ure
te-pa-che
te-pee
teph-ro-sin
tep-id
te-pid-i-ty
te-qui-la
ter-a-con-ic
ter-a-cryl-ic
ter-a-to-log-i-cal
ter-a-tol-o-gy
ter-a-to-ma
ter-bi-um
ter-cen-te-nar-y
ter-e-ben-thene

te-reb-ic
ter-e-bin-thi-nate
ter-e-bin-thine
ter-eph-thal-ic
ter-gite
ter-gi-ver-sa-tor
ter-ma-gant
term-er
ter-mi-na-ble
ter-mi-nal
ter-mi-na-tor
ter-mi-nol-o-gy
ter-mi-nus
ter-mite
ter-mit-ic
ter-na-ry
ter-op-ter-in
ter-pene
ter-pe-nyl-ic
ter-pi-nene
ter-pin-e-ol
ter-pin-o-lene
ter-pi-nyl
terp-sich-o-re
terp-si-cho-re-an
ter-ra-pin
ter-rar-i-um
ter-raz-zo
terre-plein
ter-res-tri-al
ter-ri-bly
ter-rif-ic
ter-rig-e-nous
ter-ri-to-ri-al
ter-ror-ism
ter-tian
ter-ti-ar-y
ter-tile
tes-sel-lat-ed
test-a-ble
tes-ta-ceous
tes-ta-men-ta-ry
tes-ta-tor
test-er
tes-ter (canopy)
tes-tic-u-lar
tes-ti-fy
tes-ti-mo-ni-al
tes-ti-ness
tes-tos-ter-one
te-tan-ic
tet-a-no-gen-ic
tet-a-nus
tet-a-ny

te-tar-toi-dal
teth-ered
tet-ra-bro-mo
tet-ra-cene
tet-ra-chlo-ro
te-trac-id
tet-ra-co-sa-no-ic
tet-ra-cy-cline
tet-rad
te-trad-ic
tet-ra-eth-yl
tet-ra-gon
tet-rag-o-nal
tet-ra-he-dral
tet-ra-hy-dro-fu-ran
tet-ra-kis-a-zo
te-tral-o-gy
tet-ra-mine
tet-ra-ni-tro-meth-ane
tet-ra-ple-gi-a
tet-ra-ploi-dy
te-trar-chic
te-trar-chy
tet-ra-som-a-ty
tet-ra-thi-o-nate
tet-ra-va-lent
tet-ra-zine
tet-ra-zo-li-um
te-traz-o-lyl
tet-ra-zone
tet-ri-tol
te-tron-ic
tet-rose
te-trox-ide
tet-ryl
Teu-ton-ic
Tex-an
tex-tile
tex-tu-al
tex-tur-al
Thai-land
thal-a-mot-o-my
thal-as-som-e-ter
thal-lif-er-ous
thal-line
thal-li-um
than-a-to-sis
thau-ma-site
thau-ma-tur-gy
the-a-ter
the-at-ri-cal
the-mat-i-cal-ly
then-o-yl
the-oc-ra-cy

the-o-crat-ic
the-od-o-lite
The-o-do-si-a
the-o-lo-gian
the-ol-o-gy
the-oph-a-gy
the-o-rem
the-o-re-mat-ic
the-o-ret-i-cal
the-o-re-ti-cian
the-o-rize
the-os-o-phy
ther-a-peu-ti-cal-ly
ther-a-pist
the-ri-at-rics
ther-mal
therm-i-on-ic
therm-is-tor
Ther-mit
ther-mo-chro-mism
ther-mo-du-ric
ther-mog-ra-pher
ther-mo-graph-ic
ther-mol-y-sis
ther-mo-lyt-ic
ther-mom-e-ter
ther-mo-met-ri-cal-ly
ther-mom-e-try
ther-moph-i-ly
ther-mo-scop-ic
ther-mo-stat
ther-mo-ther-a-py
the-sau-rus
the-sis
thes-pi-an
the-tin
the-ve-tin
thi-am-ide
thi-am-i-nase
thi-a-mine
thi-a-naph-thene
thi-an-threne
thi-a-zole
thi-az-o-line
thi-a-zol-sul-fone
thick-en-ing
thiev-ish
thi-mer-o-sal
think-er
thi-o-fla-vine
thi-o-naph-thene
thi-on-ic
Thi-o-nine
thi-o-ni-um

115

thi-oph-e-nine
thi-o-u-ra-cil
thi-o-u-re-a
thirst-i-ness
thir-ti-eth
this-tle
thith-er
thi-u-ro-ni-um
thix-ot-ro-py
Thom-as
Tho-mism
thon-zyl-a-mine
tho-rac-ic
tho-rac-i-co-lum-bar
tho-ra-co-scope
tho-ra-cos-to-my
tho-ri-ate
tho-rif-er-ous
tho-rite
tho-ri-um
tho-ron
thor-ough
thou-sand
thrash-er
thread-er
threat-en-ing
thre-i-tol
thre-node
thren-o-dy
three-o-nine
thresh-er
thresh-old
thrift-i-ness
thrill-er
throat-i-ness
throm-bin
throm-bo-an-gi-i-tis
throm-bo-cy-to-sis
throm-bo-plas-tin
throm-bo-sis
throm-bot-ic
throm-bus
throt-tled
thrust-er (one that
  thrusts)
thrus-tor (machine)
thu-co-lite
thu-ja-pli-cin
thu-jyl
thu-li-um
thump-er
thun-der-ous
thu-ri-ble
thu-rif-er-ous

thy-mi-dine
thy-mi-dyl-ic
thy-mine
thy-mol-phthal-ein
thy-mo-nu-cle-ic
thy-mus
Thy-ra-tron
thy-rite
thy-roi-dal
thy-roid-ec-to-my
thy-roid-i-tis
thy-ro-nine
thy-rot-ro-phin
ti-ar-a
Ti-bet-an
tib-i-al
tick-et-er
tick-i-ci-dal
tick-lish
tid-al
ti-di-ness
ti-ding (news)
tid-ing (tide)
Ti-flis
ti-ger-ish
tight-en-er
tig-lal-de-hyde
ti-gnon
ti-go-nin
ti-gress
ti-grine
ti-grol-y-sis
till-a-ble
till-age
till-er
tilt-er
tim-bered
tim-brel
tim-er
tim-id
ti-mid-i-ty
tim-o-rous
tim-o-thy
tim-pa-nist
tin-cal-co-nite
tinc-to-ri-al
tinc-ture
tin-der
tin-gled
tin-ker
tin-kling
tin-seled
tint-er
tin-tin-nab-u-lous

tint-om-e-ter
tip-ster
ti-queur
ti-rade
ti-rail-leur
Tish-chen-ko
ti-ta-nate
ti-tan-ic
ti-ta-nif-er-ous
ti-ta-ni-um
ti-ter
tith-er
Ti-tian
tit-il-late
ti-tled
ti-trat-a-ble
ti-tra-tion
ti-trim-e-ter
ti-tri-met-ri-cal-ly
tit-u-lar-i-ty
toast-er
to-bac-co-nist
to-bog-gan-er
to-col-o-gy
to-coph-er-ol
toc-sin
tod-dler
to-geth-er
tog-gler
To-go-lese
toil-er
toi-let-ry
to-ken
To-ky-o
tol-bu-ta-mide
tol-er-a-ble
tol-er-a-tion
tol-i-dine
tol-u-ene
to-lu-i-dine
tol-u-ol
to-lu-ric
tol-u-yl-ene
tol-yl-ene
to-mat-i-dine
tom-a-tine
to-men-tose
to-mog-ra-phy
ton-al
to-nal-i-ty
to-neme
ton-er
to-net-ics
tongu-er

tongu-ing
ton-ic
to-nic-i-ty
to-nite (explosive)
ton-neau
ton-o-log-i-cal
to-nom-e-ter
ton-o-met-ric
to-nom-e-try
ton-sil-lec-to-my
ton-sil-li-tis
ton-sil-lot-o-my
ton-so-ri-al
ton-tine
to-nus
tool-er
to-paz-ine
to-pec-to-my
to-per
to-pi-ar-y
top-i-cal
to-pog-ra-pher
top-o-graph-i-cal
to-pog-ra-phy
top-o-log-i-cal
to-pol-o-gy
to-pon-y-my
top-sy-tur-vy
tor-chon
to-re-a-dor
to-ric
to-rin-gin
tor-men-tor
tor-na-do
to-roi-dal
tor-pe-do
tor-pid-i-ty
tor-por-if-ic
torqu-er
torqu-ing
torque-me-ter
tor-ren-tial
tor-si-bil-i-ty
tor-si-om-e-ter
tor-sion-al
tor-ti-lla
tor-som-e-ter
tor-toise
tor-tu-os-i-ty
tor-tu-ous
tor-tur-ous
tos-yl-ate
tot-a-ble
to-tal-i-tar-i-an-ism

to-tal-i-ty
to-tal-iz-er
to-ta-quine
to-tem-ism
tou-ché
tough-en
tou-pee
tour-ist
tour-ma-line
tour-na-ment
tour-ni-quet
tou-sled
tout-er
tow-age
to-ward
tow-eled
tow-ered
tox-e-mi-a
tox-e-mic
tox-ic-i-ty
tox-i-co-log-i-cal
tox-i-col-o-gist
tox-i-co-sis
tox-if-er-ous
tox-i-ge-nic-i-ty
tox-in
trac-er-y
tra-che-al
tra-che-i-tis
tra-che-ot-o-my
tra-cho-ma
tra-chyt-ic
trac-ing
track-age
trac-ta-ble
trac-tile
trac-tor
trad-er
tra-dev-man
tra-di-tion-al
tra-duc-er
tra-duc-i-ble
traf-fic-a-ble
traf-fick-er
trag-a-can-thin
tra-ge-di-an
tra-ge-di-enne
trag-e-dy
trag-i-cal
trail-er
train-ee
trai-tor-ous
trai-tress
traj-ect (n.)

tra-ject (v.)
tra-jec-tile
tra-jec-to-ry
tram-meled
tramp-er
tram-po-line
tran-quil-iz-er
tran-quil-li-ty
trans-ac-tion
trans-am-i-nase
trans-at-lan-tic
trans-ceiv-er
tran-scend-ent
tran-scen-den-tal
tran-scrib-er
tran-script
trans-duc-er
trans-duc-tor
tran-sect
trans-fer-a-ble
trans-fer-ase
trans-fer-ee
trans-fer-ence
trans-ferred
trans-for-ma-tion
trans-form-er
trans-fus-a-ble
trans-gres-sor
tran-sient
tran-sil-ience
tran-sis-tor
tran-sit-er
tran-si-tion
tran-si-tive
tran-si-to-ry
tran-si-tron
trans-la-tive
trans-la-tor
trans-lit-er-a-tor
trans-lu-cen-cy
trans-mis-si-ble
trans-mis-som-e-ter
trans-mit-ta-ble
trans-mog-ri-fy
trans-mut-a-ble
tran-som
tran-son-ic
trans-par-ent
trans-spir-a-ble
tran-spi-ra-tion
tran-spire
tran-spi-rom-e-ter
trans-plan-ta-tion
trans-pon-der

117

trans-**por-ta-tion**
trans-pose
trans-ship
trans-u-da-tion
trans-ver-sal
trans-vers-er
trans-vert-er
trans-vert-i-ble
tra-pe-zi-um
trap-e-zoi-dal
trau-mat-ic
trau-ma-tism
trav-ail
trav-eled
trav-el-er
trav-el-og
tra-vers-a-ble
tra-vers-al
trav-erse (n.)
tra-verse (v.)
trav-er-tine
trav-es-ty
trawl-er
treach-er-ous
treach-er-y
trea-cle
trea-dle
trea-son-a-ble
treas-ur-a-ble
treas-ur-er
treas-ur-y
treat-er
trea-tise
tre-bled
tre-foil
tre-ha-lose
trel-lised
Trem-a-to-da
trem-bling
tre-men-dous
trem-e-tol
trem-o-lo
trem-or
trem-u-lous
trench-ant
tren-cher (board; cap)
trench-er (digger)
tre-pan
tre-phine
treph-o-cyte
treph-one
trep-i-da-tion
tre-pid-i-ty
trep-o-ne-ma-to-sis

trep-o-ne-mi-ci-dal
tres-pass-er
tres-tle
tri-an-gu-lar
tri-ar-yl-meth-ane
tri-a-zine
tri-az-i-nyl
tri-a-zole
tri-az-o-lyl
trib-al
tri-bom-e-ter
tri-bro-mo-eth-yl
trib-u-la-tion
tri-bu-nal
trib-une
trib-u-tar-y
trib-ute
tri-chi-a-sis
tri-chi-na
trich-i-no-sis
tri-chit-ic
tri-chlo-ride
tri-chlo-ro-meth-ane
trich-o-mo-ni-a-sis
tri-cho-sis
tri-chot-o my
trick-er-y
trick-ster
tri-cli-no-he-dric
tri-cy-cle
tri-dec-yl-ene
tri-dent
tri-eth-a-nol-a-mine
tri-far-i-ous
tri-fling
trig-o-nal
tri-go-ni-tis
trig-o-nom-e-ter
trig-o-no-met-ric
trig-o-nom-e-try
tri-ha-lide
tri-he-dral
tri-hy-dric
tri-ke-tone
tri-lo-bite
tri-log-ic
tril-o-gy
tri-mer-ide
tri-mes-ic
tri-meth-yl-ene-tri-ni-
   tra-mine
tri-met-ro-gon
tri-na-ry
Trin-i-dad

tri-ni-tro-tol-u-ene
trin-i-ty
trin-ket
tri-no-mi-al
Tri-o-nal
tri-part-i-ble
tri-par-tite
tri-phen-yl-ene
tri-phib-i-ous
triph-thong
tri-ple-gi-a
tri-plet
trip-li-cate
trip-loi-dy
tri-pod
trip-o-dal
tri-pod-ic
trip-tych
tri-so-mic
tri-syl-lab-ic
tri-thi-o-nate
trit-i-um
trit-u-ra-tor
tri-tyl
tri-um-phant
tri-um-vi-rate
tri-va-lent
triv-et
triv-i-al
tro-car
tro-chan-ter
tro-che
troch-e-am-e-ter
troch-le-ar
tro-choi-dal
tro-chom-e-ter
trog-lo-dyte
Tro-jan
trom-bi-di-a-sis
tro-mom-e-ter
tro-nom-e-ter
troop-er
tro-pane
tro-pe-ine
troph-ic
tro-phy
trop-i-cal
tro-pism
trop-o-lone
tro-pom-e-ter
tro-po-sphere
trop-tom-e-ter
tro-pyl
trou-ba-dour

trou-bled
trou-blous
trou-sers
trous-seau
tro-ver
trow-eled
tru-an-cy
Truck-ee
truck-ling
truc-u-lent
trump-er-y
trum-pet-er
trun-cat-ed
trun-cheon
trun-dle
truss-ing
trust-ee
tru-xi-llic
tryp-a-no-ci-dal
tryp-a-no-so-ma
tryp-ar-sa-mide
tryp-o-graph
tryp-sin-o-gen
tryp-to-phan
tset-se
tsu-nam-i
tsu-tsu-ga-mu-shi
tu-bec-to-my
tu-ber-cle
tu-ber-cu-lar
tu-ber-cu-lo-sis
tu-ber-cu-lous
tu-ber-os-i-ty
tu-bi-fa-cient
tub-ing
tu-bo-cu-ra-rine
tu-bu-lar
Tuc-son
tu-fa-ceous
tuff-a-ceous
tuft-er

Tui-ler-ies
tu-la-re-mi-a
tu-lip
tum-bler
tum-bling
tum-brel
tu-me-fa-cient
tu-mes-cent
tu-mid
tu-mor
tu-mul-tu-ous
tun-a-ble
tung-sten
tung-stite
tu-nicked
Tu-ni-si-an
tun-neled
tun-nel-er
tu-pe-lo
tu-ran-ose
tur-ban
tur-bi-dim-e-ter
tur-bi-di-met-ric
tur-bid-i-ty
tur-bi-nate
tur-bine
tur-bi-nec-to-my
tur-bo-charg-er
tur-bu-la-tor
tur-bu-lence
tu-reen
tur-ges-cence
tur-gid-i-ty
tur-key
Turk-ish
tur-mer-ic
tur-nip
tur-pen-tine
tur-pi-tude
tur-quoise
tur-tle

U

ul-ti-ma-cy
ul-ti-ma-tum
ul-tra-ma-rine
ul-tra-son-ic
ul-u-late
U-lys-ses
um-bel-lif-er-one
um-ber
um-bil-i-cal
um-bil-i-cus
um-bra-geous
um-brel-la

tu-te-lage
tu-tored
tu-to-ri-al
Tu-tu-i-lan
tu-yere
tweet-er
tweez-ers
twen-ti-eth
twin-kling
twist-er
Twitch-ell
ty-ing
tym-pan-ic
tym-pa-nist
tym-pa-num
tyn-dall-om-e-ter
typ-a-ble
typh-li-tis
ty-phoi-dal
ty-phoon
ty-phus
typ-i-cal
typ-i-fy
ty-pog-ra-pher
ty-po-graph-ic
ty-pog-ra-phy
ty-po-nym
ty-poth-e-tae
ty-ra-mine
ty-ran-ni-cal
ty-ran-nize
tyr-an-ny
ty-rant
ty-ro-ci-dine
Ty-rode
Ty-ro-le-an
Tyr-o-lese
ty-ro-sin-ase
ty-ro-sine
ty-ro-sin-o-sis

u-biq-ui-tous
u-biq-ui-ty
u-dom-e-ter
U-gan-dan
U-krain-i-an
u-ku-le-le
ul-cer-a-tive
ul-nar
ul-na-re
u-lot-o-my
ul-ster
ul-te-ri-or

u-mo-ho-ite
um-pire
u-na-nim-i-ty
u-nan-i-mous
u-na-ry
un-cial
un-ci-na-ri-a-sis
un-ci-nate
un-cle
unc-tu-ous
un-dec-yl-ene
un-dec-y-len-ic

119

un-der-tak-er
un-du-la-to-ry
un-guen-tous
un-gui-nous
u-ni-bi-va-lent
u-nic-i-ty
u-ni-corn
u-ni-fi-ca-tion
u-ni-form-i-ty
un-ion-ism
u-nip-a-rous
u-nip-o-tent
u-nique-ly
u-ni-son
u-nit-a-ble
u-ni-tar-i-an
u-ni-tar-y
u-nit-ed
u-nit-ize
u-ni-va-lent
u-ni-ver-sal-i-ty
u-ni-ver-si-ty
u-niv-o-cal
un-prec-e-dent-ed
un-re-quit-a-ble
up-heav-al
up-hol-ster-er
Up-per Vol-tan
up-roar-i-ous
u-ra-chus
u-ra-cil
u-ra-nate
U-ra-ni-an
u-ran-ic
u-ra-nif-er-ous
u-ra-nin-ite
u-ra-nite

u-ra-ni-um
u-ra-nog-ra-phy
u-ra-nol-o-gy
u-ra-nom-e-try
u-ra-nos-co-py
u-ra-nous
U-ra-nus
u-ra-nyl
u-ra-zine
ur-ban-i-ty
ur-bi-cul-ture
ur-chin
u-re-am-e-ter
u-re-mi-a
u-re-om-e-ter
u-re-ter-i-tis
u-re-thane
u-re-thra
u-re-thri-tis
u-ret-ic
u-re-yl-ene
ur-gen-cy
u-ri-col-y-sis
u-ri-co-lyt-ic
u-ri-nal-y-sis
u-ri-nar-y
u-ri-nate
u-ri-no-cry-os-co-py
u-ri-nol-o-gy
u-ri-nom-e-ter
u-ro-bi-lin-o-gen
u-ro-fla-vin
u-ro-gen-i-tal
u-rog-ra-phy
u-ro-leu-cic
u-ro-li-thi-a-sis
u-ro-li-thol-o-gy
u-ro-log-ic

u-rol-o-gist
u-ro-poi-e-sis
u-ro-poi-et-ic
u-ro-por-phy-rin
u-ros-co-py
u-rot-ro-pine
ur-si-gram
ur-ti-car-i-a
us-a-ble
us-que-baugh
us-ti-la-gin-e-ous
u-su-al-ly
u-su-fruct
u-su-rer
u-su-ri-ous
u-sur-pa-tion
u-surp-er
u-su-ry
U-tah-an
u-ten-sil
u-ter-ine
u-ter-og-ra-phy
u-ter-us
u-til-i-tar-i-an
u-til-i-ty
u-ti-li-za-tion
u-ti-liz-er
u-to-pi-an
u-tri-cle
u-tric-u-lar
u-ve-i-tis
u-vi-ton-ic
u-vu-la
ux-or-i-cide
ux-o-ri-ous
u-zar-i-gen-in
u-za-rin

V

va-can-cy
vac-ci-na-tor
vac-il-la-tion
vac-u-ist
va-cu-i-ty
vac-u-om-e-ter
vac-u-um
va-de me-cum
vag-a-bond-age
va-gar-i-ous
va-gar-y
va-gi-na
vag-i-nal
vag-i-nec-to-my
vag-i-ni-tis

val-e-tu-di-nar-i-an
val-iant
val-i-da-tion
va-lid-i-ty
va-line
va-lise
val-or-i-za-tion
val-or-ous
val-u-a-ble
val-vate
val-vu-lar
val-vu-li-tis
val-vu-lot-o-my
va-nad-ic

va-got-o-my
va-gran-cy
va-guish
val-ance
val-e-dic-to-ri-an
va-lence
va-len-ci-a
Va-len-ci-ennes
va-lent
val-en-tine
val-er-ate
va-le-ri-an
va-ler-ic
va-le-ryl
val-et

van-a-dif-er-ous
va-na-di-um
Van-cou-ver
van-dal-ism
va-nil-la
van-ish
van-i-ty
van-quish-er
van-tage
vap-id
va-pid-i-ty
va-pog-ra-phy
va-por-im-e-ter
va-por-i-za-tion
va-por-iz-er
va-por-ous
var-i-a-bil-i-ty
Var-i-ac
var-i-ant
var-i-at-ed
var-i-a-tion
var-i-co-cele
var-i-cose
var-ied
var-i-e-gat-ed
va-ri-e-tal
va-ri-e-ty
var-i-o-lite
var-i-o-loid
var-i-om-e-ter
var-i-ous
var-is-tor
Var-i-typ-er
var-nish-er
vas-cu-lar
vas-ec-to-my
vas-e-line
vas-o-dil-a-tin
vas-o-di-la-tor
vas-o-mo-tor
vas-sal-age
vas-ti-tude
Vat-i-can
va-tic-i-nal
vaude-ville
vec-to-ri-al
veg-e-ta-ble
veg-e-tar-i-an
veg-e-ta-tive
ve-he-mence
ve-hi-cle
ve-hic-u-lar
vel-lum
vel-o-cim-e-ter

ve-loc-i-pede
ve-loc-i-ty
ve-lom-e-ter
ve-lours
ve-lum
vel-vet-een
ve-nal-i-ty
ve-na-tion
vend-ee
vend-er
ven-det-ta
vend-i-ble
ven-dor
ve-neer-er
ven-e-nif-er-ous
ven-er-a-ble
ve-ne-re-al
ve-ne-re-ol-o-gy
ven-er-y
Ve-ne-tian
venge-ance
ve-ni-al
ve-ni-re fa-ci-as
ven-i-son
ven-om-ous
ve-nous
ven-ter (abdomen)
vent-er (utters)
ven-ti-la-tor
ven-tom-e-ter
ven-tral
ven-tri-cle
ven-tric-u-lar
ven-tri-lo-qui-al
ven-tril-o-quism
ven-tril-o-quist
ven-tur-er
ven-tu-ri
ven-tur-ous
ven-ue
ven-ule
ven-u-lose
Ve-nu-si-an
ve-ra-cious
ve-rac-i-ty
ve-ran-da
ver-a-scope
ver-a-tral-de-hyde
ver-a-tram-ine
ve-rat-ric
ve-rat-ro-yl
Ve-ra-trum
ver-a-tryl-i-dene
ver-bal (adj.)

verb-al (n.) (part of speech)
ver-bal-i-ty
ver-bal-iz-er
ver-ba-tim
ver-be-na
ver-be-na-lin
ver-bi-age
ver-bile
ver-bos-i-ty
ver-bo-ten
ver-dant
ver-di-gris
ver-dur-ous
verg-er
ver-i-fi-a-ble
ver-i-fi-ca-tion
ver-i-si-mil-i-tude
ver-i-ta-ble
Ver-i-tas
ver-i-ty
ver-mi-cel-li
ver-mi-ci-dal
ver-mic-u-lar
ver-mic-u-lite
ver-mi-form
ver-mif-u-gal
ver-mi-fuge
ver-mil-ion
ver-mi-no-sis
ver-min-ous
Ver-mont-er
ver-mouth
ver-nac-u-lar
ver-nal
ver-ni-er
ve-ron-i-ca
ver-ru-co-sis
ver-sa-til-i-ty
ver-sic-u-lar
ver-si-fi-ca-tion
ver-si-fi-er
ver-sus
ver-te-bra
ver-ti-cal
ver-tic-i-ty
ver-tig-i-nous
ver-ti-go
ves-i-cant
ves-i-ca-to-ry
ves-i-cle
ve-sic-u-lar
ves-per-al

121

ves-tal
vest-ed
ves-tib-u-lar
ves-ti-bule
ves-ti-bu-li-tis
ves-tig-i-al
ves-ti-ture
ves-try
ves-tur-al
Ve-su-vi-us
vet-er-an
vet-er-i-nar-i-an
vex-a-tious
vi-a-bil-i-ty
vi-a do-lo-ro-so
vi-a-duct
vi-bran-cy
vi-bra-to-ry
vib-ri-o-sis
vi-brom-e-ter
vi-bur-num
vic-ar-age
vi-car-i-ous
vice-ge-rent
vice-roy
vi-ce ver-sa
Vi-chy-ite
vi-chys-soise
vi-ci-a-nin
vi-ci-a-nose
vic-i-nage
vic-i-nal
vi-cin-i-ty
vi-cious
vi-cis-si-tude
vic-tim-ize
vic-to-ri-an
vic-to-ri-ous
vict-ualed
vict-ual-er
vi-cu-na
vi-de-li-cet
vid-e-o
Vi-et-nam-ese
vig-i-lance
vig-i-lan-te
vig-i-lan-tism
vi-gnette
vi-gnet-ter
vig-or-ous
vi-king
vi-la-yet
vil-i-fi-er
vil-lag-er

vil-lain-ous
vi-na-ceous
vin-ai-grette
vin-ci-ble
vin-cu-lum
vin-di-ca-ble
vin-di-ca-to-ry
vin-dic-tive
vin-e-gar
vin-er-y
vin-i-cul-tur-al
vi-nif-er-a
vin-ol-o-gy
vin-om-e-ter
vi-nous
vin-tag-er
vint-ner
vi-nyl-a-tion
vi-nyl-ene
vi-nyl-i-dene
Vi-nyl-ite
vi-nyl-o-gous
vi-o-la-ble
vi-o-la-ceous
vi-o-lan-throne
vi-o-la-tor
vi-o-lence
vi-o-les-cent
vi-o-lin-ist
vi-o-lon-cel-lo
vi-o-lu-ric
vi-os-ter-ol
vi-per-ous
vi-ra-go
vi-ral
vi-re-mi-a
vi-res-cence
vir-gin-al
Vir-gin-ian
vir-gin-i-ty
vir-gin-i-um
vir-i-al
vi-ri ci-dal
vi-rid-i-ty
vir-ile
vi-ril-i-ty
vi-rol-o-gy
vi-ro-sis
vir-tu-al
vir-tu-os-i-ty
vir-tu-o-so
vir-tu-ous
vir-u-lent
vi-rus

vis-aged
vis-cer-al
vis-cid-i-ty
Vis-co-liz-er
vis-com-e-ter
vis-co-scope
vis-cose
vis-co-sim-e-ter
vis-cos-i-ty
vis-cous
vis-i-bil-i-ty
vi-sion-ar-y
vi-sioned
vis-it-ant
vis-it-a-tion
vis-i-tor
vi-sor
vis-ta
vis-u-al
vis-u-al-i-ty
vis-u-al-iz-er
vi-tal-i-ty
vi-tal-ize
vi-ta-min-ol-o-gy
vi-ta-scope
vi-tel-lin
vi-ti-at-ed
vit-i-cul-ture
vit-i-li-go
vit-rain
vit-re-ous
vi-tres-cence
vi-tres-ci-ble
vit-ri-fi-a-ble
vit-ri-fi-ca-tion
vit-ri-ol
vit-ri-o-lat-ed
vit-ri-ol-ic
vi-tu-per-a-tive
vi-va-cious
vi-vac-i-ty
vi-van-dier
vi-vant
vi-var-i-um
vi-va vo-ce
viv-id
vi-vid-i-ty
viv-i-fi-ca-tion
viv-i-par-i-ty
vi-vip-a-rous
viv-i-sec-tion
vix-en-ish
vi-zier
Vlad-i-vos-tok

vo-ca-ble
vo-cab-u-lar-y
vo-cal-ist
vo-cal-iz-er
vo-ca-tion
voc-a-tive
vo-cif-er-ous
voic-ing
void-ance
vol-a-til-i-ty
vol-a-til-i-za-tion
vol-can-ic
vol-ca-no
vo-cod-er
vo-lem-i-tol
vo-li-tion
volt-age
vol-ta-ic
vol-tam-e-ter
volt-am-me-ter
vol-u-bil-i-ty

vol-ume
vol-u-me-nom-e-ter
vo-lu-me-ter
vol-u-met-ric
vo-lu-mi-nous
vol-un-tar-i-ly
vol-un-teered
vo-lup-tu-ar-y
vo-lup-tu-ous
vo-lute
vol-u-tin
vol-vu-lus
vo-mer-ine
vom-it-er
vom-i-tus
voo-doo
vo-ra-cious
vo-rac-i-ty
vor-tex
vor-ti-ces

vor-tic-i-ty
vot-a-ble
vo-ta-ry
vot-er
vo-tive
vouch-er
vow-el
vox po-pu-li
voy-ag-er
voy-a-geur
vul-can-ite
vul-can-i-za-tion
vul-can-iz-er
vul-gar-i-an
vul-gar-ism
vul-gar-i-ty
vul-ner-a-ble
vul-pine
vul-pin-ic
vul-tur-ous
vul-vi-tis

W

wad-dled
wad-er
wa-fer
waf-fle
waft-age
wa-ger (bet)
wag-er (competitor)
wag-es
Wag-ne-ri-an
wag-on-er
wag-on-ette
wain-scot-ing
wait-er
wait-ress
waiv-er
wak-en-er
walk-er
wal-lop-er
Wal-tham
waltz-er
wam-pum
wan-der
wan-gled
wan-ton
wap-i-ti
war-bler
war-den
ward-er
war-fa-rin
war-i-ness
warm-er

warp-age
war-rant-ee
war-rant-er
war-ran-tor (law)
war-ran-ty
war-ri-or
wash-a-ble
Wash-ing-to-ni-an
wasp-ish
was-sail
Was-ser-mann
wast-age
wast-er
was-trel
wa-ter-me-ter
watt-age
wave-me-ter
wa-ver (sway)
wav-er (waving)
Wa-ver-ley
wax-en
weak-ened
weak-ling
weap-on-eer
wear-a-ble
wea-ri-ness
wea-ri-some
wea-seled
weath-ered
weath-er-om-e-ter
weav-er
Web-er

Web-ste-ri-an
Wechs-ler
wed-ding
Wedg-wood
Wednes-day
weed-er
weep-er
wee-viled
weight-i-ness
Weight-om-e-ter
Wei-mar-an-er
weld-er
wel-kin
welsh-er
wel-ter
welt-er (worker on
  shoes, etc.)
Wes-ley-an
west-er-ly
west-ern-er
West-min-ster
West-pha-li-an
weth-er
whal-er-y
wharf-age
wheat-en
whee-dled
wheel-er
wheez-i-ness
wher-ev-er
wheth-er

123

whi-lom
whim-pered
whim-si-cal
whim-sy
whirl-er
whirl-i-gig
whisk-ered
whis-kies
whis-ky
whis-pered
whis-tler
whis-tling
whit-en-ing
whith-er
whit-ish
whit-tled
whor-tle-ber-ry
wick-ed-ly
wick-ered
wick-et
wick-i-up
wid-en
widg-eon
widg-et
wid-ow-er
wie-ner schnit-zel
Wies-ba-den
wie-sen-bo-den
wild-er
wil-der-ness
Wil-helms-ha-ven

Wil-helm-stras-se
Wil-lam-ette
will-ful-ness
Wil-liam
Wil-ton
wind-age
wind-er
wind-i-ness
win-dow
wind-row
Wins-low
win-some
win-ter-ize
win-try
wip-er
wir-i-ness
Wis-con-sin-ite
wise-a-cre
wis-tar-i-a
Wis-te-ri-a
witch-er-y
with-al
with-ered
wit-ti-cism
wiz-ard-ry
wiz-ened
wob-bu-la-tor
woe-ful-ness
wolf-ra-min-i-um
wolf-ram-ite
wol-las-ton-ite
wol-ver-ine

wom-an
wom-bat
wom-en
won-dered
won-drous
wood-en
woof-er
wool-en
wool-ly
Worces-ter
word-ster
work-er
wor-ri-some
wor-shiped
wor-ship-er
wor-sted
wor-thi-ly
wor-thy
wo-ven
wran-gler
wreck-age
wres-tler
wres-tling
wretch-ed
wring-er
wrin-kled
wrist-let
writ-er
Wy-an-dotte
Wyc-liffe
Wy-o-ming-ite

X

xan-tha-mide
xan-thate
xan-the-nyl
xan-thine
xan-tho-gen-ate
xan-tho-ma
xan-tho-ma-to-sis
xan-thom-a-tous
xan-thom-e-ter
xan-tho-phyll
xan-thop-ter-in
xan-thous
xan-thox-y-le-tin
xan-thy-drol
Xa-ve-ri-an
xe-ni-al
xen-o-lith

xe-non
xen-o-pho-bi-a
xen-yl
Xe-res
xe-ric
xe-ro-gel
xe-ro-graph-ic
xe-rog-ra-phy
xe-ro-phyte
xe-ro-phyt-ic
xe-ro-sis
xiph-oid
xi-phop-a-gus
xy-lem
xy-lene
xy-le-nol
xy-le-nyl

xy-lic
xy-li-dine
xy-lin-de-in
xy-lo-graph-ic
xy-log-ra-phy
xy-loid
xy-lol-o-gy
xy-lom-e-ter
xy-loph-a-gous
xy-lo-phone
xy-lo-side
xy-lot-o-my
xy-lo-yl
xy-lu-lose
xy-lyl-ene
Xy-ris

Y

Yak-i-ma
Yak-u-tat
ya-men
Yan-kee
Ya-qui
yard-age
yaw-me-ter
Ya-zoo
year-ling
yelp-er

Yem-en-ite
yeo-man
yes-ter-day
yield-a-ble
yo-del-er
yo-gurt
yo-him-bine
yo-kel
yon-der

Yo-sem-i-te
young-ster
y-per-ite
yp-sil-i-form
yt-ter-bi-um
yt-ter-bous
yt-trif-er-ous
yt-tri-um
yt-tro-tan-ta-lite
Yu-go-slav

Z

Zach-a-ri-ah
Zam-bi-an
za-ni-ness
za-pa-te-a-do
zeal-ot
zea-lot-i-cal
zeal-ous
ze-a-xan-thin
ze-bra
ze-nith
ze-nog-ra-phy
ze-o-lite
ze-ol-i-tize
zeph-yr
Zep-pe-lin
ze-ro-ize
ze-ros
zib-el-lne
zinc-ate
zinc-if-er-ous
zin-cog-ra-phy
zinc-oid
zin-ger-one
zin-gi-ber-ene
Zi-on-ism
zirc-ite

zir-con-ate
zir-co-ni-um
zir-co-nyl
zith-er
Ziz-i-phus
zlo-ty
zo-an-thro-py
zo-di-ac
zo-di-a-cal
Zo-is-i-a
zois-it-i-za-tion
Zoll-ver-ein
zon-al
zon-ar-y
zon-ate
zo-nif-er-ous
zo-og-a-my
zo-o-gen-ic
zo-ol-a-ter
zo-o-log-i-cal
zo-ol-o-gy
zo-om-e-ter
zo-on-o-sis
zo-o-phyte

zo-os-co-py
zo-os-ter-ol
zo-ot-o-my
Zo-ro-as-tri-an
Zou-ave
Zo-ys-i-a
zu-mat-ic
zun-yite
zwie-back
zwit-ter-i-on
zyg-a-de-nine
zy-gal
zy-go-mat-ic
zy-gote
zy-got-ic
zy-mase
zy-min
zy-mo-gen-ic
zy-mog-e-nous
zy-mo-hy-drol-y-sis
zy-mol-o-gy
zy-mom-e-ter
zy-mo-sis
zy-mos-ter-ol
zy-mos-then-ic
zy-mur-gy